What they're saying about . . .

Ecstasy: The MDMA Story

"A remarkably complete, courageous and well-researched work."
—*American Book Review*

"It is possible Bruce Eisner's book will play a role in dispelling misconceptions about MDMA. The book is a splendid summary of the drug's history, usage and effects."
—Stanley Krippner, Ph.D.
author of *Healing States, Dream Working, Personal Mythology*

"Bruce Eisner has spent time in both the world of academic psychology and as a journalist covering the psychedelic scene. He has written a masterly book about an important new mind-changer which is scholarly and readable. I enthusiastically recommend it!"
—Timothy Leary, Ph.D.
performing philosopher

"The first compendium of the pertinent MDMA data. Eisner's book is helpful, wise and balanced."
—Peter Stafford
author of *Psychedelics Encyclopedia*

"Bruce Eisner has created an excellent study of how hysterical and ignorant bureaucrats create drug problems while trying to solve drug problems. Before we plunge headlong into a totalitarian state, I wish every American citizen would read this book."
—Robert Anton Wilson

"This book presents the significant findings concerning MDMA, or 'Ecstasy' . . . The very large numbers of people who now self-experiment with this drug should benefit from the wealth of information—including the fact that longer-term effects on the brain are still unknown . . .

"It is absolutely certain that a new world is dawning in which alterations of brain function and states of consciousness will b accepted and of great value . . . A subst reminiscent as it is of Homer's Nepen now 'normal woes' of everyday life."

co-author of *The Variet* Games

ECSTASY

The MDMA Story

Expanded Second Edition

Bruce Eisner

Foreword by Stanley Krippner, Ph.D.
Introduction by Peter Stafford
Chemical Synthesis by Alexander Shulgin, Ph.D.

Published by Ronin Publishing, Inc.

Ecstasy: The MDMA Story
Second Edition
ISBN: 0-914171-68-2
ISBN: 978-0-914171-68-3
Copyright 1989, 1994 by Bruce Eisner

Project Editors: Sebastian Orfali, Dan Joy, Ginger Ashworth
Manuscript Readers: Alexander Shulgin, Lester Grispoon,
    Timothy Leary, Ralph Metzner, Claudio Naranjo
Typography: Peter Stafford, Aiden Kelley
Cover: Copyright 1992: LordNose! (Mark Franklyn)
Chemical Drawing: C.hristopher and Kim Workdelay
Half-tones: Norman Mayell

Disclaimer:
Neither author nor the publisher condone or encourage the possession, use, manufacture of any illegal substances. The material herein is presented for reference and informational purposes only. The author and publisher advise against breaking the law and against any action involving hazard to person and/or property. Consult your attorney and physician. Readers are urged to support, authorized research and to work for more intelligent drug laws.

U.S. Library of Congress Cataloging in Publication Data
Bruce Eisner
Ecstasy: The MDMA Story
    Includes Appendix, Bibliography & Index
    1. Psychology. 2. Hallucinogenic drugs. 3. Drug Lawsd
    4. Psychopharmacology. I. Title.

Dedication

To David Banton

Acknowledgements

To *Peter Stafford*, who typeset this book three times and read it at least 17 times;

Alexander Shulgin, who offered generous help and guidance;

Kim and *Christopher Workdelay* for chemical drawings and comment.

Sebastian Orfali, who patiently guided me through the steps from manuscript to volume;

Claudio Naranjo, to whose Gurdjieff I attempt to play Ouspensky;

Irene Ehrlich, for support and encouragement;

Will Penna, for editing and suggestions on the second edition;

and to the many therapists, anonymous pamphlet writers and other brave explorers who first ventured into the territories I have mapped.

The author has made every effort to trace the ownership of all copyright and quoted material presented. In the event of any question arising as to the use of a selection, he offers his apologies for any errors or omissions and will make the necessary corrections in future printings.

Thanks are due to the following:

Ralph Metzner, *Through the Gateway of the Heart*, (© 1985) Four Trees Press

Timothy Leary, Ph.D., "Ecstatic Electricity," *New York Talk*, 1985

Claudio Naranjo, M.D., *The Healing Journey* (© 1973)

Joe Klien, "The New Drug They Call Ecstasy: Is It Too Much to Swallow?" (© 1988) New America Publishing, Inc. Reprinted with the permission of *New York* magazine

Alexander T. Shulgin, Ph.D., "Twenty Years on My Ever-Changing Quest," *Psychedelic Reflections* (© 1983)

George Greer, M.D. and Requa Tolbert, R.N., "MDMA: A New Psychotropic Compound and Its Effects in Humans" (© 1986)

George Greer, M.D. "Using MDMA in Psychotherapy," Big Sur, California, March 10–15, 1985 (© 1986)

"Getting High on Ecstasy," (© *Newsweek*, April 15, 1985)

Peter Stafford, *Psychedelics Encyclopedia* (© 1983, 1992) Ronin Publishing, Inc.

Cynthia Robins, "The Ecstatic Cybernetic Amino Acid Test," *San Francisco Examiner Image*, February 16, 1992

Contents

List of Illustrations

*Young people dancing at a New Year's Eve rave
organized by Toon Town in San Francisco*

Prologue:
Ecstasy Revisited

THE FIRST EDITION of this book, published in February 1989, chronicled the introduction of a powerful psychoactive entity into the world. Nicknamed "Adam" after the primordial being, but known in chemical nomenclature as MDMA, this substance (methylenedioxy-N-methylamphetamine) is the most prominent member of a new generation of mind-altering compounds with family roots in the psychedelics. But unlike its predecessors such as LSD, mescaline, and psilocybin, this chemical has a personality that is precise, predictable—and almost universally pleasant. By the time this book made its appearance, these qualities had already made Adam—or "Ecstasy," as it is now commonly called—a favorite among spiritual seekers, "yuppies," and psychotherapists alike.

Release of the first edition occurred during perhaps the single most turbulent week in the history of the drug war. Headlines focused on the appointment of a new drug "czar" and stories appeared about marijuana dealers who reportedly ate their babies. Fear about Ecstasy and its possible effects on the brain was spreading. Around this time, recreational MDMA use—which had been on a rapid upswing—began to drop drastically and rumors about its dangers abounded.

My first appearances on talk shows and at public lectures reflected these concerns. Frequently, two or three different audience members or call-ins would confront me with the same questions during a single appearance: "Does Ecstasy drain your spinal fluid?" "Is it true that MDMA causes Parkinson's disease?" There was hardly time to talk about Ecstasy's positive uses and benefits.

Four years later, the climate has changed. The curtains have closed on Act One of the Ecstasy drama and have opened on another—with new scenes, fresh characters, and unexpected twists of plot.

Several exciting developments have taken place since the publication of the first edition. The National Institute on Drug Abuse study of recreational use of MDMA, the burgeoning international "rave" or "Acid House" youth movement, and Ecstasy's declining purity on the street are all covered here. Also included are brief overviews of new information regarding MDMA's alleged toxicity and of research efforts recently initiated in Switzerland and the U.S., two subjects given a more detailed treatment in Rick Doblin's Appendix. This Prologue also features an explanation of the synthesis of MDMA by psychopharmacologist Alexander Shulgin, an update of the original edition's "Guide for Users," and closes with further thoughts on the future of this breakthrough compound.

The NIDA Study

The most memorable seminar on the topic of MDMA in which I participated after this book's initial launch took place at Will Nofke's Shared Visions seminar center in Berkeley in 1989. Co-leading the event was Jerome Beck, primary author of the National Institute on Drug Abuse study that served as the basis for his doctoral dissertation at the University of California, Berkeley (Beck's book *In Pursuit of Ecstasy* should be available soon).

Almost every time I summarized an observation from my book, Beck would leap in with confirmations from his study. I don't recall a single point of disagreement between the two of us—even though Beck's research hadn't even commenced when my book was written and was still under way when it was published. I was gratified by the discovery that an independent empirical study had validated many of the ideas put forth in the 1989 edition—which would have been greatly enhanced had Beck's results been available for inclusion at the time of publication. For instance, Beck's topography of the stages of an MDMA trip was congruent with my own—but was documented in his study by reports from a broad cross-section of users spanning diverse social categories.

Titled "Exploring Ecstasy: A Description of MDMA Users," the 253-page study lists Beck as project director; Marsha Rosenbaum, Ph.D. and Patricia A. Morgan, Ph.D. as principle investigators; and Deborah Harlow, Douglas McDonnell, and Lynne Watson as co-authors. Employing a primarily sociological methodology, the NIDA report bases its conclusions on intensive interviews with 100 MDMA users and supplemental interviews with MDMA distributors.

The NIDA study makes fascinating reading in large part because of the authors' use of excerpts from their interview transcripts to illustrate each point. It focuses on the reports of the users themselves to demonstrate that MDMA—because of the unusual social strata in which its use occurs and the extraordinarily low frequency of addictive behavior associated with it—is a truly unique phenomenon among "recreational" drugs.

Despite the many places where this book and the NIDA study dovetail, there are three significant subjects explored by the report that are barely touched upon in these pages: extreme abuse of MDMA; the sociological terrain covered by MDMA use; and the history of its dissemination.

The authors of the NIDA study divide the abuse of MDMA into two types: "binge use" and "frequent use." They point out the striking parallels between abusive consumption of MDMA and syndromes more commonly associated with cocaine and amphetamines. By way of example, I was surprised to receive a letter after the publication of this book from a binge user who reported on his "addictive" use of MDMA. Once he started, he was compelled to continue using the drug for its stimulant properties. Even though he was besieged by mounting side effects, he could not stop for days on end. Beck and I concur that such abuse patterns occur very rarely because of their unpleasant and rapidly felt consequences.

The NIDA study also observed that MDMA users could be grouped according to six social categories: college students, "new age" spiritual seekers, gays, Deadheads, participants in the "Acid House" scene, and the mid-'eighties contingent from Dallas, where use of Ecstasy exploded when large amounts of the compound became available. The report documents similarities and differences in patterns of use among these various social arenas, and concludes that usage was abating in all of these spheres at the time the research was being conducted.

The researchers' examination of distribution channels adds depth to our understanding of the spread of the Ecstasy phenomenon. It confirms this book's account of the massive jump in volume that occurred around 1984 when the primary channels of distribution shifted to the "Texas Group" from the small, quiet cadre of users that had largely monopolized the drug in the late 'seventies and early 'eighties. This transition played a crucial role in the criminalization of MDMA. The NIDA study also offers a discussion of the personal motivations and experiences of distributors drawn from extensive interview material.

The report concludes by stating, "Given how much we really know about MDMA and its users, the obvious recommendation forthcoming from this exploratory study is for more research exploring all facets of this substance." Such research is just now getting underway.

Although a rich exploration of early recreational use of MDMA, the NIDA study, published on September 15, 1989, was somewhat premature in its conclusion that the "Acid House" phenomenon had failed to catch on. In the intervening four years, the "rave" underground has rapidly blossomed into a full-blown youth subculture whose development has been accompanied by a new upsurge in the use of MDMA.

The Rave Scene in England

According to some accounts, the rave scene began in 1987 when working youth from England began to hold parties on the Spanish island of Ibiza. These gatherings featured all-night dancing to a propulsive, trance-inducing, heavily electronic, new form of music. The new sound was dubbed "Acid House" after the "House" music of Chicago, from which it borrowed the practice of "acid burn"—using snippets or "samples" of previously recorded music to build a throbbing sonic collage. While the "acid" in "Acid House" originally bore no reference to LSD, the psychedelic was often used to fuel a night of dancing 'til dawn.

Later, the drug of choice became MDMA, and the celebrations spread to England, where raves—as Acid House parties then came to be known—became a huge phenomenon. Perhaps most remarkable about the early English gatherings was the camaraderie evident among members of diverse ethnic, social, and economic groups—no doubt at least partially stimulated by the presence of empathogens. The true import of this breakdown of cultural barriers can only be understood in the context of the relatively rigid stratification of traditional British society.

With large numbers of young people taking illegal drugs, it wasn't long before Parliament had passed a number of increasingly harsh laws against MDMA and against raves themselves. To avoid police harassment, raves moved from traditional nightclub venues to less predictable locations such as empty warehouses and open fields along the "Orbital," the highway encircling London. In *X Magazine*, Christian Barthodsson reports:

Ardent dancers come flocking from all the surrounding cities, often up to 30,000 dedicated ravers. To make it a little bit harder for the police to raid, the place where the party is held is kept secret until the very last moment. Then it's up to the raver to find out where it is, and the standard way is to dig your way though a certain number of phone "hotlines" that give you the needed information. However, the bigger the raves are, the easier it is to track them down. According to legend, James Hamilton once drove around London late at night headed for Heathrow Airport, when he saw rotating floodlights, and heard a distant rumble. Convinced that it was the airport, he drove along the road only to suddenly find himself in the middle of an ongoing rave . . .

Since the raves began, the increase in the use of Ecstasy in the U.K. has continued—albeit along a rather twisted path. In January of 1992, my publisher forwarded to me the following letter from England:

I am not a doctor or anything, just a curious 20 year old, who got involved with MDMA back in July last year. I decided to find out about the drug and what it was doing to me after I read a book called *The Vitamin Bible* by Earl Mindell that basically showed me that if you are taking drugs, you need to be taking vitamin and mineral supplements as well (which you rightly pointed out in your book).

Basically I am telling you this, as I greatly need your help. There is widespread use of Ecstasy in this country among the young (some users as young as 14). And abuse of the drug is growing all the time. While I don't expect any of them to stop (I'm not into preaching), I do believe they ought to know the score. As you must know there are now lots of different types of Ecstasy tabs with names like White Doves (mostly MDMA), and Triple X's (to put it frankly, full of crap). Some of them don't have any MDMA, and many have cocaine, smack, and concentrated caffeine (the last one is a guess) so nowadays taking Ecstasy is like playing Russian roulette with your life. Already youngsters have died (obviously from something put in the drug or from some negative synergy). I can honestly say I don't think that would have happened if MDMA was legal and I think your argument on that is completely right.

       Yours Hopefully,

       Claire Henderson

After receiving the letter, I corresponded with Claire, who supplied me with articles from the U.K. press. Gradually what was happening in England came into focus. The clippings she has sent remind me strongly of the stories that emerged about LSD in the 'sixties in the U.S. Although over one-half million people are said to take their "tablet" on any given weekend, there have been a few deaths at raves in England. The press has used these incidents to condemn both raves and MDMA use.

When Claire first wrote to me, the reasons for these deaths were not known. Medical authorities have now determined that these deaths are related to heatstroke caused by a combination of high temperatures in rave clubs, continuous dancing, and dehydration. It seems that some rave promoters in England turn off the water in bathrooms and at drinking fountains in order to sell more drinks. Young ravers, their financial resources tapped by increasingly expensive admission prices and therefore unable to afford equally over-priced drinks, have suffered the consequence of the exploitation by a greedy few of a subculture which, as British musician-producer Brian Eno has noted, was originally characterized by a refreshing lack of cynicism.

To put the English situation in perspective, it has been estimated that the average individual in England is 10 times more likely to die in a car accident, and for those who play soccer 33 times more likely to die on the soccer field, than an individual who uses Ecstasy is likely to die from taking the drug. While there have been some deaths directly attributed to this compound, the victims who have allegedly taken MDMA may well have ingested substitutes or combinations of drugs. With thousands of people dying every year due to tobacco- and alcohol-related causes, Ecstasy turns out to be safe by comparison.

Raves in the U.S.

With the pressures from English authorities growing ever greater, some of the most idealistic rave promoters and DJs traveled to California. In early 1991, one of the first large U.S. raves was held by a group called Toontown in San Francisco. Toontown ballooned in size to gatherings in excess of 7,000 people and sparked dozens of other events. On any given weekend night, there may be as many as a dozen raves occurring simultaneously in San Francisco and Los Angeles. Cynthia Robins offers this account of one such event in the February 16, 1992, issue of the *San Francisco Examiner Image* magazine:

By five minutes after midnight, New Year's Eve, the music has been going for three hours. But the party is just starting to build. By 2 A.M., 6000 bodies are shoehorned into a cavernous space below San Francisco's Fashion Center, buffeted, embraced, and engulfed by sound and lights caroming off the concrete walls, floors and ceilings.

Like the sorcerer's apprentice in *Fantasia*, the DJ directs the flow of energy with controlled waves of sound. Prancing like a high priest in front of dual turntables and a control panel whose decibel levels constantly violate the red line, he weaves a seamless skein, a solid blanket of sound. He is an electronic shaman. No one escapes his spell. Relentless, the music is almost all bass—a *boom* da *boom* da *boom* da *boom* da *boom* da *boom* cranked to marrow-boiling levels, plunging ahead at fetal heartbeat cadence. An incessant 118–126 beats per minute tickled incidentally by featureless vocals and snatches of sampled riffs and melody. The beat soaks your shoes, enters your feet like a tidal surge and then charges up your body to attack your groin. If you have one ounce of rhythm, you gotta dance. If you don't, you gotta leave.

The lights synch with the sound—pulsing, whipping, whirling. Video screens televise live crowd shots overlaid with psychedelic fractal patterns. Laser-green light rays explode on the floor like shattered snakes. Smoke machines spew faux fog through which Intellebeam spots direct shards of color and white light, fragmenting on bodies, walls and ceilings like an ak-ak barrage in Baghdad.

The total sensory environment wraps the dancers in a techno-cocoon. It is disco inferno, psychedelic apocalypse.

All around you are heaving bodies. Belles in leather and lace. Beaux in jimmy-mams and exaggerated Dr. Seuss Cat-in-the-Hats. Men in garter belts. Women stripped down to jeans and bras. Drag queens. Gender benders. Hoary-headed hipsters. The straight, the gay, the old, the young. Mostly young. A phantasmagoria hurled from the bar scene in *Star Wars*.

Their arms stretch heavenward. Eyes roll back, looking not at the fusillade of imagery, but inward. They dance like lone wolves, occasionally entering another intimate space, rubbing bodies, making connections, clocking new perso-nae—but only in an incidental way. This is not the brittle, predatory hip-club-cruise scene. Nobody's exchanging numbers. The air is charged with sexual energy, but nobody's thinking about getting laid. Not while the dance is so in-toxicating. A trance dance of random patterns and thrashing extremities and faces bathed in sweat and bliss—blank, glazed, open, innocent. Is it rapture? Or is it the drugs?

Certainly it must be a little of both. Like the English Acid House scene before it, the U.S. rave culture features the use of psychedelics and Ecstasy as an integral element. This is one of the many simi-larities between 'nineties' raves and the love-ins, be-ins, and Acid Tests of the 'sixties. But the ravers are trying to do things differ-ently—most importantly through their embrace of technology.

Toontown organizer Mark Heley describes this new interface between psychedelia and high technology with the word "techno-shamanism." In "One World One Party" by Evelyn McDonnell in the January 29, 1992 *S F Weekly*, he elaborates:

There's something that we're moving toward that's be-yond time . . . . We're connecting contemporary society with the mythic roots of humanity. Shamanism is beyond time. It's a primal spirit. And technology is the interface between what exists now and what is coming into existence.

The tribal cultures that gave birth to shamanism are known for holding rites of passage for young people. I believe that raves can best be viewed as contemporary mutations of these traditional initiations, which played a vital role in the psychic transition from youth to adulthood. It is important for the young to gather together, to dance their dances, to sing their chants, to remain awake through the night, to take their drugs and have their visions—activities that were all important components of the ancient rites. And until now, American society has provided no context for such ceremonies.

However, using Ecstasy *exclusively* at raves—while certainly a fascinating and useful experience—is to forego unique opportunities that can only be provided by more intimate environments. The deep insights and interpersonal connections described in this book tend to occur in small groups or in conditions of solitude, and are difficult to achieve in a crowd setting. Those who have used it only at raves perhaps cannot imagine the true potential of MDMA.

Ravers in the United States, like their British brothers and sisters, are beginning to complain of a decline in the rave scene. As is inevitable with any youth phenomena, commercialism is setting in; rave fashions are now appearing at Macy's. And with time, some raves are beginning to look less like avant-garde happenings and more like high-school parties.

This pattern parallels the evolution of the counterculture of the 'sixties. But as the rave subculture grows into a more mainstream youth movement, it will certainly gain impact upon the media and the values and visions of the youth of America. There are many who see this new culture as providing a bridge into the next millennium. Dan Mapes, founder of Digital Media (a multimedia production company in Santa Cruz, California that produces visuals for raves as well as psychedelic videotapes), told Cynthia Robins:

> There are evolved kids, and it's important to tune into that. This is where art and technology and evolution are all linked. We evolve through our art and technology.

> We're laying the foundation for the 21st-century society and things like raves are an expression of it. Think about New Year's Eve [the Toontown rave described by Robins above]—7,200 people and no fights. That's incredible. There's a lot of people who were harmonious with

each other. And for them, it's an expression of living in the world they want to live in—a microcosm of a possible future world. For a moment in time, hang out with a large number of people and you're grooving with them. That's very evolutionary. That's very healing."

Decline in Purity

Claire Henderson's comments about the misrepresentation and questionable purity of underground MDMA are accurate. When a drug becomes illegal, the material available to those who wish to use it inevitably suffers a decline in quality. Manufacture of the drug is taken over, at least to some extent, by people more concerned with profit than the more idealistic early distributors, who are driven from their mission by draconian laws. This trend was predicted in the first edition of my book and came to pass as soon as MDMA was scheduled. Add the increasing demand for the drug resulting from the rave scene and the result: Availability and purity of MDMA has taken a turn for the worse.

With the distribution of certain precursor chemicals now monitored by the Drug Enforcement Agency, producing real MDMA entails greater risks for chemists using standard routes of synthesis. Much of what has been seen on the streets in the U.S. is amphetamine, or amphetamine combined with other drugs. In England, matters are much worse, with reliable reports that much of what is represented as Ecstasy is actually ketamine (an anesthetic with hallucinogenic properties) or sometimes just over-the-counter medicine. Now that street-drug analysis is unavailable in this country, the motto *caveat emptor*, "may the buyer beware," is the rule of the day. With only a white powder, a tablet, or a capsule in front of you, there is no reliable way of knowing what you have. Two questions to ask yourself: "Have my sources taken this product themselves?" "Have my sources ever taken real MDMA so they can accurately evaluate what they have given me?"

This Is Not Spinal Tap...
Questions about MDMA Neurotoxicity

Of more concern to many people than the question of purity is the possible neurotoxicity of MDMA. Let's take a look at some of the rumors and then consider the question directly.

As I mentioned previously, one question I hear repeatedly is, "Does Ecstasy tap your spinal fluid?" This odd rumor has circulated since the early 'eighties, probably as a result both of complaints about backaches or neck aches after a long evening of Ecstasy and of confusion generated by the fact that researchers have tapped spinal fluid in order to assess MDMA's effects on levels of serotonin, a chemical that transmits nerve impulses between brain cells.

The question of MDMA's neurotoxicity was first raised in 1985, when George Ricaurte and Charles Schuster at the University of Chicago performed an experiment in which rats were administered intravenously with the equivalent of ten times the human dose of MDA, a compound structurally similar to MDMA, at four-hour intervals for two days. Changes were noted in the terminals where serotonin interfaces with brain cells. Researchers quickly brought this effect to the attention of the Drug Enforcement Administration, which used it as a pretext for placing MDMA on the Schedule I list. After the ban, the experiment was repeated with MDMA and showed similar results.

Later, Ricaurte and, in a separate study, Dr. Stephen Peroutka of Stanford University, both administered spinal taps to determine if MDMA use causes a decrease in serotonin levels in humans. Peroutka's study showed no difference between MDMA users and the control groups. Ricaurte's experiment showed lowered serotonin in the MDMA group, but the study was criticized because the control group consisted of people suffering from back pain, a factor that might itself have some bearing on serotonin levels. This study is now being repeated with improved methodology. But so far, no solid conclusions can be drawn from spinal-tap studies.

Researchers ran a humorous ad in various alternative newspapers in an effort to find subjects for their spinal-tap studies. It bore the headline "This Is Spinal Tap." An unfortunate consequence was the amplification of rumors already in circulation that MDMA "taps your spinal fluid" or "drains your spinal fluid." In reality it does neither.

Another frequent question: "Does MDMA cause Parkinson's disease?"

Again, the answer is a resounding "No." This rumor was caused by a chain of misunderstandings. First, Ecstasy is often mislabeled a "designer drug." Designer drugs are, by definition, new compounds designed by chemists to circumvent the drug laws. There was no such intention behind the original synthesis of MDMA, which occurred in Germany in 1914.

In the late 'seventies, a designer drug called Fentanyl or "China White" was developed as a legal substitute for heroin. A substance known as MPTP, a by-product of the synthetic process, found its way into some batches of China White. In at least one case, MPTP was linked to a Parkinson's-like syndrome. A false connection was made with MDMA, not a true designer drug, and MPTP, a completely different chemical.

What then is the truth about MDMA's alleged neurotoxicity? There are no definitive answers; but, as of this writing, it appears increasingly likely that the neurotoxicity issue represents the U.S. government's attempt to justify its policy toward MDMA in a manner reminiscent of the completely unfounded "Chromosome Scare" surrounding LSD in the 'sixties.

First, it might be noted that the same experiment that Schuster and Ricaurte did with MDMA and MDA—giving huge and frequent doses to rats—was also performed with fenfluramine, used in treating eating disorders. Fenfluramine shows up as three times more "neurotoxic" on these tests. Fenfluramine is given to patients every day and has been prescribed by doctors for over 25 years. Adverse effects have not been observed from its use, and people who took it quite frequently many years ago still exhibit no brain damage or other problems. Fenfluramine is still prescribed even though MDMA was quickly banned; and modifications of fenfluramine are currently going through FDA's approval process without regard to any alleged "neurotoxicity."

Another important point is that lowered serotonin levels produce no known behavioral changes in humans. One study showed a very slight change in performances of rats on one of many tests given to them after huge and repeated doses of MDMA produced dramatic changes in serotonin levels. More important is a recently published study by George Ricaurte, in which normal human doses were administered to primates every two weeks for four months, resulting in no evidence of neurotoxicity.

With millions of people having taken MDMA over a 20-year period, some more than several hundred times, there has never been a confirmed case of MDMA brain damage. Not as of this writing.

MDMA Guide Update

There are a few guidelines followed by knowledgeable users in planning an MDMA experience. Some of these are mentioned in the "Guide to Users" but are repeated here for emphasis.

Smart users drink plenty of fluids and watch their level of exertion. If they are dancing, they take frequent rest breaks and make sure the fluids they drink are cool. They avoid extreme temperature changes; saunas or sweatlodges on cold days may be inadvisable. They make sure to get plenty of sleep both the night before as well as after the trip. (Prescription tranquilizers such as Valium or Xanax are used to help to induce sleep by relieving muscle tension and post-MDMA stimulation—but these drugs can be highly addictive.) When they wake up, they eat a healthy meal. Many instances of "burn-out" may simply be the result of prolonged lack of food intake.

Neurotoxicity research has not provided a guarantee of safety. Many users take a capsule of the prescription anti-depressant Prozac within four hours after ingesting Ecstasy. Prozac is reported to block the process suspected to be responsible for MDMA's "neurotoxic" effects.

San Diego researcher Leonard Enos reports that the use of anti-oxidants for several days before and after the ingestion of MDMA can help to alleviate post-MDMA fatigue and lowering of mood. He recommends Superoxidase Demutase by Kal or Oxi-Quenchers, a Twinlabs product.

New anecdotal evidence indicates that the use of calcium-magnesium supplements as suggested in the "Guide to Users" may not be particularly effective.

The MDMA experience is a two-day process. Smart users plan on taking the second day to rest, reflect, and integrate the experience. They don't, as P. J. O'Rourke put it, "Turn on, tune in and go to work late on Monday."

For those curious about the "shelf life" of MDMA, here is a report sent over the sfraves UseNet Group by Howard Berkey:

Safrole (very similar in structure to MDMA) decomposes under prolonged exposure to UV radiation (e.g., sunlight). This is true of many organic chemicals although MDMA should be more stable in this respect than safrole (with the methylamine group replacing the allyl group's double bond). Unless you've been keeping it in the dark and

cold (like in the freezer) it's probably (a) decomposed somewhat and (b) absorbed things (water, etc.) from the air. My
advice would be to trash MDMA that's two years old.

However, reports from people who have stored the material for
long periods of time indicate that it can remain remarkably fresh.

Many people report diminished effects with repeated use of Ecstasy. Less—not more—is reportedly better, in terms of both dosage and frequency of use.

Revival of Therapeutic Research

With the conclusion of the Last Act of our drama, the curtain
closed abruptly on research into MDMA's potential as a therapeutic agent as well as on other avenues of inquiry involving administering MDMA to humans.

With the banning of MDMA in 1985 it appeared as if it would be
a very long time before anyone would ever again take the drug
legally in the United States. Researchers had exhausted their efforts
to overturn the DEA's placement of MDMA in Schedule I—the
same status assigned to heroin.

Nevertheless, the first rays of light have recently begun to shine
forth. In Switzerland, research into the therapeutic use of MDMA
is currently underway, while in the U.S. the Food and Drug Administration has approved a project using human subjects.

Albert Hofmann, former research chemist at Sandoz Pharmaceutical Company in Basel, Switzerland and discoverer of many
important compounds including LSD, disclosed some exciting news
for the psychedelic community during a 1988 visit to Los Angeles.
Speaking to the Los Angeles St. James' Club, Hofmann announced
that a special exemption to the Swiss narcotic laws had been enacted,
allowing specially trained physicians to prescribe LSD, MDMA,
and other psychoactive compounds. The ban that had existed for
more than two decades on psychedelic research had been lifted.

Since that time, five Swiss physicians have been granted permits
to prescribe psychedelics, and many more have been trained and
are expected to receive permits in the near future. MDMA and
other mind changers are administered to patients in the course of
therapy, usually in group settings. In *MAPS Newsletter*, Vol. III,
No. 3, project administrator Samuel Widmer, M.D., reports:

In our work with MDMA in psychotherapy so far, we
have not observed any negative effects, either of a psychological or physical kind. The tremendous usefulness in
healing severe psychological disturbances outweighs the
occasional stress to the organism through these substances.
Most importantly, no addictions to MDMA have been observed after the use of MDMA. To the contrary, we have
been able to confirm what had already been documented by
others, that other addictions (alcohol, medical drugs, heroin,
etc.) were greatly reduced by MDMA-supported therapy
and even led to significant reduction of these addictions in
patients. . . .

The suspicion of possible toxicity to the nervous system, which had been considered a possible side effect of
MDMA, was not substantiated by our therapeutic dosage
of this substance. This finding is confirmed by recent scientific research, not yet published, by George Ricaurte, USA:
Following treatment of primates with therapeutic dosages,
no damaging effects to the nervous system were observed.

In our opinion, psychoactive drugs such as MDMA,
LSD, and others that have proven therapeutic application,
have been erroneously placed on the list of Schedule I. We
are working to correct this mistake on the international
level, and even though in Switzerland it is possible under
current law to obtain exemption permits, these procedures
could be greatly simplified. In our opinion, psychoactive
substances such as MDMA do not belong to the category
of narcotics, since no narcotic effect is in evidence, but
rather, on the contrary, facilitate the laying bare of emotional structures. They can thus help in bringing clarity
and insight into unconscious mechanisms, a realm hardly
reached by conventional methods. They have been of such
great help in our psychotherapeutic work that we see tremendous loss if these substances are not made available on
a broader scale.

The research environment for MDMA and other psychedelics has
begun to open up. As Sarah Pekkanen of States News Service
reported on July 27, 1992:

Faced with evidence that some illicit hallucinogenic drugs may benefit certain patients, the federal government is on the verge of lifting its near-ban on LSD and Ecstasy for therapeutic purposes.

The push to reevaluate the government's policy has come from researchers who concluded that under carefully controlled conditions, hallucinogens have been shown to benefit the terminally ill, alcoholics, and some psychiatric patients.

This change of affairs came to pass through meetings in Washington coordinated among two government agencies. It represents a triumph for the steadfast efforts of Rick Doblin, founder of the Multidisciplinary Association for Psychedelic Studies (MAPS), who has worked for years to facilitate and fund research with psychedelics (see Doblin's new Appendix for this edition for further details on these events as well as other recent progress in MDMA research).

First, NIDA convened a technical review on "hallucinogens," its first in fourteen years. On July 13 and 14, 1992, 20 scientists met and discussed the status of psychedelic research. The body concluded that there were significant scientific benefits to resuming human research with psychedelics.

Then on July 15, the FDA's Drug Abuse Advisory Committee met to discuss the general policies with regard to "hallucinogenic" research and to consider a research protocol for use of MDMA with human subjects. The committee decided that research into the medical uses of MDMA and other hallucinogens warranted the risks to subjects and society of conducting such research. It also ruled that the research be held up to the same rigorous standards for safety and efficacy that are applied to all drugs reviewed by the FDA for medical research. In other words, research was approved in principle, but it would not be easy to conduct.

In a separate decision, the Advisory Committee provided guidelines for the first sanctioned human study with MDMA. The principal investigator would be Charles Grob, M.D. of the University of California at Irvine. Grob was recently granted FDA approval for the two-part project, involving both "normal" human volunteers from the medical profession and terminal cancer patients. Only two more government agencies must clear the project before it proceeds.

The first part of the study would serve to train therapists as well as to assess the neurotoxicity risk in humans for the first time. The second part of the study would examine the impact of the MDMA experience on the mental perspectives of individuals waiting to die. Earlier studies with terminal patients using "psychedelic therapy" with LSD have demonstrated very positive effects on attitudes toward death and dying.

The Future

At the 1992 International Transpersonal Conference in Prague, Czechoslovakia, Alexander Shulgin Ph.D., psychopharmacologist and author of *PIHKAL* (a fictionalized account of his discovery of scores of new mind-changing compounds), suggested that MDMA represents the beginning of a revolution in our understanding of biochemistry and the mind. As mentioned at the beginning of this Prologue, MDMA signifies a quantum leap in the specificity of mind-changing compounds. While drugs like LSD and mescaline amplify and alter almost every aspect of mental functioning, MDMA's effects tend to focus on empathy and self-esteem.

Shulgin suggested that in the future, new compounds would inevitably be invented, "teased out of other drugs such as MDMA," that would have a higher degree of specificity for triggering human emotions such as fear of death, awareness and suppression of anger, and the feelings of guilt. If such materials are developed in the future, human beings may be able to use them to alter and improve their own consciousness and intelligence in precise and beneficial ways that we cannot yet even begin to imagine.

A collage of handbills from the early 1990's publicizing raves

Foreword

In 1984, THE U.S. DRUG ENFORCEMENT ADMINISTRATION initiated a process that ended in the classification of MDMA as a Schedule I drug, equivalent to narcotics and regarded as having no medical use. Since that time, a number of physicians, researchers, and psychotherapists have fought this classification through legal means, insisting that MDMA can make unique and valuable psychotherapeutic contributions. Although the outcome is still unsettled, it is obvious that the proponents of MDMA are fighting an uphill battle.

Even though the psychotherapeutic use of prescription mood-changing and behavior-modifying drugs permeates American society, and even though the sale of these drugs is a multimillion dollar business, there has been virtually no support for MDMA by either psychiatric organizations or by pharmaceutical companies. I would propose several reasons for this state of affairs.

In the first place, MDMA is not only capable of changing one's mood and modifying one's behavior; it can alter one's way of thinking as well. American psychiatry has found it easier to use mood-changing and behavior-modifying drugs than to utilize mind-altering substances. A client's mood usually can be calmed or stimulated through medication, and a client's behavior can be modified in fairly direct ways. Psychiatrists are pleased when a client's mood swings can be stabilized and when a client's erratic behavior can be brought under control. They admit that some individuals will show paradoxical reactions to medication, but will insist in the predictability of drugs' general outcomes.

On the other hand, most psychiatrists find it difficult to justify using substances that can produce novel ways of conceiving reality, and unusual ways of being in the world. They will use drugs that inhibit hallucinations, block disordered thought patterns, or halt repetitive verbalizations. But such mind-altering drugs as MDMA, LSD, and psilocybin have the reputation of evoking unconventional thought; as a result, it is thought justifiable to dismiss them as more trouble than they are worth.

Secondly, MDMA can intensify clients' thoughts and feelings regarding their therapist. Transference phenomena can magnify during an MDMA session and a client's relationship with his or her therapist can intensify profoundly. The ordinary problems of transference, counter-transference, and projection produce so many complications in psychotherapy that few practitioners would want to risk augmenting this predicament.

Third, the use of MDMA violates the structure of psychoanalytically oriented psychotherapy, which is geared toward a 50-minute hour, not the three- or four-hour session that the proper use of MDMA demands. These lengthy sessions are often justified with the claim that psychotherapy is accelerated as a result of MDMA. But psychiatrists usually are suspicious of any modality that claims to expedite psychotherapy in the absence of a slow unraveling of a client's defenses. Various humanistic and transpersonal approaches to psychotherapy could make allowance for the demands of MDMA, but neither orientation has permeated the highest levels of the psychiatric establishment and their influence in legal and governmental circles is negligible.

Opposition to MDMA in psychotherapy is not limited to psychiatrists. Most of those psychologists who practice behavior modification are wary of MDMA not only because of the time factor but because it admits to the possibility of quick "insights" and "breakthroughs," not the step-by-step learning and relearning that characterizes most behavioral approaches. In addition, when a psychotherapist is trained to use MDMA, part of one's apprenticeship involves taking the drug oneself. This first-hand experience is not needed before a psychologist uses behavioral techniques or before a psychiatrist employs stimulant or depressant drugs, or the other medications that are frequently employed in psychiatry. In fact, the ecstatic effects of MDMA are looked upon as "pathological" or "dysfunctional" by many psychotherapists. If someone suggests that they try MDMA themselves, they might retort that this would be tantamount to ingesting poison to learn about toxic psychoses.

Finally, psychotherapists who use MDMA often have abandoned the medical model that permeates most of contemporary psychiatry. The goal of these divergent therapists is sometimes described as facilitating the development of "fully functioning human beings" and in going "beyond adjustment" in the enhancement of "human capacities" and the "human potential." These terms are suspect to a psychiatrist trained to look at his or her clients from the model of disease, or a psychologist whose education has emphasized faulty learning as the cause of a client's maladaptive behavior.

As a result of these factors, very few psychotherapists have been interested in the therapeutic use of MDMA. As a result, pharmaceutical companies have seen no profit margin in its development, and have lacked the motivation to finance investigations into the drug's effectiveness. It is possible that Bruce Eisner's book will play a role in dispelling misconceptions about MDMA. The book is a splendid summary of the drug's history, usage, and effects. There is little likelihood that MDMA will become a major psychotherapeutic tool in the near future. However, the readers of this book may conclude that is deserves a chance to demonstrate its worth in the hands of those therapists whose sensitivity, training, and expertise have enabled them to use it to alleviate the distress of those clients who come to them seeking to be relieved from their suffering.

—Stanley Krippner, Ph.D.

Introduction

IN YOUR HANDS you hold the first book that treats the issues raised by MDMA (aka "Adam," "Ecstasy," "XTC") in a comprehensive way. MDMA is, of course, the empathy-enhancing compound that came to immense public attention in the 1980s, and then rode the crest of a fifth major wave washing psychedelia over a small, significant part of humanity.

Every mind-affecting molecule has effects unique to itself. The properties of MDMA were appropriate in these circumstances because it introduced the mass use of, and access to, a nonthreatening empathy-generating mechanism. Bruce Eisner's account places an associated intellectual fermentation in wide-ranging context, based upon first-hand acquaintance and diligent study.

❉❉❉

The *first* of the preceding waves of psychedelic enthusiasm extends all the way from prehistoric times up until the end of the 19th century, during which members of *all* societies (except for Eskimos, most of whom had no direct plant access, and also, possibly, some Polynesians) stumbled upon and ritualized use of selective vegetative matter . . . that enlarged the scope of the mind in ways that appeared both healing and inspirational.

A *second* large psychedelic wave rolled in around the start of the 20th century, once German pharmacologists isolated and then reproduced mescaline—the first synthetic of a mind-changing sort.

A *third* psychedelic wave was kicked off by Albert Hofmann's discovery of LSD's psychoactivity in 1943—a catalyzing event of such magnitude that by the late 1960s immersion in psychedelia got noticed by 'most everyone.

After that immense inundation, the 1970s saw an ebbing—which only petered out as mushrooms (containing psilocybin and psilocin) encouraged another flush of enthusiasm for psychedelia. This *fourth* incursion spread due to these mushrooms' gentleness, "naturalness," wide distribution and a leap in home production (so that those serious didn't have to travel to Mexico, as many people had supposed, but could actually grow a major psychedelic in the basement).

Such a quick rundown on a psychedelic past brings us to the present subject—MDMA's role in ushering in a *fifth* wave of fascination with these mind-changers. Located along with several hundred molecules that could be placed in a "psychedelic" category, this one stands out as unusually benign—a substance that offers users the possibility of a contrived "heart opening," and that also, as one therapist describes it, makes clients "unbelievably honest"!

* * *

As with fundamental innovations, arrival of a critical mass of people having interest in and access to MDMA framed many old questions in a new context. It also raised matters that had not come to the fore. Here I will attempt to group just over a dozen such central questions, and indicate pages in this book where Eisner lays out relevant historical–anecdotal evidence well-documented by the end of the 1980s. For starters, let's take up four prompting concerns:

1. What are the principal characteristics of MDMA experience?
2. How "natural" is MDMA?
3. Is it "psychedelic"?
4. How about "consistency" of the experience, and its overall "reliability"?

1. *MDMA's chief characteristics.* MDMA "strengthens" the ego, however you define that, as does an amphetamine, but not in a cold, strong-armed way. It softens defensiveness and gently removes obstacles to communication, so one speaks directly from the heart. Often to their surprise, users find they say what they really feel, without fear of being hurt by their honesty.

MDMA also removes walls of isolation between individuals so that even strangers speak to each other in familiar, intimate ways.

Insight and affinity-enhancing qualities evoked momentarily can be applied either to relationships and/or other matters of personal concern. These changes are subtle, but are recognized as significant by a majority of experiencers.

The de-stressing aspect is experienced mentally as well as physically; in certain instances, this can be dramatic. For most people, MDMA produces the sense of relaxation felt after several days of vacation. While the experience itself lasts only about four to six hours, an "afterglow" may linger for a few days, a week, a month, or possibly up to a whole lifetime (see pages 1–4, 6, 10, 33–34, 38–39, 42, 46–47, 51, 58, 70–71, 75).

2. *Natural substances led the way.* MDMA is a "semi-synthetic," a molecule similar to those found in nutmeg, mace, crocus, and dill, as well as the over-the-counter cold remedy Sudafed. So far we don't know of this molecule's existence in the realms of fauna and flora, but it is evident that most brains contain regions quite sensitive to it. Nutmeg and some of the others have histories as mind-alterants, but the experiences they catalyze have usually been accompanied by rather unpleasant physical effects.

Nutmeg, for instance, is sometimes described as a psychedelic of "last resort," since it has been used by prisoners and sailors when no other mind-changer has been available. Chemical manipulation—in this case, the N-methylation of an amine addition—heightens desirable aspects sought from the natural substances, while reducing such physical side effects as dryness of mouth and aching joints.

Of course, in a wider sense, everything that exists—even things produced in a laboratory—are "natural," arguably "nonartificial" (see pp. 138–139, 142–143).

3. *Is MDMA a "psychedelic"?* This special category of psychoactive substances, introduced to us by mescaline, LSD and psilocybin mushrooms—affects thinking and feeling in half a dozen major ways. One of these, the visual, is very prominent in the classic literature, and has been emphasized by the media—although most users don't think of it as the essence of the experience. In the case of MDMA, effects manifested in the visual sphere are minimal except when large amounts are taken. Thus, the MDMA experience is most often thought of as distinct from that usually accessed by "psychedelics."

Yet ways of interacting with the environment and other people are noticeably similar to many of those experienced after mediation of earlier psychedelics. In MDMA is represented another pole of the psychedelic realm, where affinity and focusing are heightened in a gentler but still powerful way.

With classic psychedelics, transformations frequently are both extreme and, for the most part, internalized, somewhat like that terrible, wonderful night during which Ebenezer Scrooge was visited by Ghosts of the Past, Present and Future, and awoke so grateful to be alive that afterwards he was a shockingly transformed individual. MDMA seems to offer a benign route to many similar consequences as are produced by the more well-known psychedelic catalysts (see pp. 3–4).

4. *A high "reliability."* Even without prompting as to effects, at least 90% of those who try MDMA experience consequences—a "heart opening," and a lessening of stress and defensiveness—that cause this compound to be of great fascination to many. This remarkable inclusiveness can, as multiple experience shows, be raised further by slight, as well as easy, environmental manipulation.

A very small group of first-time MDMA users—considerably fewer than occurs with other psychedelics—still feel somewhat ill at ease when given this "drug" (sacrament, medicine, whatever you want to call it), perceiving only the drawbacks often associated with amphetamines or cocaine, such as chill, jaw clenching or an amorphous general physical discomfort (see pp. 76, 96).

5. Is MDMA dangerous?
6. What about brain damage?
7. How about possibilities of addiction and/or abuse?

5. *Dangers.* Range between an effective dose and an overdose is much smaller in regard to MDMA than with most other psychedelics. Thus, care taken in measurement of dosage is an important consideration. Eisner correctly emphasizes that no one should ever take more than a quarter gram (250 mg.) at a time. (It should also be pointed out that although larger amounts have been used for various reasons, no death attributable to MDMA ingestion has thus far [at the time of this book's first edition] been credibly documented.)

Effects in physical respects are generally mild. The main one observable is that MDMA causes a slight rise in blood pressure (for up to about an hour and a half). Little else is of any serious consequence for those in reasonable health.

Nonetheless, in interest of safety, no one should take this substance if suffering from heart disease, high blood pressure, or epilepsy, or if taking MAO inhibitors, or if pregnant (see pp. 1, 9–10, 19–25, 113–114, 118–119, 124, 156–158).

6. Brain studies. Reports in *Science* magazine and *The Journal of the American Medical Association* have raised the spooky fear that MDMA causes neurotoxicity. As might be expected, airing of this possibility—as hedged and remote as had been suggested in original presentations—was highly trumpeted in the press.

The studies, however, have been based on immense amounts of MDMA given repeatedly to laboratory animals, and have been accompanied by the qualification that the results may not apply to ordinary human usage. Over the last two years, more careful studies indicate, preliminarily, that there seems no such risk at the human dose level, and that no negative behavioral or functional effects are as yet associated with MDMA.

Extensive animal testing as well as examination of human spinal fluid of MDMA users is currently taking place (see pp. 19–21, and Appendix II).

7. What about addiction, or other potentials for abuse? MDMA is difficult to overuse because effects diminish rapidly if taken repeatedly over any short space of time. Under such circumstances, the resulting experience also tends to enhance undesirable qualities that often accompany abuse of amphetamines or cocaine. Thus, the route of using excessive MDMA appeals to very few.

Desirable MDMA experiences just simply cannot be achieved repeatedly without spacing out use. An interval of four days is minimally necessary to do this—which, apparently, involves integration of the previous experience(s). For those with an abusive personality, MDMA would not thus likely be a "drug of choice." Its characteristics so used are quite unrewarding (see pp. 15, 18–19, 22, 26, 121).

8. What is good MDMA "set" and "setting"?

9. Is MDMA synergistic with other substances and practices?

10. How can desirable qualities be enhanced, and encouraged to linger?

8. Optimal conditions. MDMA is best taken in a comfortable, familiar setting, free of distractions and interruptions, in the presence of a trusted friend or friends—or, as still frequently happens, in a relaxed therapeutic situation.

Since this compound encourages an extraordinary honesty with little defensiveness, a session should not be casual—and those at hand should not include persons who possibly would take advantage of exposed vulnerabilities sometime later on. Attention beforehand should especially be paid to how intentions and heightened sensitivities might affect a partner or some other significant loved ones.

Music to be played during this "contrived" interval, if chosen at all, should be instrumental, "uplifting," choral or one's personal favorites. In general, "heavy metal," "heavy rock" and "heavy" classical music are best avoided, as these are dissonant with the mood that MDMA typically evokes.

MDMA is best taken on an empty stomach, since food tends to reduce its effects. Eating during the experience might also be kept to a minimum for the same reason, and because some have suggested that a possible "anesthetization" could maybe lead to choking. Most users won't be inclined to eat anyway, although they might desire fruit juices and a small amount of simple foods. Plenty of water should be at hand to counter possible dehydration.

As for recalling thoughts and interactions that might be of value later, a recorder or various writing instruments could be provided for in advance (and tested that they are operational) (see pp. 96–99, 102, 104–108, 110–112).

9. Synergies. MDMA is synergistic with most psychedelics. Effects are diminished, however, by considerable amounts of alcohol or marijuana. It may be dangerous taken together with cocaine. A glass of wine or a few tokes of grass, on the other hand, may help when "coming down," to take the "edge" off—especially for those sensitive to amphetamine-like compounds.

When used with other psychedelics, MDMA is frequently taken first and in a lessened dosage, so as to optimize a good mind-set. Because the sum is considerably greater than individual parts when things interact synergistically, dosages for each compound should be less than when used normally.

Much experience shows that MDMA also intensifies almost any exploration of spiritual disciplines or techniques, such as meditation and yoga. Again, when used with a partner, trust usually has to be established, given that MDMA frequently points up fundamental disagreements that may before have been covered over superficially (see pp. 122–126).

10. *Strengthening effects.* To get the most possible out of this experience, delay normal routines to the extent reasonably possible—hopefully leaving the following day sufficiently free so as to allow a mulling over of new considerations that arise. Here is given a chance to put one's life more in order, best done as gracefully, delicately and thoughtfully as possible.

Supplements of potassium, magnesium and zinc, plus tyrosine (an amino acid), a high-protein meal and a good night's sleep, are also often recommended after a session (see pp. 89, 100–101).

11. What questions does MDMA raise for society?

12. What does it tell us about "stress" and "grace"?

13. Finally, what are left as unanswered concerns?

11. *Societal concerns.* The "mini-vacations" provided by MDMA illuminate pressures that we all may well have learned to ignore in order to get on and "muddle through" our ordinary lives. They also show that we are operating under deprivations not nearly as evident to us in "an ordinary" state of mind—such as a fair amount of lack of compassion and empathy for others.

Integration of MDMA-prodded insights into our daily lives has to come step-by-step, and is not likely to be as easy as might have been envisioned during the experience itself. As a psychiatrist, Rick Ingrasci, whom you'll hear from later, expressed this: "MDMA is like getting a glimpse of the picture on the box of the jigsaw puzzle of life. You still have to put the pieces together." (See pp. 26, 59, 67, 126–133.)

12. Acceptance of this "gratuitous grace." The chance to give in via MDMA to one's "underlying mysticism," sense of wonder, and feelings of love for a fellow human and/or one's "fate" is frequently overwhelming—so much so that some users may try to deny the validity of the evoked experience . . . when later back in their usual states of mind and their everyday routines. It may seem "unfair," for an instance, that such a level of exultation could have been achieved via mind molecules without the exertions and deprivations that accompany traditional methods for "enlightenment." This attitude may arise especially among those imbued with the "Protestant ethic," and/or various religious notions of an essential sinful condition predestined for humans.

Alternative views opened up by MDMA can thus be troublesome to the individual user, as well as society. It appears now that an eventual integration will come about only after a considerable amount of conflict. To express a factor in this briefly, the idea of a "free lunch" is not all that easily accepted—even when it comes as first-hand experience (see pp. 59, 66–67, 90, 93).

13. Unanswered questions. At present, it is not known why MDMA is "an access code" to largely unused or undeveloped aspects of personality that many people would like to experience with greater regularity. How does it reduce mental, emotional, and physical stress? When does it open the user's heart? (See pp. 135, 145.)

*＊＊

Discussion above and evidence to be presented ahead, if these have any validity at all, indicate that scheduling MDMA into the most banned drug category of all may well have been one of the most criminal acts of our recent U.S. government. A fairly immense amount of money—not, although, billions!—was spent taking depositions from highly credentialed witnesses in a charade, as it turned out, in which evidence presented was then entirely ignored. With a signature, the administrator of the DEA was empowered to, and did, sweep aside what bulked up to ten volumes of testimony and a 90-page decision from its own judge based on a hundred solid "findings."

This is unfortunate, given abundant evidence in this book alone as to how beneficial this MDMA substance can be for both its user and for society as a whole. While it is true that such evidence is "merely" first-hand, and largely not presented with "scientific rigor," it should at least be remarked that much more can be substantiated for the transformative qualities of MDMA than for that of psychoanalysis. Reasons for this have been summarized by Debby Harlow, a San Francisco MDMA researcher: "It is virtually impossible to prove the efficacy of any form of psychotherapy or personal growth method (with or without chemical adjuncts) since the benefits accrued are largely happiness, personal growth and interpersonal fulfillment."

***

Examples from MDMA research already have illuminated areas in which whole population segments of suffering humanity could be helped. Use of MDMA for alleviation of the stresses produced by incidents of rape, and for that experienced among war veterans, recalls for me one of the most charged sentences to come from Freud: "For psychoanalysis to change neurotic suffering to ordinary human misery is no small event."

Progress clearly available from MDMA is now curbed by our government and cannot even be researched. Think about that!

The same can be said for aid that MDMA has to offer psychotherapy. No other tool to date offers such an increase in (1) rapport, and (2) access to relevant personal data, and yet for reasons Krippner describes in his foreword to this book, this priceless advance has been thrown away. Testimony provided by Eisner shows what has been lost.

Driving this marvelous tool to underground usage guarantees an increasingly perverse edge to the delicate but robust potentials it once had. Adulteration, contamination, surreptitious use and dosing, subjecting users to more haphazard conditions—in the future millions of trips will carry added weight after the criminalizing of this profoundly human experience. Explorations will, nonetheless, continue . . . due to MDMA's inherent worth.

As a final point, effects so far have been such that what MDMA does, and is famous for, now carries on by itself. This extraordinary compound has raised such questions and possibilities as to shift a significant amount of contemporary thinking. That will continue, even if MDMA were banished from the face of the earth tomorrow.

—Peter Stafford

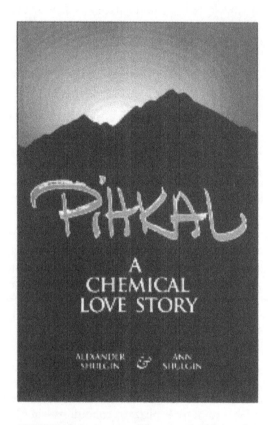

"*PIHKAL* is a compelling novel. Given the autobiographical nature of the story, the subject matter—psychedelic biochemistry and sexual chemistry—is daring indeed."
                              —Marilyn Ferguson

Chemical Synthesis for MDMA
by Alexander Shulgin
Excerpted from *PIHKAL: A Chemical Love Story*

#109 MDMA; MDM; ADAM; ECSTASY; 3,4-METHYLENEDIOXY-N-METHYLAMPHETAMINE

Synthesis

(From MDA) A solution of 6.55 g of 3,4-methylenedioxy-amphetamine (MDA) as the free base and 2.8 mL formic acid in 150 mL benzene was held at reflux under a Dean Stark trap until no further H_2O was generated (about 20 h was sufficient, and 1.4 mL H_2O was collected). Removal of the solvent gave an 8.8 g of an amber oil which was dissolved in 100 mL CH_2Cl_2, washed first with dilute HCl, then with dilute NaOH, and finally once again with dilute acid. The solvent was removed under vacuum giving 7.7 g of an amber oil that, on standing, formed crystals of N-formyl-3,4-methylenedioxyamphetamine. An alternate process for the synthesis of this amide involved holding at reflux for 16 h a solution of 10 g of MDA as the free base in 20 mL fresh ethyl formate. Removal of the volatiles yielded an oil that set up to white crystals, weighing 7.8 g.

A solution of 7.7 g N-formyl-3,4-methylenedioxyamphetamine in 25 mL anhydrous THF was added dropwise to a well-stirred and refluxing solution of 7.4 g LAH in 600 mL anhydrous THF under an inert atmosphere. The reaction mixture was held at reflux for 4 days. After being brought to room temperature, the excess hydride was destroyed with 7.4 mL H_2O in an equal volume of THF, followed by 7.4 mL of 15% NaOH and then another 22 mL H_2O. The solids were removed by filtration, and the filter cake washed with additional THF. The combined filtrate and washes were stripped of solvent under vacuum, and the residue dissolved in 200 mL CH_2Cl_2. This solution was extracted with 3x100 mL dilute HCl, and these extracts pooled and made basic with 25% NaOH. Extraction with 3x75 mL CH_2Cl_2 removed the product, and the pooled extracts were stripped of solvent under vacuum. There was obtained 6.5 g of a nearly white residue which was distilled at 100–110 °C at 0.4 mm/Hg to give 5.0 g of a colorless oil. This was dissolved in 25 mL IPA, neutralized with concentrated HCl, followed by the addition of sufficient anhydrous Et2O to produce a lasting turbidity. On continued stirring, there was the deposition of fine white crystals of 3,4-methylenedioxy-N-methylamphetamine hydrochloride (MDMA) which were removed by filtration, washed with Et2O, and air dried, giving a final weight of 4.8 g (from 3,4-methylenedioxyphenylacetone). This key intermediate to all of the MD-series can be made from either isosafrole, or from piperonal via 1-(3,4-methylenedioxyphenyl)-2-nitropropene. To a well-stirred solution of 34 g of 30% hydrogen peroxide in 150 g 80% formic acid there was added, dropwise, a solution of 32.4 g isosafrole in 120 mL acetone at a rate that kept the reaction mixture from exceeding 40 °C. This required a bit over 1 h, and external cooling was used as necessary. Stirring was continued for 16 h, and care was taken that the slow exothermic reaction did not cause excess heating. An external bath with running water worked well. During this time the solution progressed from an orange color to a deep red. All volatile components were removed under vacuum which yielded some 60 g of a very deep red residue. This was dissolved in 60 mL of MeOH, treated with 360 mL of 15% H_2SO_4, and heated for 3 h on the steam bath. After cooling, the reaction mixture was extracted with 3x75 mL Et2O, the pooled extracts washed first with H_2O and then with dilute NaOH, and the solvent removed under vacuum. The residue was distilled (at 2.0 mm/108–112 °C, or at about 160 °C at the water pump) to provide 20.6 g of 3,4-methylenedioxyphenylacetone as a pale yellow oil. The oxime (from hydroxylamine) had a mp of 85–88 °C. The semicarbazone had a mp of 162–163 °C.

An alternate synthesis of 3,4-methylenedioxyphenylacetone starts originally from piperonal. A suspension of 32 g electrolytic iron in 140 mL glacial acetic acid was gradually warmed on the steam bath. When quite hot but not yet with any white salts apparent, there was added, a bit at a time, a solution of 10.0 g of 1-(3,4-

methylenedioxyphenyl)-2-nitropropene in 75 mL acetic acid (see the synthesis of MDA for the preparation of this nitrostyrene intermediate from piperonal and nitroethane). This addition was conducted at a rate that permitted a vigorous reaction free from excessive frothing. The orange color of the reaction mixture became very reddish with the formation of white salts and a dark crust. After the addition was complete, the heating was continued for an additional 1.5 h during which time the body of the reaction mixture became quite white with the product appeared as a black oil climbing the sides of the beaker. This mixture was added to 2 L H_2O, extracted with 3x100 mL CH_2Cl_2, and the pooled extracts washed with several portions of dilute NaOH. After the removal of the solvent under vacuum, the residue was distilled at reduced pressure (see above) to provide 8.0 g of 3,4-methylenedioxyphenylacetone as a pale yellow oil.

To 40 g of thin aluminum foil cut in 1 inch squares (in a 2 L wide mouth Erlenmeyer flask) there was added 1400 mL H_2O containing 1 g mercuric chloride. Amalgamation was allowed to proceed until there was the evolution of fine bubbles, the formation of a light grey precipitate, and the appearance of occasional silvery spots on the surface of the aluminum. This takes between 15 and 30 min depending on the freshness of the surfaces, the temperature of the H_2O, and the thickness of the aluminum foil. (Aluminum foil thickness varies from country to country.) The H_2O was removed by decantation, and the aluminum was washed with 2x1400 mL of fresh H_2O. The residual H_2O from the final washing was removed as thoroughly as possible by shaking, and there was added, in succession and with swirling, 60 g methylamine hydrochloride dissolved in 60 mL warm H_2O, 180 mL IPA, 145 mL 25% NaOH, 53 g 3,4-methylenedioxyphenylacetone, and finally 350 mL IPA. If the available form of methylamine is the aqueous solution of the free base, the following sequence can be substituted: add, in succession, 76 mL 40% aqueous methylamine, 180 mL IPA, a suspension of 50 g NaCl in 140 mL H_2O that contains 25 mL 25% NaOH, 53 g 3,4-methylenedioxyphenylacetone, and finally 350 mL IPA. The exothermic reaction was kept below 60 °C with occasional immersion into cold water and, when it was thermally stable, it was allowed to stand until it had returned to room temperature with all the insolubles settled to the bottom as a grey sludge. The clear

yellow overhead was decanted and the sludge removed by filtration and washed with MeOH. The combined decantation, mother
liquors and washes, were stripped of solvent under vacuum, the
residue suspended in 2400 ml of H_2O, and sufficient HCl added to
make the phase distinctly acidic. This was then washed with 3x75
mL CH_2Cl_2, made basic with 25% NaOH, and extracted with
3x100 mL of CH_2Cl_2. After removal of the solvent from the combined extracts, there remained 55 g of an amber oil which was
distilled at 100–110 °C at 0.4 mm/Hg producing 41 g of an off-
white liquid. This was dissolved in 200 mL IPA, neutralized with
about 17 mL of concentrated HCl, and then treated with 400 mL
anhydrous Et2O. After filtering off the white crystals, washing
with an IPA/Et2O mixture, (2:1), with Et2O, and final air drying,
there was obtained 42.0 g of 3,4-methylenedioxy-N-
methylamphetamine (MDMA) as a fine white crystal. The actual
form that the final salt takes depends upon the temperature and
concentration at the moment of the initial crystallization. It can be
anhydrous, or it can be any of several hydrated forms. Only the
anhydrous form has a sharp mp; the published reports describe all
possible one degree melting point values over the range from 148–
153 °C. The variously hydrated polymorphs have distinct infrared
spectra, but have broad mps that depend on the rate of heating.

DOSAGE: 80–150 mg.

DURATION: 4–6 h.

Qualitative Comments

(with 100 mg) "MDMA intrigued me because everyone I asked,
who had used it, answered the question, 'What's it like?' in the
same way: 'I don't know.' 'What happened?' 'Nothing.' And now
I understand those answers. I too think nothing happened. But
something seemed changed. Before the 'window' opened completely, I had some somatic effects, a tingling sensation in the
fingers and temples—a pleasant sensation, not distracting. However, just after that there was a slight nausea and dizziness similar
to a little too much alcohol. All these details disappeared as I
walked outside. My mood was light, happy, but with an underly-

ing conviction that something significant was about to happen. There was a change in perspective both in the near visual field and in the distance. My usually poor vision was sharpened. I saw details in the distance that I could not normally see. After the peak experience had passed, my major state was one of deep relaxation. I felt that I could talk about deep or personal subjects with special clarity, and I experienced some of the feeling one has after the second martini, that one is discoursing brilliantly and with particularly acute analytical powers."

(with 100 mg) "Beforehand, I was aware of a dull, uncaring tiredness that might have reflected too little sleep, and I took a modest level of MDMA to see if it might serve me as a stimulant. I napped for a half hour or so, and woke up definitely not improved. The feeling of insufficient energy and lack of spark that I'd felt before had become something quite strong, and might be characterized as a firm feeling of negativity about everything that had to be done and everything I had been looking forward to. So I set about my several tasks with no pleasure or enjoyment and I hummed a little tune to myself during these activities which had words that went: 'I shouldn't have done that, oh yes, I shouldn't have done that, oh no, I shouldn't have done that; it was a mistake.' Then I would start over again from the beginning. I was stuck in a gray space for quite a while, and there was nothing to do but keep doing what I had to do. After about 6 hours, I could see the whole mental state disintegrating and my pleasant feelings were coming back. But so was my plain, ornery tiredness. MDMA does not work like Dexedrine."

(with 120 mg) "I feel absolutely clean inside, and there is nothing but pure euphoria. I have never felt so great, or believed this to be possible. The cleanliness, clarity, and marvelous feeling of solid inner strength continued throughout the rest of the day, and evening, and through the next day. I am overcome by the profundity of the experience, and how much more powerful it was than previous experiences, for no apparent reason, other than a continually improving state of being. All the next day I felt like 'a citizen of the universe' rather than a citizen of the planet, completely disconnecting time and flowing easily from one activity to the next."

(with 120 mg) "As the material came on I felt that I was being enveloped, and my attention had to be directed to it. I became

quite fearful, and my face felt cold and ashen. I felt that I wanted to go back, but I knew there was no turning back. Then the fear started to leave me, and I could try taking little baby steps, like taking first steps after being reborn. The woodpile is so beautiful, about all the joy and beauty that I can stand. I am afraid to turn around and face the mountains, for fear they will overpower me. But I did look, and I am astounded. Everyone must get to experience a profound state like this. I feel totally peaceful. I have lived all my life to get here, and I feel I have come home. I am complete."

(with 100 mg of the "R" isomer) "There were the slightest of effects noted at about an hour (a couple of paresthetic twinges) and then nothing at all."

(with 160 mg of the "R" isomer) "A disturbance of baseline at about forty minutes and this lasts for about another hour. Everything is clear by the third hour."

(with 200 mg of the "R" isomer) "A progression from an alert at thirty minutes to a soft and light intoxication that did not persist. This was a modest +, and I was at baseline in another hour."

(with 60 mg of the "S" isomer) "The effects began developing in a smooth, friendly way at about a half hour. My handwriting is OK but I am writing faster than usual. At the one hour point, I am quite certain that I could not drive, time is slowing down a bit, but I am mentally very active. My pupils are considerably dilated. The dropping is evident at two hours, and complete by the third hour. All afternoon I am peaceful and relaxed, but clear and alert, with no trace of physical residue at all. A very successful ++."

(with 100 mg of the "S" isomer) "I feel the onset is slower than with the racemate. Physically, I am excited, and my pulse and blood pressure are quite elevated. This does not have the 'fire' of the racemate, nor the rush of the development in getting to the plateau."

(with 120 mg of the "S" isomer) "A rapid development, and both writing and typing are impossible before the end of the first hour. Lying down with eyes closed eliminates all effects; the visual process is needed for any awareness of the drug's effects. Some teeth clenching, but no nystagmus. Excellent sleep in the evening."

Extensions and Commentary

In clinical use, largely in psychotherapeutic sessions of which there were many in the early years of MDMA study, it became a common procedure to provide a supplemental dosage of the drug at about the one and a half hour point of the session. This supplement, characteristically 40 milligrams following an initial 120 milligrams, would extend the expected effects for about an additional hour, with only a modest exacerbation of the usual physical side-effects, namely, teeth clenching and eye twitching. A second supplement (as, for instance, a second 40 milligrams at the two and a half hour point) was rarely felt to be warranted. There are, more often than not, reports of tiredness and lethargy on the day following the use of MDMA, and this factor should be considered in the planning of clinical sessions.

With MDMA, the usual assignments of activity to optical isomers is reversed from all of the known psychedelic drugs. The more potent isomer is the "S" isomer, which is the more potent form of amphetamine and methamphetamine. This was one of the first clear distinctions that was apparent between MDMA and the structurally related psychedelics (where the "R" isomers are the more active). Tolerance studies also support differences in mechanisms of action. In one study, MDMA was consumed at 9:00 A.M. each day for almost a week (120 milligrams the first day and 160 milligrams each subsequent day) and by the fifth day there were no effects from the drug except for some mydriasis. And even this appeared to be lost on the sixth day. At this point of total tolerance, there was consumed (on day #7, at 9:00 A.M.) 120 milligrams of MDA and the response to it was substantially normal with proper chronology, teeth clench, and at most only a slight decrease in mental change. A complete holiday from any drug for another 6 days led to the reversal of this tolerance, in that 120 milligrams of MDMA had substantially the full expected effects. The fact that MDMA and MDA are not cross-tolerant strengthens the argument that they act in different ways, and at different sites in the brain.

A wide popularization of the social use of MDMA occurred in 1984–1985 and, with the reported observation of serotonin nerve changes in animal models resulting from the administration of the structurally similar drug MDA, an administrative move was launched to place it under legal control. The placement of MDMA into the

most restrictive category of the Federal Controlled Substances Act
has effectively removed it from the area of clinical experimentation
and human research. The medical potential of this material will
probably have to be developed through studies overseas.

A word of caution is in order concerning the intermediate 3,4-
methylene-dioxyphenylacetone, which has also been called
piperonylacetone. A devilish ambiguity appeared in the commer-
cial market for this compound, centered about its name. The controversy focused on the meaning of the prefix, piperonyl, which
has two separate chemical definitions. Let me try to explain this
fascinating chaos in non-chemical terms. Piperonyl is a term that
has been used for a two-ring system (the methylenedioxyphenyl
group) either without, or with, an extra carbon atom sticking off of
the side of it. Thus, piperonylacetone can be piperonyl (the two-
ring thing without the extra carbon atom attached) plus acetone (a
three carbon chain thing); the total number of carbons sticking out,
three. Or, piperonylacetone can be piperonyl (the two-ring thing
but with the extra carbon atom attached) plus acetone (a three
carbon chain thing); the total number of carbons sticking out, four.

Does this make sense?

The three carbon sticking out job gives rise to MDA and to
MDMA and to many homologues that are interesting materials
discussed at length in these Book II comments. This is the usual
item of commerce, available from both domestic and foreign sup-
pliers. But the four-carbon sticking out job will produce totally
weird stuff without any apparent relationship to psychedelics,
psychoactives or psychotropics whatsoever. I know of one chemical supply house which supplied the weird compound, and they
never did acknowledge their unusual use of the term piperonyl.
There is a simple difference of properties which might be of value.
The three carbon (correct) ketone is an oil with a sassafras smell
that is always yellow colored. The four carbon (incorrect) ketone
has a weak terpene smell and is white and crystalline. There should
be no difficulties in distinguishing these two compounds. But un-
principled charlatans can always add mineral oil and butter yellow
to otherwise white solids to make them into yellow oils. *Caveat
emptor.*

Ecstasy, by Maxfield Parish

Preface: Ecstatic Easter

Gretchen INVITED ME by letter to meet her in La Jolla, a fashionable beach community north of San Diego, California.

She would be visiting her son there in early April 1978, flying in from Woodstock, New York, where she had run a boutique.

I had met Gretchen the year before in Santa Cruz. At age 66, her personal history would make a fascinating biography. Included would be this gray-haired Jewish Austrian's escape from Nazi Germany, her marriage to a wealthy businessman, and her socialite years as well as her interest in Eastern philosophy that led her to seek out an acquaintance with Alan Watts. From there, her life-road led to setting up lectures for Timothy Leary during the heyday of psychedelia in the mid-'sixties.

I spent the night in the small house that her son had rented for this visit. We spent the evening talking about a series of interviews she was doing. She also talked about a new drug her son had taken, called MDMA, which was similar to a drug I had tried, MDA.

Indeed, in the ten years prior to my La Jolla visit, I had taken a variety of psychedelic substances. My roots were in the 'sixties counterculture. At this time, I was enrolled at the University of California, Santa Cruz, where I later completed a B. A. in Psychology.

"What is the drug like?" I asked Gretchen. "Is it just like MDA?"

"I'm not sure exactly what it's like, but my son told me that it is somewhat different than MDA. It lasts for a shorter time, it's legal, and it's supposed to help people communicate in a unique way."

"I'd like to try it," I volunteered enthusiastically.

"Well, my son is bringing some in the morning. I'll ask him to bring you some, too."

We awoke about 8 A.M. on Easter Sunday. Gretchen switched on a radio program by one of her recent interviewees, Gabriel Wisdom. The "Joyful Wisdom Hour" was a program local to the San Diego area, consisting of an upbeat combination of futurist news and New Age gossip by host Wisdom, as well as music and interviews. My introduction into a new environment, renewing my acquaintance with Gretchen, and the optimistic tone of the program provided an upbeat mind-set for the experience I was to have. Gretchen's son— a handsome, young man in his early thirties, a recent Ph.D. in Cognitive Psychology from University of California, San Diego, currently involved with artificial intelligence and computer research—arrived at Gretchen's apartment. He briefed me a bit further about the effects of MDMA. He told us that he would not take it himself, but would instead be a guide for us during the experience. We took the small white capsules and set off by car for San Diego's Pico Park. It was a sunny, blue-skied spring day.

La Jolla is a tourist town, full of specialty shops and restaurants and people on vacation. We arrived at the park and plunged into the woodsy expanse by foot. After about five minutes of walking, I began to feel the effects of the MDMA. The first sensation was breathless awe. It was as if I were seeing the world for the first time, crisp and clear and new. This feeling reminded me of my initial experience with LSD. But this time there were no visual changes. Everything appeared as it did before, but different somehow—more intense, fresh, novel.

Gretchen also began showing the effects of the MDMA. We began to talk excitedly as her beaming son led us to the botanical gardens. As we examined exotic flora marked by signs with Latin names, we kept up a lively conversation covering a wide range of topics and people. The tone was consistently optimistic.

Our next stop on the park tour was at the Space Museum. We strolled past exhibits of space capsules past and present (this was pre-Space Shuttle 1978). The space jewelry in the gift shop caught our attention. Especially alluring were the necklaces and earrings with holograms (our first look at this sort of high-tech adornment).

From the museum, we walked close to the far end of the park, with what both of us agreed was an unusual amount of energy. We then sat on a grassy hill overlooking a playground.

Families of U.S. Marines sat on picnic benches around the play area, as their children frolicked in the sun.

Gretchen, who enjoys small children, sat smiling and contemplating the scene beneath us. Normally, I abhor military people, especially Marines, because of my background in the anti-Vietnam War movement. But the crew-cut, khaki-clad Marines and their families seemed transformed in this MDMA-inspired state. They were no longer stereotypes, but human beings, men and women sharing a quiet Easter Sunday in the park. With my normally judgmental outlook suspended, I felt nothing but love and compassion for everyone I saw—including Marines.

With this insight came a peacefulness, a meditative calm. No anticipation of future events, no regrets from the past marred the experience of the moment.

As we walked back to the car, the peacefulness continued, as it would for the remainder of the day. We talked excitedly about our adventure, and the wonders of this new mind-altering substance.

In the ten years since the experience that Sunday in the park, I have continued to use MDMA periodically. None of the subsequent experiences quite duplicated the wonderment of the first. However, the nature and direction of the experiences began to shift into new avenues of insight.

These concerned powerful new connections and communication with friends and lovers. The focus of my life seemed to turn, as the result of my experiences, away from concern with transcendental spirituality and toward interpersonal relationships and the wonders of day-to-day life. The ability to communicate in a direct manner with people that I encountered during my sessions stayed with me.

Also during this decade, I have witnessed many people, in groups or one-on-one, take their first dose of MDMA and open up. The experiences I observed have given me a new appreciation of the good side of human nature. People have sent me short papers or pamphlets, reports of sessions, or guides to the use of Adam, Ecstasy, or some other colorful alias for MDMA. I have integrated this material into the book you are about to read.

I have attempted here to weave all this data, along with personal exploration and participation with others, into the first comprehensive overview of MDMA. In it, you will find the history, the psychology, the chemistry, the biology, the methods of use, and the possible future of this interesting new substance and its descendants.

Chapter I. Introducing Adam

You discover a secret doorway into a room in your house that you did not previously know existed. It is a room in which both your inner experience and your relations with others seem magically transformed. You feel really good about yourself and your life. At the same time, everyone who comes into this room seems more lovable. You find your thoughts flowing, turning into words that previously were blocked by fear and inhibition.

After several hours, you return to your familiar abode, feeling tired but different, more open. And your memory of your mystical passage may help you in the days and weeks ahead to make all the other rooms of your house more enjoyable.

This metaphorical door exists in the form of a new and experimental mind-changing compound. It goes by many names, "Ecstasy (XTC)," "Adam," "Presence," "Clarity," "Zen," and "M," but the initials of its chemical name are MDMA (or the also correct MDM).

Early History

Although it has come to public attention only recently, MDMA is not a newly synthesized compound. It was originally developed in 1914, the first year of W.W.I. in Germany. It was patented by Merck Pharmaceutical Company, then for the most part forgotten for the next forty years.

In 1953, the Army Chemical Center (supporting research at Michigan) gave MDMA to guinea pigs, rats, mice, monkeys, and dogs, in order to find out how toxic it might be. It was found to be less so than its chemical cousin, MDA, with which it is often compared. (The history of MDA is much fuller than that of MDMA, and will be covered in Chapter V).

It wasn't until 1976 that the first report was published which indicated the psychoactivity of MDMA in humans. The journal article was by Alexander Shulgin and a collaborator, D.E. Nichols. We will come across Shulgin's name several times in this book, especially when discussing the future of mind-changing drugs. He is a research biochemist, whose revelatory experience with mescaline sulphate in the mid-'Sixties put him on an "ever-changing quest of curiosity," developing and personally exploring a wide range of psychoactive substances. Nichols, who is now at the Department of Medical Chemistry of Purdue University, has also contributed much to this field, and we will also encounter his name throughout this book.

Shulgin and Nichols conclude:

> Within the effective dosage range, 75-150 mg orally, the effects are first noted very quickly, usually within a half-hour following administration. With most subjects, the plateau of effects is reported to occur in a half-hour to one hour. The intoxication symptoms are largely dissipated in an additional 2 hours except for a mild residual sympathiomimetic stimulation which can persist for several additional hours. There are few physical indicators of intoxication and psychological sequelae are virtually non-existent. Qualitatively, the drug appears to evoke an easily controlled altered state of consciousness with emotional and sensual overtones.

Yet even before the publication of the Shulgin/Nichols report, the diffusion of MDMA into society had begun. Some reports of early underground batches of MDMA start as early as 1970. Among those who noted the compound's promise, there was fear that MDMA might become a "street drug" as LSD had, and be quickly banned. LSD had been mainly a research tool of psychotherapists for the first twenty years after its psychoactive effects had been discovered. When publicized by the Harvard Psychedelic Research group, it became the "sacrament" of the Hippies and the recreational drug of the Youth Culture. The use of this powerful mind-changing agent by several million inadequately prepared users, often taking improperly made LSD, led to some well-publicized "bad trips." For this reason, as well as others we will discuss later in the chapter, possession of LSD was made a felony.

Learning from these earlier mistakes, those who experimented with MDMA, many of them psychotherapists, attempted to control the dissemination of information about the drug as well as the substance itself. They hoped that enough informal research could be done before it became public to keep it from suffering a fate like that of LSD and mescaline.

Differences Between MDMA and Major Psychedelics

Aside from this attempt at secrecy, another factor—the differences between MDMA and its predecessors—helped keep things quiet. MDMA is a member of a new generation of psychoactive substances which are, in many respects, different from major psychedelics. Indeed, some refuse to consider it a psychedelic drug at all. They would rather use descriptors like "feeling enhancer" or "empathogen." The latter term, coined by Ralph Metzner, is explored more fully in Chapter II.

How does MDMA differ from LSD, mescaline, or its close chemical relative, MDA, for that matter? Perhaps the most important distinction between MDMA and the others is that MDMA is more specific in its effects.

Stanislav Grof, M.D., former National Institute of Mental Health (NIMH) LSD researcher and author of three books reporting the results of his experiments, has classified LSD as a "non-specific amplifier of brain functions." By this, he means that LSD tends to enhance almost every aspect of mental experience, from amplifying and distorting any or all of the senses and the revelation of the contents of the unconscious mind. The LSD taker is bombarded with more of almost everything, positive as well as negative. This is, for the most part, also true for the other major psychedelic drugs.

MDMA does not produce many of the effects attributed to these major psychedelic drugs. It is not hallucinogenic in normal doses, and it does not disrupt "ego-integrity," a term psychologists use to describe our ability to function in the world. Coordination is not lost during the MDMA experience, and there are no disorganizing effects on thought processes.

Instead, MDMA focuses selectively on a few of the many mental functions that LSD may affect, including emotional ecstasy, capacity for empathy, serenity, self-awareness, and "noetic" feelings. The last, noetic feelings, are the experience of seeing the world in a fresh way, as if for the first time—as a child sees it.

The LSD experience is sometimes referred to by psychologists as involving "depersonalization." That is, the experience of existing as a separate personality or "ego" is disrupted by LSD. MDMA does not normally produce depersonalization. Instead, the effects are ego-strengthening.

MDA is closer in its effects to those of the major psychedelics (LSD, psilocybin, mescaline). It has some depersonalizing qualities as well as mild hallucinogenic effects. The latter are much less pronounced than with LSD. At the same time, it promotes emphathetic communication and interpersonal exploration in the same manner as MDMA, although, again, not to the same degree. MDA appears to be a less selective, more globally active representative of the family of phenethylamines of which it is a member, whereas MDMA is a more specific enhancer of empathetic awareness. In fact, MDMA might be considered the prototype of a new class of psychoactive compounds, the "empathogens," as we will discover in the next chapter.

As a result of these differences between MDMA and its predecessors, the experiences catalyzed by MDMA are nearly always positive. The set (expectations of the user) and the setting (the environment in which the drug is taken) have much less influence on the outcome of the MDMA experience than is true for LSD. The depersonalizing, hallucinatory experience of LSD requires much more preparation and structuring than MDMA does to produce a favorable outcome. And even with the most careful planning and environment, the dramatic consciousness changes produced by LSD can be frightening or even shattering for some people.

When large numbers of people on bad LSD trips appeared at hospital emergency rooms during the 'Sixties, the phenomenon attracted the attention of the government and the media. But only eight people in the entire country sought treatment in hospital emergency rooms after using MDMA during the four years from 1977 (when the drug first appeared on the street) to 1981, according to the government's Drug Abuse Warning Network (DAWN). More are admitted for alcohol-related problems in any two hours of a single day than in those four years. Between 1981 and 1985, not a single admission to any of the DAWN-monitored hospital emergency rooms was reported.

Dissemination of MDMA into Society

The benign nature of the MDMA experience, along with the purposeful efforts of those who used it to keep things quiet, contributed to the low profile that MDMA exhibited from its introduction in 1977 until 1984.

During that time, MDMA spread through underground channels which included psychotherapists, psychiatrists, long-time psychedelic drug explorers, yuppies, and a remarkable assortment of individualists of all kinds. The main uses of MDMA were as a facilitator for interpersonal exploration and communication between lovers and friends, and, among the professionals, as a tool for psychotherapy. For these purposes, MDMA turned out to be quite reliable. By this time, it was

Alexander T. Shulgin, Ph.D., first reported on the effects of MDMA.

called "Adam" or "Ecstasy" by many of those who used it.

Ralph Metzner, Ph.D., who named this class of compound "empathogens," has noted in the unpublished "The Nature of the MDMA Experience & Its Role in Healing, Psychotherapy & Spiritual Practice":

> Perhaps the most interesting code name for MDMA, that seems to have originated with a group of therapists on the West Coast, is the term "Adam," by which is meant not Adam as man, but rather Adam-and-Eve as androgynous ancestor.
>
> The figure of Adam is a highly important symbolic figure in Gnostic and Hermetic writings, and C.G. Jung wrote extensively about it. He represents "primordial man," the "original being," the "man of Earth," the condition of primal innocence and unity with all life, as described in the Bible's account of the Garden of Eden. Feelings of being returned to a natural state of innocence, before guilt, shame and unworthiness arose, are common in these Adamic ecstasies; and so are feelings of connectedness and bonding with fellow human beings, animals and all the forms and energies of the natural world.

The other popular name for MDMA, "Ecstasy," was chosen for obvious reasons. The man who first named it "Ecstasy" told me that he chose the name "because it would sell better than calling it 'Empathy.' 'Empathy' would be more appropriate, but how many people know what it means?" In mid-1984, the calm waters of MDMA use began to feel some ripples, forerunners of the waves of the storm that was to follow. Hardly a word had been written about Adam until Bill Mandel's flippant piece, "The Yuppie Psychedelic," appeared in the June 10, 1984, edition of the *San Francisco Chronicle*:

> Shades of Timothy Leary! A defrocked Harvard professor appeared on the Marin County intelligentsia circuit a few months ago preaching the wonders of a new psychedelic drug.
>
> Called "Adam," it has been turning up recently in rather unlikely circles. Adam is spreading faster than a secret restaurant tip among educated professionals in their 30's and 40's, non-kooky baby boomers who experimented with psychedelics 15 years ago and then forsook them for careers and family.
>
> Could this be the last hurrah of the '60's, a final nostalgic

harkening to a golden age when "bald spots" were on ski slopes, not one's scalp? Back then, Leary and Richard Alpert (who later became Ram Dass) left psychology professorships at Harvard to become guides on the LSD Magical Mystery Tour.

No, Adam is very definitely of the '80's. According to people who've taken it, this new psychedelic isn't supposed to teach you anything or take you anywhere. It was designed simply to stimulate the pleasure centers of the cerebral cortex . . .

Many who used Adam were relieved to find that its chemical name was incorrectly given in this slick mix of fact and fallacy, a combination which was to typify much of the media coverage that was to follow. Mandel says, "The name 'Adam' is probably derived from the chemical name, methyloxy-methylene-dioxy-amphetamine (MMDA)." MMDA is one of Adam's close chemical cousins, and had been scheduled by the Comprehensive Controlled Substance Act of 1970—which contains lists of drugs prohibited by the federal government—along with MDA. By specifying the wrong name in the article, attention to MDMA was averted.

But this respite was to be short-lived. The next month, the World Health Organization asked of its member governments about the use of more than twenty known psychoactive substances of the chemical class called phenethylamines. MDMA was on the list. Checking records of drug seizures, WHO identified MDMA as the only drug on the list found a significant number of times.

After a year of collecting data and planning in collaboration with the Food and Drug Administration, the Drug Enforcement Administration (DEA) published a notice in the July 27, 1984, edition of the *Federal Register*, that it intended to include MDMA in the Comprehensive Substances Act as a Schedule I drug, equivalent to a narcotic and deemed to be without medical use.

The DEA could not have anticipated what happened next. A group of self-described "physicians, researchers, therapists, and lawyers" was established under the name of a Florida-based nonprofit corporation formed earlier by proponents of Buckminster Fuller, Earth Metabolic Design Laboratory. Concurrently four individuals, Professor Thomas B. Roberts, Ph.D., George Greer, M.D., Professor Lester Grinspoon, M.D., and Professor James Bakalar, retained a Washington D.C. attorney, Richard Cotton. Cotton, on Sept. 10, 1984, sent a letter to Francis

Mullen, Administrator of the DEA, requesting that a hearing be held to determine whether MDMA should be scheduled, and if so, what schedule it should be placed in.

The initial hearing was held on February 1, 1985, in a room on the twelfth floor of the Washington, D.C., Drug Enforcement Administration offices. Presiding was administrative law justice Francis Young. Also present were two DEA attorneys, Richard Cotton, and a pharmaceutical company attorney not interested in MDMA, but interested in a procedural question discussed in the *Federal Register* with regard to the hearings about whether a drug could be placed in a category other than Schedule I of the Controlled Substance Act if there was no currently accepted medical use.

In the hearing, it was decided that three future hearings would be held, one in Washington, D.C., another in Kansas City, Missouri, and the third in Los Angeles. These hearings would try to address five questions decided by general agreement of the contending parties: (1) Is there accepted medical use of MDMA? (2) Is there lack of accepted safety for MDMA when used under medical supervision? (3) What is the relative abuse potential of MDMA? (4) If there is no accepted medical use of MDMA, can it be placed in a category other than Schedule I? (5) If MDMA can be placed somewhere other than Schedule I, where should it be scheduled, if at all?

Judge Young commented that the decision process could take up to a year. Those who were interested in using the drug therapeutically hoped that during this period, much more research could be done with human subjects to prove the efficacy of MDMA for psychotherapy. But events of the next several months placed a dark cloud over these expectations.

California Conference

Esalen Institute, perched on cliffs above the surging Pacific Ocean, is eleven miles south of the small town of Big Sur, California. The site of hot mineral springs, it was once the residence of the Esselen Indians, who considered its waters to have remarkable healing properties. Since its founding in the mid-'Sixties, Esalen has been a vortex for new ideas and methods involving humanistic psychotherapies and consciousness sciences.

Esalen has also been the base of operations for Stanislav Grof, M.D., who has conducted research on LSD for nearly thirty years, both in his native Czechoslovakia and with funding from the National Institute of Mental Health in Bethesda, Maryland. Grof, and Esalen co-founder Dick

Price, both interested in the promise of MDMA, opened up Esalen as a grounds for a conference of researchers in the field.
Co-sponsored by Earth Metabolic Design Foundation, the conference was held from March 10-15, 1985. It was reported on by George Greer, M.D., in the Spring 1985 issue of *Advances: Journal for the Institute for the Advancement of Health*. Some of this report is excerpted:

> Among the 35 participants at the meeting were 5 veteran researchers on psychoactive drugs (Francesco DiLeo, M.D., Stanislav Grof, M.D., Robert Lynch, M.D., Claudio Naranjo, M.D., and Richard Yensen, Ph.D.) and 4 psychiatrists who use MDMA in their clinical practice. On the fourth day of the meeting, George Greer, one of the psychiatrists, directed a session in which 13 participants took MDMA; each person was monitored separately by a physician or psychiatrist. Among the professionals present, the combined clinical experience in using MDMA during the past several years totaled over a thousand sessions . . .
>
> Psychiatrists Joseph Downing, M.D., and Philip Wolfson, M.D., presented results of an unpublished, recently completed toxicity study of 21 human subjects, all of whom had taken MDMA in the past. Other than a brief and moderate rise in pulse and blood pressure, the researchers found no significant abnormalities before ingestion or up to 24 hours afterward . . .
>
> The reports on the benefits of MDMA, although anecdotal, were uniformly positive. In the discussion of MDMA's effects, the clinicians using it felt it possessed a unique action that enhanced communication, especially in couples in therapy. The drug reduced defensiveness and fear of emotional injury, thereby facilitating more direct expression of feelings . . .
>
> Reports of MDMA's facilitation of individual psychotherapy were also favorable. Many subjects experienced the classic retrieval of lost traumatic memories, followed by the relief of emotional symptoms. Victims of child abuse and sexual attack experienced the most dramatic benefits. Wolfson also reported having multiple MDMA sessions with psychotic individuals and their natal families, leading to improvements in the patient's functioning and ego integration . . .

None of those that took MDMA had any complications; some found the session emotionally intense. The two days remaining in the conference allowed for follow-up discussion and analysis. The people who took MDMA regarded the experience positively and felt the drug encouraged self-insight . . .

The group favored assigning MDMA to a lower Schedule, reserved for drugs with moderate-to-low abuse potential, thus allowing for prosecution for illicit trafficking and the continuation of ongoing studies of MDMA's therapeutic potential. In support of this position, it was pointed out that the Drug Abuse Warning Network—a federally funded national clearinghouse of information—had listed only 8 emergency-room visits as a result of MDMA and that since the drug's appearance in the 1970's, no deaths in conjunction with MDMA use had been established. The participants agreed that although MDMA was not a proven therapeutic agent, its supervised experimental use with full informed consent was medically acceptable and safe.

MDMA Goes Public

Newsweek, in the April 15, 1985, issue, printed in its Life/Style section an article titled, "Getting High on 'Ecstasy'." It began:

This is the drug that LSD was supposed to be, coming 20 years too late to change the world. It is called MDMA—or "Ecstasy"—and users say it has the incredible power to make people trust one another, to banish jealousy and to break down barriers that separate lover from lover, parent from child, therapist from patient. Yet unlike LSD, it does not also break down one's ability to distinguish between reality and fantasy, so that it appears free of many of that drug's unfortunate side effects. A New York writer who tried it compares it to "a year of therapy in two hours." A Benedictine monk from Big Sur, Brother Steindl-Rast, says "a monk spends his whole life cultivating the same awakened attitude it gives you." Of course, not everyone is taking it for the insights it provides. It has become popular over the last two years on college campuses, where it is considered an aphrodisiac. Drug-abuse clinics have begun seeing kids who take a dozen or more doses a day to achieve an amphetamine-like high. Apparently the nation is on the verge either of a tremendous breakthough or a lot more kids too strung out to come in from the rain.

The next major media exposure for the suddenly publicized drug was on network television's "Phil Donahue" show, which turned out to be a rollicking free-for-all taped before a vocal New York audience.

The show began with Donahue poking fun at MDMA by first suggesting that the Iranians might dump it in the water supply. Then, as Ayatollah Khomeini lands at the Washington Airport, we welcome him with open arms—rendered open and loving by the new drug.

As Donahue sampled audience opinion, the immediate reaction was that they didn't like the idea of a new drug. Donahue then gave an appeal for the information to be heard, since much of the false information given in the drug scare of the late 'Sixties had resulted in kids being told that heroin was the same as marijuana.

On the panel was Rick Ingrasci, M.D., who used MDMA in his Massachusetts medical practice; Mel Riddle of Straight, Inc., a drug abuse center; Gene Haslip, Deptuty Director of the DEA; and Charles Schuster of the Drug Abuse Research Center, University of Chicago.

Ingrasci said that he did not consider the drug a panacea, and was not advocating that people take it all the time. He was simply suggesting that it be used in therapeutic circumstances to help people work through difficult emotional problems and improve their quality of life.

Mel Riddle spoke next, with a strongly anti-drug line, suggesting that many kids who come to him have used the drug, and some were completely messed up after just one dose.

Gene Haslip was introduced by Donahue with a lecture on the problems that the hard-line policy of the Reagan administration toward drugs has created. Haslip replied with a statement that he wanted to get MDMA off the street and made a Schedule I drug.

Charles Schuster of the Drug Abuse Research Center, University of Chicago, took what at first seemed a moderate position, suggesting that the drug be held out of Schedule I until research was done with it, as is done with other drugs which are being tested for possible medical use.

However, this was followed by a rather sensational statement. Schuster announced that he and two other researchers from the Drug Abuse Research Center had found that MDA, the "parent compound" for MDMA, caused brain damage in rats, and therefore might also in humans (oddly, the research paper they published in *Science* stated their position in much more conservative language, as we will see later in this chapter).

However, the tone of the program was changed by the articulate testimony of several patients of Rick Ingrasci, who spoke from the audience. The first case history was from a woman whose marital problems were helped by an MDMA session in the context of psychotherapy (this case is detailed in Chapter III). The second to talk, Diane Watson, a cancer patient, spoke emotionally about how MDMA had helped her deal with the diagnosis that she had terminal cancer and only six months to live. MDMA, she said, was a catalyst to help her deal with the anger and the pain of her terminal disease. She stated, "MDMA is not an ecstasy drug. It allows you to see the world more clearly and to heal yourself. You realize that you don't need negative emotions, old emotions any more, and you can let them go."

There were many testimonials from the audience, pro and con. Advocates and "anties" were given time to make brief statements. Clearly, the statements by those helped by MDMA therapy made a deep impression on the studio audience, but still there were many who remained skeptical of the advent of another new drug.

BY GARRY TRUDEAU

Doonesbury

The floodgates had now opened, and a deluge of media copy and videotape spilled forth. An article appeared in the May issue of *Psychology Today*, by Jack Shafer, a reporter writing a book about the increase in synthetic drugs appearing in the drug underground. His previous magazine publication, in the March 1985 issue of *Science '85*, "Designer Drugs," portrayed the dangers of synthetic heroin substitutes such as alpha-methyl fentanyl, also known as China White. In this article, "MDMA: Psychedelic Drug Faces Regulation," Shafer attempted to present both sides of the controversy of another designer drug, the much safer MDMA.

On the lighter side, Doonesbury's Uncle Duke hosted a conference entitled "Ecstasy: Whither the Future" at Baby Doc College. The comic events were depicted by Gary Trudeau:

Doonesbury takes off on MDMA. (DOONESBURY Copyright 1985 G. B. Trudeau. Reprinted with Permission of Universal Press Syndicate. All rights reserved)

Ron Siegel, Ph.D., a pharmacologist who researches psychoactive drugs at the UCLA School of Medicine under grants from the National Institute of Drug Abuse (NIDA), emerged as the major representative of the DEA's attack upon the safety and usefulness of Adam. He was featured in *Psychology Today* as well as in subsequent articles in *Time, Life,* and *New York.*

Rick Doblin, a 31-year-old co-founder of Earth Metabolic Design Laboratories, became the major pro-MDMA figure in the media coverage, although he was subjected to heavy criticism by his more conservative colleagues in the organization because of differences in strategies of action.

Doblin first tried MDMA in 1985 and quickly became an activist for the substance. Wrote Joe Klien of *New York* Magazine:

> Even before the Federal Government entered the picture, Rick Doblin sensed that MDMA would become a political issue. "Compassion has political implications. Empathy has polical implications," he says. Doblin decided to contact various government agencies, to show good faith by *telling* them all about MDMA and asking guidance. He contacted Nancy Reagan's anti-drug group, the National Federation of Parents for Drug Free Youth. He contacted the Food and Drug Administration and the National Institute on Drug Abuse and the United Nations. He proposed cooperation. He proposed joint research into MDMA. He proposed to the United Nations that MDMA be used in a project called "Shaping a Global Spirituality While Living in the Nuclear Age."

Currently, Doblin is beginning graduate work at Harvard and working on a proposal to set up a pharmaceutical company—Orphan Pharmaceuticals, Inc. This pharmaceutical company would conduct animal tests, human tests, and clinical trials in an effort to establish the therapeutic efficacy of MDMA.

During the beginning of 1985, another development that would affect the fate of MDMA also occurred. A laboratory in Texas, which first began operating in 1983, started producing unprecedentedly high amounts of MDMA. Ron Siegel, in the *Psychology Today* article, estimated that 30,000 doses of MDMA were being made each month. This laboratory was said to be producing a kilogram—8,000 doses—per day or 240,000 doses per month. These were made into tablets and sold in brown bottles labeled "Sassyfras."

"Sassyfras" brand MDMA was being sold, according to the DEA, at parties in which "pyramid sales" were organized. Participants paid $20 for a sample tablet and were recruited to find other sellers. This prompted Senator Lloyd Bentsen, a Democrat from Texas, to write to John C. Lawn, "Acting Administrator of the DEA," asking for an emergency ban on MDMA.

Indeed, Congress had given the DEA the power to place any drug in Schedule I for one year, because of the deaths and crippling disease attributed to the synthetic heroin nicknamed China White.

On May 31, 1985, a news conference was held in Washington by the DEA. John C. Lawn, in an Associated Press dispatch published in the June 1 *New York Times*, states, "All the evidence the DEA has received shows that MDMA abuse has become a nationwide problem and it poses a serious health threat. This emergency action is a stopgap measure to curb MDMA abuse until the administrative process can be completed." The story goes on to bluntly state, "Officials of the drug agency said their intention was to replace the emergency ban on MDMA with a permanent ban within one year."

The Problem with the DEA's Handling of the Drug Problem

The actions that the DEA took in this matter are typical of its past patterns of action on other newly popular drugs. This "hardball" approach to drugs—smear publicity, severe penalties, kick-down-doors enforcement—has not eradicated problems with drugs in the U.S. Indeed, all it has created is public confusion about drugs and a huge black market.

There is no question that there is a serious drug problem in America. The most widely abused drugs are not even thought of as drugs at all. The addictive drug known as nicotine, sold legally in cigarettes, is clearly the most commonly abused drug. Next in popularity is one of the most dangerous and certainly the most lethal of all drugs sold, alcohol—found in liquor, beers, and wines. This drug is legal and sold even in grocery stores.

If you don't like any of the list of government-approved mind-alterants, you might choose one of the banned alternatives. But then you risk the wrath of the Drug Enforcement Administration. The DEA is the latest in an alphabet-soup series of agencies, beginning with the Federal Bureau of Narcotics, that have attempted to enforce the nation's drug laws. These drug laws cover an increasingly long list of drugs, and their penalties become relentlessly more severe.

Of course, the reason that alcohol is now legal is that the 18th Amendment to the Constitution, which instituted Prohibition in this country, did not work. In fact, there are few laws against any drug at any time in history that have worked. Edward M. Brecher and the editors of *Consumer Reports* in 1972 published *Licit and Illicit Drugs*, an excellent account depicting the consequences of instituting such repressive legislation.

Particularly fascinating is the section on heroin and the opiate drugs. The account begins with the situation with respect to morphine and the opiates that existed in the nineteenth century. At that time, these Schedule I narcotics were available over the counter. Because the opiates are highly addictive, many people who tried them got hooked on the preparations then available.

Although the opiates and heroin are addictive, they are not damaging physically. They are in no way as destructive physically as alcohol, for example, which has been demonstrated to cause brain and liver damage. They are psychologically dangerous, however, in that they put people into a dull stupor.

More severe problems with heroin and the opiates arose after the Harrison Narcotic Act was passed in 1914 and began to be enforced. This action created a black market in heroin. Because of the government sanctions, prices of heroin on this black market are a thousand times as high as the drug costs from a pharmacy. The high cost forces those addicted to heroin to steal or prostitute themselves in order to pay for their drugs. Heroin's price also brings huge profits into the hands of criminal syndicates.

In addition, much of the black-market heroin is cut (diluted) with other materials, some of which are toxic. Occasionally, dangerous synthetic drugs are substituted for heroin; these can cause severe physical impairment or even be lethal. Yet heroin users, once addicted, have a poor prognosis for recovery.

The case of heroin demonstrates the consequences to be expected when a drug is made illegal.

First, the price of the drug goes up, and its distribution is taken out of the hands of experts and put into the hands of criminals.

Second, it criminalizes a group of people who use a particular substance. For heroin, penalties can range up to life in prison.

Third, making a drug illegal usually leads to adulteration of the substance or its being replaced by another compound.

Another account in *Licit and Illicit Drugs* illustrates the mishandling of drug use and misuse in this country—the case of LSD. Prior to 1963, LSD was a little-known but promising tool for psychotherapy.

In 1963, there was a media blitz publicizing the ouster of Timothy Leary and Richard Alpert from Harvard University because of their experimentation with psychedelic substances. LSD became, almost overnight, a household word, and a subculture of users arose.

Because of the increase in use, and because it became associated with the counterculture which included hippies and anti-Vietnam war activists, a polarization of the country on the question of LSD use developed.

In 1966, sensational media stories accentuated this division. One concerned a 5-year-old baby in Brooklyn who accidentally swallowed an LSD sugar cube. She had her stomach pumped and recovered quickly, with no lasting psychological harm. The other was about a murderer who claimed that he had killed while on LSD. Subsequently, it was revealed that the man was a paranoid schizophrenic. But initial headlines—"LSD MURDER" and "BABY HOSPITALIZED ON LSD"— are what stick in public memory, and these two sensationalized stories were catalysts for the institution of felony penalties for the possession, sale, and manufacture of LSD.

Subsequently, the media became increasingly hostile to LSD use. In 1967, TV and newspapers were filled with reports that LSD broke chromosomes. It was speculated that deformities in children, similar to the Thalidomide scandal of 1962, would be the result of LSD use. But subsequent investigations found no abnormalities in the offsprings of LSD users. Many of those who refrained for a while from using LSD returned to it, becoming skeptical of any negative media stories regarding drugs.

Some researchers felt and still believe that the promise of LSD and other proscribed psychedelic drugs such as mescaline and psilocybin was not allowed sufficient exploration by researchers. *Psychedelics Reconsidered* by Lester Grinspoon and James Bakalar presents the case for the reopening of research with these potentially useful substances.

All of the media attention to LSD and its hazards had two effects. First, it increased usage dramatically. From a small number of relatively sophisticated and dedicated users, LSD use spread until it became a recreational drug in high schools and colleges and even among Vietnam soldiers.

It has been repeatedly demonstrated that almost any publicity about a psychoactive drug, negative or positive, will stimulate use of that substance. Expectations about an LSD experience strongly influence the nature of the experience. The drug makes a person suggestible, and prior beliefs about its effects govern the course of the experience. Prior to 1962, there were very few negative experiences reported by those who experienced LSD.

But with the polarization of attitudes toward the drug, those with an interest in seeing LSD banned played up every negative experience. Soon, the number of bad trips and even LSD suicides rose sharply.

As with heroin, making LSD a black market drug led to impurely manufactured and adulterated LSD. This also produced more negative reactions among underground users.

So the result of the incredible publicity about LSD was (1) to increase use, (2) to provoke the proverbial "LSD bummer," (3) to criminalize idealistic middle-class youth, and (4) to discourage research into promising new modes of psychotherapy.

The DEA was set up to police drug use in America. It receives its funding in relation to the severity and scope of the drug problem. Because it is involved in enforcement of drug laws, the DEA's members tend to view any drug use (other than alcohol, cigarettes, and coffee) in a negative way. The DEA also has strong economic interest in having widely used drugs made illegal. The more drug criminals there are to hunt and arrest, the more funding the DEA receives, and the larger the organization becomes. Giving the DEA the power to decide which drugs to criminalize could lead to a constantly expanding police organization always needing more tax monies.

DEA Tackles MDMA

Many of the problems of criminalizing drugs are apparent in the handling of MDMA. Also, many of the biases of the DEA have been revealed in the way it proceeded in having the drug placed in Schedule I.

During the hearings to decide whether MDMA should be made a Schedule I drug, it may have become apparent to the DEA that its case was falling apart. It was difficult to show a high potential for abuse of MDMA. It was possible to show that the drug was used, however, with exhibits of amateur fact sheets, some of which I have quoted from in this book. Many of these pamphlets are testimonials to MDMA's efficacy.

But those who testified for the Earth Metabolic Design Foundation universally affirmed that there were no people whose lives had been harmed by MDMA. Because of the rapid rise in tolerance caused by repeated use, and the buildup of unpleasant side effects, most people learn quickly that MDMA can only be used occasionally. Taking too much is just not rewarding.

For the same reasons, it can be said that MDMA is not an addictive drug. It is true that some people like to repeat the experience. But it is generally found that the less often MDMA is taken, the more meaningful the experience is. The tendency is to take it less frequently after the first two or three exposures. Also, there was little evidence that MDMA was dangerous psychologically. The data from DAWN emergency rooms cited earlier demonstrate that there are few "bad trips" on MDMA. Richard Seymour, of the Haight-Ashbury Free Clinic, reports that most of those who do have a bad time and come into his clinic are provided with a supportive environment and reorient themselves as soon as the drug is metabolized. Being nonaddictive and relatively free of negative psychological phenomena, even in unsupervised situations, MDMA looks like a remarkably safe drug, even safer than the most commonly used recreational drugs, illegal marijuana and legal alcohol.

As MDMA became popular and publicized, it was clear that the DEA was dedicated to banning the substance. In an article, "Federal Authorities Want to Ban Ecstasy," printed in the *San Francisco Examiner*, May 19, 1985, by staff writer John Flinn, this was clear: " 'We're going to ban Ecstasy within the next several months', DEA assistant administrator Gene Haslip vowed. 'By next fall, Ecstasy will be as rigidly controlled as heroin. It's extremely dangerous.' "

Then, when the DEA ban was announced on May 31, the major reason given for the evoking of the DEA's emergency powers was a study done at the University of Chicago and submitted for publication in *Science.* The study revealed that the drug *MDA* has been shown to cause brain damage in rats.

When this report was examined more closely, however, it became clear that many aspects of the report made its application to the use of MDMA by humans highly questionable.

The drug used in the study was MDA, which is chemically distinct from MDMA. While they are both empathogens with somewhat similar mental effects, they are molecularly different, and probably affect the brain in different ways.

Testimony of two hearing witnesses, medical chemist David Nichols and June Riedlinger, pharmacist, presented good evidence for the chemical distinction between the two substances. According to Nichols, there is no cross-tolerance between MDMA and MDA. If you take MDMA until it no longer has an effect, you can then take MDA and it will still have an effect, and vice versa. This points to separate sites of action in the brain.

Both Riedlinger and Nichols point out that MDA and MDMA have opposite isomer activity in their effect on the brain. Actually MDA, according to Nichols, can be thought of as two separate psychoactive drugs, with each of the stereoisomers having quite different psychological effects. MDMA has only one active (s) isomer, the opposite of the more active MDA isomer. The DEA's own report points out that there is evidence that MDA and MDMA have different pathways of action within the nervous system. (These chemical aspects will be explained more fully in the Appendix.)

Alexander Shulgin, Nichols' colleague, commented that MDA resembles MDMA, but it also resembles the over-the-counter allergy remedy Sudafed (pseudoephedrine hydrochloride). Should we place this commonly-used patent medicine on Schedule I along with MDMA?

Several other clear objections to the Chicago study are found in the following excerpt from the research report itself:

> Our study raises the question of whether MDA produces 5HT neurotoxicity in humans. Given differences in species, dose, frequency and route of administration, as well as differences in the way in which rats and humans metabolize amphetamine, it would be premature to extrapolate our findings to humans. It should also be noted that the doses of MDA required to produce 5HT neurotoxicity in the rat (5-10 mg/kg) are roughly three to five times higher than those required to produce hallucinogenic effects (approximately 1.5 to 3 mg/kg). *Hence, doses of MDA generally ingested by humans may not be sufficiently high to induce 5HT neurotoxity unless humans prove to be more sensitive than rats to the toxic effects of MDA.*

The "differences in species, dose, frequency, and route of administration" refer to the procedures followed in the experiment, in which the drug was (1) given to rats rather than humans, (2) given in the much larger doses, as noted in the subsequent sentence, (3) given every twelve hours for two days, and (4) given intravenously (injected in the vein) rather than taken orally, the usual route of administration in humans. Taking a drug orally results in smaller amounts of the drug reaching the brain than if taken by i.v. injection.

In August 1985, Intox Laboratory performed a further study in which a group of rats were given an escalating series of rather stiff doses of

MDMA. They were started off at 25 milligrams per kilogram of body weight, and the amount was increased by 25 mg./kg. each day thereafter. The average psychoactive dose taken by humans is about 2 milligrams per kilogram.

Eventually, all the animals died when the dosages reached between 150 mg./kg. and 300 mg./kg. This is about 150 times the normal human dose. When the rats were examined, there was no evidence of histological brain damage. Although the second study does not use the same techniques as the first, it must raise doubts about the evidence provided by the former study. Subsequent animal and human studies examining the toxicity question are discussed in Appendix II .

Ron Siegel's Anti-MDMA Crusade

In addition to the questionable issue of brain damage, much of the DEA's other negative evidence rests on the study of recreational users done by Ronald Siegel of the UCLA School of Medicine. Siegel has had a high profile in many media reports about MDMA. In an article in *New York*—"The New Drug They Call Ecstasy: Is it Too Much to Swallow?," by Joe Klien—some excerpts from Siegel's statements suggest the nature of Siegel's attack on MDMA.

> "My reaction is 'Here we go again'," says Dr. Ronald Siegel of the UCLA School of Medicine. "Every few years you get one of these miracle drugs that's going to save the world and make everyone feel good. My favorite was PCP. Remember what they used to call that? The *Peace* Pill. At low doses, people were reporting serene, tranquil, peaceful experiences. Then it hit the street and the name changed—it became angel dust—and dosages increased and it was cut with God knows what, and you began to get all the reports of bizarre, violent behavior. So now we have Ecstasy. If you take it, you might become a self-actualized empathetic, caring person, or you might become a nauseated person, or you might have a severe psychotic reaction. Among street users, we're seeing all of the above." . . .
>
> The effects of the drug, he says, seem very similar to those of mescaline. "They're from the same pharmacological family," he says. "You know, the molecular twists and turns that the chemists are playing with—MDA, MMDA, MDMA—raise nice, interesting academic questions, but

out on the street, the experience is the same: hallucinations, disorientation, psychotic episodes."

It is possible that because of the milder, more subtle effects of MDMA, inexperienced users are doubling and tripling the dose. It's also probable that after the recent media coverage, enterprising drug dealers are calling everything from speed to powdered sugar Ecstasy. "We're getting people who claimed to have taken this drug who are disoriented for days on end," says Siegel. "We've had people locked in fetal positions for as long as 72 hours. We had a psychotherapist that took it, disappeared, and turned up a week later directing traffic."

Siegel, in his statements, compares MDMA with two hallucinogenic drugs. PCP, which has a deservedly bad reputation, is nothing like MDMA, in either its chemical structure or its psychological effects. By linking the two, the negative reputation of PCP is pinned on MDMA. The reader is led to think, "Another PCP, huh? Let's get this stuff off the street."

Siegel also alleges that MDMA and mescaline are almost identical in their effects, and that the chemical differences are superfluous. Yet this is certainly not the case. As we explored in the preceding, MDMA is not a hallucinogen as mescaline is—even in double or triple the normal doses. If it is taken in double or triple doses, it produces unpleasant overstimulation; so high doses are normally avoided by users.

Then there are the repeated allegations by Siegel that MDMA can lead to psychotic reactions, and that sometimes these psychotic symptoms do not go away. As we discussed earlier in this chapter, the record of MDMA is one of remarkable safety. The percentage of severely negative reactions is very low. The cases that Siegel mentioned of prolonged reactions must even be rarer. Siegel is probably mentioning every horror story he has heard about the drug.

When hundreds of thousands of people take a psychoactive drug, there are bound to be a few psychotics or prepsychotics who take it, and some of these will be triggered into psychoses by it. With MDMA, unlike LSD or mescaline, the actual number of these reactions has been shown to be quite low. Ronald Siegel is employing a rhetorical trick. By mentioning every extreme case, he makes the casual reader think that MDMA produces psychotics by the score, and that they could end up crazy if they should experiment with the compound.

When Siegel mentions that "cut" and adulterated MDMA is going to be distributed, in doses that are too large, he should recognize that this is the common effect of putting any drug into the black market by enacting stiff legislation. This occurred with heroin and LSD, and since the July 1, 1985, criminalization of MDMA, the same stories of adulteration and substitution and cutting are being heard about MDMA. Until then, almost all of what was represented as MDMA actually was the real substance.

The result of making MDMA a Schedule I drug has been that experimentation with MDMA has been effectively stopped, and that people with an interest in taking it have been turned into potential felons. If it had been placed in Schedule III instead, then medical

Ronald Siegal, Ph.D., witness for the DEA.

experimentation could have continued, and only street use would have been criminalized, although not to the same extent as with Schedule I. Schedule I drugs require research protocols which are prohibitive to researchers without huge grants.

One last example of Siegel's distortions comes in an *Omni* article called "Chemical Ecstasies":

> One dealer gives written "flight instructions," promising that while XTC [Ecstasy, or MDMA] is "kissing in your veins" during the hour-long voyage, you'll experience happiness, security, peace, and freedom. That should end all wars, but secret U.S. Army tests in the 'Fifties found that it also ended the lives of experimental animals. Low doses reduce toxity, but leave subjects with clenched jaws, wiggly eyes, and high blood pressure . . .

Tom Riedlinger comments on the above in an article in the *Journal of Psychoactive Drugs:*

> Trivialization and deliberate distortions are obvious in the foregoing. Siegel is a specialist in psychopharmacology. He therefore knows perfectly well that *all* substances are toxic to humans at some dosage level. Drug experiments with animals typically include a test where dosages are increased incrementally until death occurs, in order to establish where the toxic threshold lies. Siegel chooses not to point this out, preferring instead to convey the impression that MDMA is toxic at low doses—which for humans, at least, is not true. He does acknowledge his duplicity implicitly, however, when he writes that "low [read: therapeutic] doses reduce [avoid the dangers of] toxicity." The side effects he mentions are acknowledged to occur in many patients and in different combinations, but virtually always are no more than mere vexations—acceptable risks.

More Publicity

The kind of media coverage that MDMA got for several months after its criminalization was somewhat reminiscent of the hysteria and hyperbole of the anti-LSD crusade of 1966-69.

Perhaps an extreme example of this is a column by Shari Roan printed in the July 2, 1985, issue of the Dallas *Sun Sentinel.* The column, titled "Designer Drug Dangers," is here excerpted:

A drug lauded by a small group of psychologists as a consciousness-raising aid became an illegal substance as of Monday. But federal Drug Enforcement Agency officials and drug abuse counselors fear they haven't seen the end of the controversy surrounding "Ecstasy."

After years of therapeutic use among a small group of psychologists, Ecstasy (MDMA) recently has become popular among some college students and gays. The hallucinogenic drug has less severe effects than LSD, and some therapists say it reduces anxiety and promotes empathy in patients.

DEA officials, however, say the drug is a dangerous and scientifically untested substance. The DEA called for an emergency ban on Ecstasy after University of Chicago researchers found the drug works by destroying large numbers of vital brain cells and may speed up the aging process in a manner similar to the muscle degeneration produced by Parkinson's disease. The DEA also reported 31 deaths from the drug, mostly in the San Francisco Bay area, with 26 of those deaths occurring after Aug. 1, 1984.

When I read the above newspaper clipping sent by a friend, I immediately called up Alexander and Ann Shulgin to ask them why I had not heard about all of this. Ann Shulgin answered the phone. When I read her the report, she replied, "They mixed everything up. All of those statistics and the Parkinson's disease portion is about MPTP, an unexpected by-product of MPPP."

Immediately it dawned on me that this reporter, in her fervor to get out the anti-dope news, had taken information from two sources and intertwined them in a curious fashion. A strange twist, because the law that was used to ban MDMA resulted from the scandal around synthetic heroin.

The last piece published in a national magazine during the media blitz was in the August 1985 issue of *Life* magazine. The article was generally a balanced view of the controversy. However, you would not know this by the title and accompanying bold headlines on the first page of the story. The title was "The Trouble with Ecstasy." Underneath the title, in bold black letters, is, "THE DRUG IS SEDUCTIVE, CONTROVERSIAL, DANGEROUS—AND NOW ILLEGAL." It's clear what message the casual reader would get from this sensationalistic treatment of MDMA.

Conclusions of the Hearings

The three hearings on MDMA, in Los Angeles, Kansas City, and Washington, D.C., produced ten volumes of testimony from DEA witnesses and from professionals who wished the drug to be placed on a lower and less restrictive schedule so that further research would not be curtailed.

Some highlights of this testimony included two staff members of the Haight-Ashbury Free Medical Clinic facing each other from both sides of the issue, and agreeing that they had seen little abuse of MDMA in their practice. Depositions included statements by Alexander Shulgin and David Nichols distinguishing MDMA from MDA.

Ron Siegel, who had failed to show up at the Los Angeles hearings, did later testify on behalf of the DEA in Washington D.C. He based his statements on a study of "street users." In a positive vein, Siegel stated that he did not find compulsive use patterns developing for MDMA and thought that it did not have a high potential for abuse.

Some other aspects of Siegel's testimony repeated the questionable assertions in the media. He declared MDMA a "hallucinogen" not much different from mescaline. He also told his favorite horror story about the Chicago psychologist who took MDMA once and ended up directing traffic on a busy boulevard.

In the same courtroom, one of the government's chief witnesses, John Docherty, former chief of the Psychosocial Treatment Branch of NIMH, told the court that he supported further MDMA research and that "MDMA is at the confluence of two great trends in psychiatry: psychotherapy and pharmacology," because it had been shown to enhance rapport between therapists and their clients. Studies have demonstrated that rapport is one of the few factors reliably significant in psychiatry.

On May 22, 1986, the DEA's Administrative Law Judge Francis Young in a two-part, 90-page decision recommended that the compound be placed in Schedule III. "The administrative law judge finds and concludes," he wrote, "that prior to its being proscribed effective July 1, 1985, MDMA did have a 'currently accepted medical use in treatment in the United States.' It is not presently being used in treatment because it has been proscribed." The judge itemized 100 "findings" from the testimony that had been received. On the question of abuse, he declared that "The evidence of record does not establish that, in the context of §812, MDMA has a 'high potential' for abuse."

The DEA issued several objections to the judge's decision, including a charge that he was "biased." Richard Cotton issued a sharp rejoinder. "The DEA staff has reacted with knee-jerk hostility to what are serious and real medical issues. Moreover, their position that the evidence in this record warrants a finding that MDMA has a 'high' potential for abuse is—frankly—preposterous . . . The evidence doesn't exist . . . Nevertheless, the DEA staff is determined to place MDMA in Schedule I, come hell or high water, and it isn't going to let the facts, law, or even common courtesy to the Administrative Law Judge stand in its way . . ."

One of the litigants, Lester Grinspoon, decided to appeal the DEA administrator's decision to the First District of Appeals. Richard Cotton agreed to continue as attorney on the case.

Recent Events

Thus, by mid-1986 MDMA was a Schedule I drug and no longer hot media copy. While its use continued underground and legal battles raged, the first books on the subject were published, and a major conference held.

Through the Gateway of the Heart by Sophia Adamson, a collection of first-hand experiences about 44 individual and ten group experiences, was published about this time. Some of my favorites of these experiences are excerpted in Chapter IV.

The Haight-Ashbury Free Clinic sponsored the first major conference open to the public focusing on this newly popular feeling-enhancer called "MDMA: A Multidisciplinary Conference," which presented most of the important figures in the MDMA scenario. Held May 18 and 19, 1986, in Oakland, California. The conference was well attended and especially by a large percentage of individuals in the helping professions.

Perhaps the highlight of the conference was Dr. Rick Ingrasci's passionate appeal to continue his therapeutic work with MDMA. Chemists Shulgin and Nichols were there to present chemical and pharmacological aspects. James Bakalar, George Greer, and Joseph Downing, three litigants in the MDMA scheduling challenge, gave accounts of their work. Ron Siegel tried to show he wasn't a bad guy by playing up the favorable aspects of his research. From the same side of the question, Frank Sapienza, a DEA spokesman, presented that agency's point of view. A sexual panel at the end, which was surprisingly dull despite the lively topic, concluded that MDMA was a "hug" drug rather than an aphrodisiac.

THROUGH
THE GATEWAY
OF THE HEART

Accounts of Experiences with MDMA
and other Empathogenic Substances

Compiled and Edited by
Sophia Adamson

Through the Gateway of the Heart *is an excellent book of vivid first-hand MDMA experiences.*

June Riedlinger, D.Pharm., testified at the MDMA hearings.

JOURNAL OF
PSYCHOACTIVE DRUGS

A Multidisciplinary Forum

MDMA: PROCEEDINGS OF THE CONFERENCE

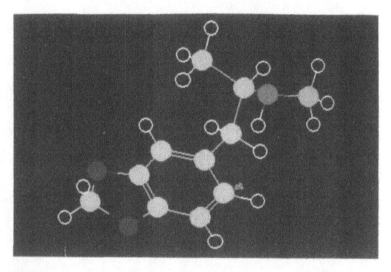

VOLUME 18   OCTOBER-DECEMBER 198ᴸ
NUMBER 4 $20.00

THEME EDITORS:
RICHARD B. SEYMOUR
DONALD R. WESSON, M. D.
DAVID E. SMITH, M. D.

EDITED BY:
E. LEIF ZERKIN
JEFFREY H. NOVEY

"Proceedings" of the MDMA Conference in May, 1986 was
published in Vol. 18, No. 6 of the Journal of Psychoactive Drugs.

A monograph entitled *MDMA* by Richard Seymour of the Haight-Ashbury clinic was given to all attendees. It provided the first, albeit brief, overview of the topic in book form (available from Haight-Ashbury Publications, 409 Clayton St., San Francisco, CA 94117, $17). Papers from the conference were collected into a special edition of the *Journal of Psychoactive Drugs* (October-December, 1986). There were articles by many of the presenters at the conference which contributed greatly to the volume of published academic information about MDMA.

With the exception of an occasional local newspaper feature or small magazine story, MDMA would now almost seem to have never existed. There was no evidence of a massive groundswell of use or abuse. Few people were arrested for it or appeared in hospitals suffering from its effects.

The DEA promised researchers that it would facilitate research for those qualified after scheduling, but researchers instead found that it was virtually impossible to get a research protocol approved; scientific studies became impossible.

Then, in September 1987, the First District Court of Appeals issued a decision. It ordered the DEA to vacate the ruling placing MDMA in Schedule I on a permanent basis.

The First Circuit Court ruled that the DEA did not lawfully follow the correct criteria for deciding whether or not MDMA met the standard for "currently accepted medical use in treatment in the United States" and for "accepted safety for use . . . under medical supervision."

With the ball back in its court, the DEA was only required to reconsider the matter administratively. The DEA decided quickly that they had been right all along and placed MDMA back again in Schedule I, effective March 23, 1988.

It appears now that this ruling will stand for a long time. Those who have fought so long against the disproportionate power and financial resources of a DEA seemingly adament in its desire to keep MDMA a scheduled drug may now give up. There is still legal recourse but every legal victory the researchers have seen has been negated by the fiat of the DEA Administrator.

And just as I am completing this saga, I am surprised to discover a story titled, "Ecstasy: Poll Says 40% at Stanford Have Tried It" on the first page of my morning newspaper, the *San Jose Mercury News*. Also today, a story with the same theme in the *San Francisco Chronicle* by Science Editor David Perlman reports:

More than a third of all Stanford University undergraduates may have used the illegal drug called Ecstasy
according to a student poll that was reported yesterday.

In a letter in the current issue of the *New England Journal
of Medicine*, Dr. Stephen Peroutka, a Stanford neurologist,
reported that 39 percent of 369 students interviewed in a
random sample said they had used the drug at least once.

Some said they had taken it 25 or more times, but four to
five times was the average use, the poll showed.

The survey [was] conducted anonymously under Peroutka's supervision by two undergraduates who stationed
themselves on Stanford's "White Plaza" to conduct their
interviews.

One last bit of recent media attention, "Tune In, Turn On, Go to the
Office Late on Monday," appeared first in *Rolling Stone* and was recently
reprinted in P.J. O'Rourke's humorous collection, *Republican Party
Reptile*. O'Rourke tries to describe the mental effects of MDMA:

If you think of your mind as an animal act (as good a
metaphor as any, since bugger-all is known about how
psychoactive drugs work in the brain), Ecstasy gets right in
the cage and bangs the anxiety bear on the head with a lead
pipe. It has the big cats up on their footstools making like
stuffed carnival prizes. And it brings on the adorable fox
terriers in party hats who walk on their hind legs, ride on
ponies, and jump through the hoops for four hours.

And so, hopefully with a smile, ends my story of the discovery and
history of the key to the door to that other room I pictured in the
beginning of this chapter. In the following chapters we will explore the
dimensions of our "alternative state of consciousness" room as well as
the use and possible future of this new key to ecstasy.

Chapter II.
What is an Empathogen?

"To empathize is to see with the eyes of another, to hear with the ears of another, and to feel with the heart of another."
—an anonymous English author, quoted by Alfred Adler

Enhanced communication and the exploration of interpersonal relationships are two of the most talked-about effects when MDMA comes up in conversation among users. Indeed, it is this quality that must distinguish MDMA and its chemical relatives from all other drugs. True, ampthetamines and cocaine push people to talk a lot, but oftentimes meaning gets lost in the chatter. Also, these stimulants orient the individual toward self-absorption. Talking becomes a means for self-gratification rather than a means of communication.

The unique quality which the MDMA family possesses can be summed up in one word: empathy. In fact, Ralph Metzner, Ph.D., Dean of the California Institute of Integral Studies, proposed this new name for a group of substances in an address at a 1983 Conference at the University of California, Santa Barbara, on "Psychedelics and Spirituality."

Another group of drugs are the phenethylamines, of which MDA is an example. Instead of calling these "psychedelic drugs," I'd like to suggest the name "empathogenic." Empathogenic means "empathy generating." Everyone I've mentioned this name to thinks it is a good one. These drugs don't produce visions as LSD does. They don't produce multileveled thinking or objectivity toward your mind as LSD and the psychedelics do. They generate a profound state of empathy for self and other in the most general and profound terms. A state of empathy where the feeling is that the self, the other, and the world is basically good, is all right. This state can be referred to as the ground of being, the core of our being, a still point of our being.

Then individuals using these substances in therapy can look at their own problems from the standpoint of stillness and empathy. They are able to do changework on themselves very rapidly, compared to ordinary therapy.

In this chapter, we will explore the interpersonal nature of the MDMA experience. This dimension can be characterized as "empathetic," but will also touch on other aspects of the interpersonal encounter, including those of a sensual or sexual nature. The next chapter will discuss the intrapersonal facet of MDMA sessions, perhaps best represented by chemist David Nichols' term "entactogen."

What is Empathy?

The modern use of the word "empathy" began in 1897, when the German psychologist Theodore Lipps published a description of a process of aesthetic appreciation. Lipps used the term "Einfuhlung" to designate losing self-awareness on the part of an observer, as that individual views a painting or a piece of sculpture. Further, it denotes the tendency of the subject to fuse with the object that absorbs his attention. Edward B. Tichner, a psychologist at Cornell University, then introduced "empathy" as the English equivalent for the original German.

According to Katz, who wrote a book on the subject, "When we experience empathy, we feel as if we were experiencing someone else's feelings as our own. We see, we feel, we respond, and we understand as if we were, in fact, the other person."

Empathy means projecting our imagination outside of ourselves and into another human being. The experiencing of someone else's lifespace might be either physical, imaginary, or perhaps both.

At this juncture, you might be asking, "Empathy. So what? What is the value of taking a substance that can help you go beyond yourself and understand how others think and feel?"

Empathy is both enjoyable and a useful experience for healthy people to have. And for those emotionally troubled, it can be invaluable as therapy. In the direction of growth and self-actualization, the experience of empathic contact offers the strengthening, deepening, or revitalization of existing relationships as well as helping in the formation of new ones. In terms of therapy, empathy promises to teach people to be kind to each other, to love one another rather than hurting.

When the emotionally troubled can get out of their selfish way of seeing the world and stand, for a moment, in someone else's shoes, they begin to realize that others have feelings and senses and hurt, just like they do. This may go a long way to deter them from violence. In a world of too little love and too much violence, any tool accentuating the former and reducing the latter is worth looking into.

Empathy also helps in healing close relationships. MDMA has been used in family therapy and marital counseling to get meaningful dialogue going within these relationship systems. MDMA sessions enhance intimacy and allow for direct, loving, and honest verbal communication of what is real and meaningful between participants.

Using Empathy in Couples Therapy

The following is an account of the work of Rick Ingrasci, M.D., a Massachusetts physician from an article by Joe Klien in *New York* magazine:

> The first time Bob Littlehale took MDMA under Dr. Rick Ingrasci's supervision, he experienced an epiphany. "I realized I loved my wife. It was an enormous feeling, it just filled my chest," says Littlehale, a prominent Massachusetts physician. "I had to pick up the phone and call her. She was at work. It didn't matter. That feeling has stayed with me, too. This stuff won't let you forget."
>
> "He sounded totally joyful," Marie Littlehale recalls. "He didn't sound spaced or dull or buzzed. It was pretty embarrassing."
>
> Though they have taken the drug together since Bob's epiphany, the Littlehales are quick to point out that MDMA hasn't saved their marriage; after 24 years of sporadic warfare, it may not be salvageable. "But it *has* made us a lot more aware of the issues at stake," Marie says: "It's really helped us along in the process of figuring out what we want to do."
>
> "It's not a panacea," says Ingrasci. "It won't save an unhappy marriage. But I've found it to be incredibly useful."
>
> Before he learned about MDMA from friends, Ingrasci had built a sucessful practice based upon holistic principles, emphasizing the connection between mental and physical health. He was especially well known for his work with people who suffered from serious illnesses. In fact, Marie

Littlehale first visited Ingrasci because she believed she was in the early stages of multiple sclerosis. The Littlehales spent about a year in therapy, individually and as a couple, before Ingrasci suggested MDMA as a possibility.

"I took the drug before I ever gave it to a patient," Ingrasci says, "and experienced an enormous sense of well being. I don't recommend it for everyone. Usually, I'll simply suggest that mind-altering drugs are one of several possible therapeutic strategies. If the patient decides that's what he or she wants, I'll set a two-hour appointment for them and tell them to come an hour early to take the drug."

Ingrasci gets his MDMA from a local chemist. He administers it either in capsules or as a powder mixed in fruit juice.

Rick Ingrasci, M.D., a Boston therapist who used MDMA in couples-therapy.

"About half the people have a mild physical reaction—tightened jaw, nausea, some anxiety—that passes pretty quickly," he says. "Usually people just begin to talk, but sometimes I have to take a more active role. With couples especially, sometimes they'll just want to sit here hugging or rocking back and forth, and I'll have to say, 'Listen, folks, let's get down to the business at hand.' "

Drug-Induced Empathy?

A question that may arise here is: *How can a drug, a chemical substance we ingest, produce a human experience like empathy?*

Drugs don't produce experiences; experiences occur in people. MDMA changes the electrochemical balance of the brain in ways that we still do not understand. By changing the chemical nature of the brain, it is as if a neurological switch were flipped, providing the MDMA user with access to an alternative state of consciousness. As the individual "opens up" in this new state, normal defense patterns are temporarily suspended. In this changed mental posture, empathy and some other characteristic experiences are more likely to occur.

This whole area of "drug affects experience" touches on a complex philosophical and psychological issue: the relationship between the brain and the mind. Without attempting to answer this classic enigma, we can see that what empathogenic compounds do is trigger the experience of empathy within the body/mind (whether body and mind are the same thing or just interrelated).

Experimental Empathy

Empathy and its effects were a major theme in the report on the first formal study of MDMA with humans carried out by George Greer, M.D., and Requa Tolbert, R.N. George Greer is a psychiatrist and Requa Tolbert is a psychiatric nurse. They are married and living in New Mexico, and they used MDMA in his psychotherapy practice until it was criminalized. New Mexico and California are two states that permit a physician to use drugs in their treatment of patients, and allow them to manufacture the drugs themselves with peer review and informed consent.

In order to investigate the effects and usefulness of MDMA, Greer and Tolbert initiated a pilot study of MDMA. They used none of his private-practice patients in the study, instead recruiting a group of 29 subjects by word of mouth. The group was screened to exclude serious psychiatric problems and contraindicated medical problems, such as heart disease or hypertension. They reported on this pilot investigation in the *Journal of Psychoactive Drugs*, Oct.-Dec. 1986:

> Every subject experienced some benefit from MDMA during his or her session. 27 felt closer and more intimate with anyone present. (The other 2 had solo sessions.) All 21 subjects who had sessions in couples or groups experienced more closeness and/or enhanced communication. And 2 found it easier to receive compliments or criticism . . .

> It is our general conclusion that the single best use of MDMA is to facilitate more direct communication between people involved in a significant emotional relationship.

> Not only is communication enhanced during the session but afterward as well. Once a therapeutically motivated person has experienced the lack of true risk involved in direct and open communication, it can be practiced without the assistance of MDMA. This ability can not only help resolve existing conflicts but also prevent future ones from occurring due to unexpressed fears or misunderstandings.

> Regardless of the mechanism, most subjects expressed a greater ease in relating to their partners, friends and coworkers . . .

Norman Zinberg, associated with the Harvard Medical School, did a study of MDA as an investigation "in the phenomenology of consciousness change." His results were published in the January-March 1976 issue of the *Journal of Psychedelic Drugs*.

In his study, Zinberg conducted several MDA sessions. He observed, "It was the repeated insistence on empathic awareness of what others were thinking that fascinated me."

Zinberg attempted to find out more about the nature of these empathic sensations by speaking separately to individuals having such experiences. He reports:

> Not only was such a subject able to describe what others felt, e.g. "A is thinking of sex with B" or "I think C is lost in childhood memories or relationship fantasies with D," but they were also able to say something about the cues that led to these conclusions—the way somebody was now dripping with sand, the way the lines formed around a person's mouth, or the way somebody looked over there and then looked away. These cues were ones that I had not noticed until they pointed them out to me. However, the intermediate steps of how the cues led to the final, empathic

awareness could not be articulated. I would then drift over to the person we had been talking about, and asked what s/he had been thinking. 80% of the time my original respondent was correct down to quite fine details.

It was remarkable, and it gave me some sense of why some psychedelic users of my acquaintance had become interested in ESP. I asked particularly if this empathy was based on unusual closeness to a particular individual and usually was told, "No." In fact, it seemed to operate as effectively with people who were not close friends.

Although Zinberg's study was done with MDA, it is relevant in our discussion. I pointed out earlier that MDMA is a more pure empathogen than MDA; if MDA displays empathic effects, certainly MDMA would. I will use data from MDA studies throughout this book. It should be understood that the two substances do not have identical effects. They are, however, in the same family. Information gathered from any of the members of this family are true, to a certain extent, about all of them.

Opening Up

The initial phase of the MDMA experience occurs about half an hour after ingestion. This period leasts from 15 to 25 minutes. It is at this time that the sensation of "opening up" is felt most intensively. Claudio Naranjo, M.D., author of *The Healing Journey* and an early collaborator in Shulgin's research, called this period of the session, "a brief, fleeting moment of sanity." During this "peak," unexpressed feelings or emotions flow freely between participants in the session. B. Van Alstyne, in "Some Personal Observations on the 'Adam' Experience," states:

> The major effect we have noticed is definitely RELA-TIONAL [author's caps] in nature. That is, the XTC tends to dissolve the barriers people normally interpose between themselves and others, and thereby allows the true feelings present at the heart level to manifest themselves. This is immediately felt when the drug first comes on. Upon looking at your partner's eyes, you will no doubt find that you are seeing her or him in a way that you have never experienced before, or perhaps only rarely or partially. There is a sense of incredible beauty and perfection in your perception of the other person, and a feeling of absolutely unconditional love. Social factors which may have con-

ditioned your love for that person, such as considerations about the person's opinions, goals, habits and particularly FEARS about the state of the relationship or its eventualities, are felt in a completely different light, if at all. Communication becomes effortless, even when worries or differing feelings are expressed. There is the certainty that the other individual is perfect and infinitely beautiful just as he or she is, even when the differences expressed have been issues in the relationship up to the present. IT SEEMS possible ONLY TO BE IN A TRUTHSPACE [note: relating truthfully] during the XTC experience and the truth experienced is the truth that grows out of unconditional love.

Unconditional love refers to the sort of love which places no expectations on the beloved. It comes from a total acceptance of the individual just as they are. It can be seen as an interpersonal reflection of the feeling of the "all rightness of the universe"—seeing just the basic fact of being alive as sufficient for happiness, with all of life's troubles and cares—experienced on MDMA intrapersonally. This experience of unconditional love is similar to the unconditional positive regard that Carl Rogers recommends that therapists have toward their clients.

In fact, MDMA has been consistently heralded by therapists as facilitating an open relationship between therapist and client, in which material that might normally be withheld can be expressed. This makes it useful, for example, in a diagnostic interview early in therapy. Therapists call this sort of approach "breaking down the walls" between therapist and client or "good transference."

A possible use for good transference would be in hypnotherapy. For deep hypnotic trance, it is essential that there be trust established between hypnotist and subject. MDMA may facilitate conditions of trust. This has been corroborated by anecdotal information from hypnotherapists I know, who have attempted trancework using MDMA. They have found that MDMA facilitates induction of trance and results in deeper trances.

Another concept relevant to the special kind of relating we are talking about is what theologian Martin Buber called the "I-Thou" relationship. Buber contrasted the "I-Thou" with the "I-It" relationship. The former is authentic contact between two people in which each respects the other's basic humanness. The "I-It" relationships are interactions which reduce each of the partners to lifeless objects. In the vernacular of the time, it is the difference between "fucking" (I-It) and "making love" (I-Thou).

The MDMA experience often has this same quality of enhanced authenticity. Interaction between partners turns away from superficial issues and toward a deeper "soul" connection, away from "I-It" and toward "I-Thou." David Robinette, a hypnotherapist from Santa Cruz, California, comments on MDMA's effects on relationship formation.

> The therapeutic value of "ecstasy" (MDMA) may lie in its capacity to act upon the heart center, expanding the feeling/sensory/emotional body into higher, more subtle realms. It also acts upon the perceptual center in the fore-brain, metaphorically called the "third eye," amplifying perceptions of the finer permutations of human interactions.
>
> This can allow for a deeper bonding process to take place in relationships where for some reason the natural bonding process has been prevented from occurring. Bonding is the capacity to connect meaningfully on a deeper feeling level to one's self or another in a relationship of trust. The bonding capacity is ordinarily developed at birth. It is the secure, trusting relationship with the mother that allows for mature pair bonding late in life. Where that capacity has been co-opted by a system that does not regard the infant as a fully developed human being nor sees the necessity of early infancy and childhood bonding, MDMA holds promise of allowing a healing to take place on those primary feeling levels.

A useful model of what occurs during the MDMA experience can be found in the psychology of Wilhelm Reich. Reich, a student of Sigmund Freud, developed a theory centered on the body and movements of biological energy within the body. In a normal, healthy individual (a rare bird in our society), the energy moves throughout the body in pulsations. In this state of free-flowing energy, which Reich labeled "orgastic potency," a person is capable of expressing emotions and of full sexual orgasm.

However, for most of us, the traumas involved in growing up in our society, with its restriction on sexual expression, leads to blockages of bioenergy in the body, which Reich called "character armor." This muscular armoring occurs in certain parts of the body. These regions of armoring include the pelvis, the chest, and the face. Orgasm is restricted to the genital region and does not extend throughout the body, as in a healthy person. Reich departed from Freud's verbal couch therapy by actually attempting to manipulate the body in order to break down the armoring. It appears that MDMA might also accomplish the same goal. Alfred Scopp, Ph.D., a clinical psychologist, observed, "MDMA is analgesic. The effect of MDMA is to relax the muscular armoring. This results in the bringing to the surface of associated psychological trauma, defense or mental pain, which is then easily released."

To speculate a bit, perhaps the bubble-bursting phenomenon noted above is the process by which repressed negative emotional exeriences from the past can be brought to the surface. On an interpersonal level, this results in direct expressions of previously repressed feelings and a way of behaving which is freed from habitual patterns.

Sexuality

The following is from an article, "Psychiatrists Defend New Street Drug for Therapy" by Miles Corwin in the *Los Angeles Times*, Monday, May 27, 1985.

> [MDMA] is known as "the love drug" on college campuses where it is considered to be an aphrodisiac, but users who were interviewed said it precipitates emotional, not sexual feelings.
>
> "You can't sleaze with it," said student Jeff Manning, who has taken the drug several times for the "experience." "Your true emotions come out and nobody's going to do something they don't want to do."

The question of whether MDMA is an aphrodisiac is perhaps one of the most fascinating and complex aspects of its interpersonal effects. This is because MDMA both intensifies and changes the nature of lovemaking.

The answer to the aphrodisiac question hinges upon what definition is used for the term "aphrodisiac." James Gawin, in the *Journal of Psychedelic Drugs*, July-Oct. 1978, points to a disparity between the classical definition of aphrodisiac, used in scientific studies, which emphasizes the enhancement of sexual drive or libido, and a broader notion of aphrodisiac, which includes the substance's effect on subjective pleasure experienced in sexual activity, without considering its effects on libido.

When the classical definition of aphrodisiac is used, then no such substance has thus far been developed or discovered. Gawin suggests "expanding the definition of aphrodisiacs to include an effect of a pharmacological substance on the subjective pleasure of sexual experience, independent of any effect at all on what is commonly considered libido or sexual drive."

Once this new meaning for aphrodisiac is accepted, then many psychoactive substances can be examined as such aphrodisiacs. Gawin goes on to describe MDMA's chemical relative, MDA:

> Perhaps the most significant potential for sexual benefit through the use of pharmacologic substances rests with MDA (3, 4-methylenedioxyamphetamine). MDA has gained some underground notoriety as a sexual stimulant of sorts and has also been proposed as an adjunct to psychotherapy . . . It seems to unite some of the sexual enhancement and increased pleasure derived from stimulants with the ability to enhance affect, facilitate self-insight and enhance interpersonal empathy in a manner common to the hallucinogens but without the perceptual alterations, depersonalizations or disturbances in thought which often prevent the hallucinogens from being useful therapeutically or as consistent aphrodisiacs . . . Several authors . . . have noted that MDA brings feelings of deep interpersonal needs and of effects described as "love" to the surface. In all, it appears that the "enhancing stimulant" and "emotional components" of the drug actions may merge in sexual situations to produce an "affective" aphrodisiac.

Several individuals have looked at the relationship between MDA or MDMA and sexuality. Zinberg, in another observation from his previously mentioned MDA study, notes:

> Sexual relationships were possible, especially as the drug waned, but during the height of the high, people described a greater interest in general, diffused sensualism than in specific sexuality, such as intercourse or masturbation.
> (Although two subjects told me that when they had taken the drug alone, and only then, did they become sexually preoccupied and masturbate frequently.) This sensualism showed itself in a wish to touch others or to feel the sand, grass, water, flowers or the like. Again, the desire to touch or pleasure in touching was specifically pansexual, and often not connected to everyday closeness.

Another early explorer of the effects of this group of mind-changers is Andrew Weil. Weil, reporting on the effects of MDA in the *Journal of Psychedelic Drugs:*

> Participants may feel very loving toward one another, but the feelings are not explicitly sexual because MDA tends to decrease the desire for orgasm. For many people the experience of enjoying physical contact and feeling love for others in the absence of a specific hunger for sex is unique and welcome.

A third view of the sexual experience, this time specifically about MDMA, is offered by B. Van Alstyne in his unpublished "Some Personal Observations on the 'Adam' Experience":

> Probably the most striking and beautiful experience for us, as well as for many others who have utilized Adam as a relational tool, was the way in which our sexuality integrated into this heart-consciousness. Adam is NOT an "aphrodisiac" in that it has no direct stimulative effect on the sexual channels. In fact, I noticed that my ability—and, more significantly, my desire—to build up a charge of ORGASMIC [author's caps] energy in the usual manner was noticeably inhibited. What does occur, however, is a complete dissolution of any artificial barriers to the expressions of LOVE. So when it FEELS appropriate to express love sexually, there are no BARRIERS TO DOING THIS. (During and after our first trip, we scarcely got out of bed for two days.)
>
> But the QUALITY of the lovemaking experience is what is so completely transformative. There is the feeling of being CONSCIOUS about the fact that you are here, now, making love with your bodies. We found a wonderful and magical naturalness about using our bodies in this way, and especially about using our senses to appreciate our bodies and what we were doing with them. I discovered a completely uninhibited fascination with touching my partner's body intentionally, slowly, consciously, using all my senses wide-open, watching our bodies intently with rapt fascination and wonderment. Again, the incredible ORDINARINESS of it all was quite amazing to me . . .
>
> We both had the feeling that the only factors affecting whether people would become sexually interactive during the Adam experience were 1) their own level of sexual

orientedness with people in general, and 2) the perceived appropriateness ON A HEART LEVEL (rather than a socio-cultural level) of being sexual with a given other or others. More simply, we don't see that there would likely be a lot of internalized stress or struggle going on as part of this experience; if two or more people involved in an Adam trip felt a desire to be sexual with each other as an expression of their immediate feelings of love and connectedness, they

Andrew Weil, M.D., author of The Natural Mind.

would probably do so quite spontaneously and naturally. The point is that the experience of Adam deletes both COMPULSION and INHIBITION, whichever is present, with regard to sexuality.

In an article published in the October 1985 *Journal of Psychoactive Drugs*—the first survey of MDMA's effects on human sexuality, "MDMA and Human Sexual Function"—John Buffum, Pharm.D., and Charles Moser, Ph.D., summarized their findings.

> It appears that MDMA does not increase sexual excitation or sexual desire in a majority of individuals. For both males and females, MDMA enhances the sensual aspects of sex. This may be due to the increased feelings of emotional closeness.
>
> Almost half of the males and a third of the females indicated that they felt more receptive to being sexual while under the influence of MDMA, but this effect was not paralleled by an increased interest in initiating sexual activity in either the men or the women. While a majority indicated that they would use MDMA as a sexual enhancer, most of the subjects who had used MDMA during sex reported increased emotional closeness. It is curious that a drug, which can increase emotional closeness, enhance receptivity to being sexual and would be chosen as a sexual enhancer, does not increase the desire to initiate sex.
>
> The subjects who were surveyed found that MDMA makes orgasm more difficult to achieve, especially for males. Erectile ability was decreased in almost half the males. No other sexual effects occurred in a majority of subjects.

The preceding observations allow us to generalize about MDMA, its close relative MDA, and their relationship to sexuality, as follows:

Both substances can be classified as aphrodisiacs under Gawin's definition of the term. These empathogens seem to encourage physical contact, yet make that contact less specifically sexual. The need to achieve orgasm is decreased, but the pleasurable feelings associated with body contact are increased. This diminished drive toward orgasm has some interesting correlates. Reich's example of the individual who has reached orgastic potency is one of these. The orgastically potent are not locked into mechanical fixation on their genitals during sexuality. Perhaps, then, experiences on empathogens might provide a model for orgastic potency.

An Oriental parallel to this is to be found in the tantric yoga of the Hindus and the Buddhists. In tantric yoga, the sex partners attempt to lie quietly in sexual union without movement for long periods of time. They are advised to avoid orgasm, instead focusing on the energy exchanged between them. There is an attempt made to turn the sexual act into a sacred ritual. Here, again, the substances we are examining provide an experiential model.

Another common theme found in accounts looking at MDMA and sexuality stress that it demands authenticity in love-making unlike cocaine, alcohol, and Quaaludes which have a reputation as seduction drugs. Some promiscuous gays in the New York bar scene who use cocaine in one-night sexual pickups found MDMA to be an unsatisfactory substitute. Sleazy, selfish motives become transparent under its influence. Because MDMA encourages expression of deep feelings, it is difficult to put up a phony front during the experience.

Is the Experience "Real"?

Taking MDMA so dramatically affects interpersonal behavior that there is a constant question asked of the experience: "Were the expressions of love, caring, and sex real, or was it just the drug?"

This resembles the question posed in the oft-told parable by the Chinese sage Chuang Tsu. Chuang Tsu once had a dream about becoming a butterfly and flying through meadows filled with flowers. He awoke from the dream, and asked, "Am I a man who dreamed he was a butterfly, or a butterfly who is now dreaming he is a man?"

It is this sort of question that compels me to use the term "alternative state of consciousness" rather than "altered state of consciousness." Our ordinary reality or the reality we agree upon by consensus is seen as just one possibility among a wide range of alternatives.

The MDMA experience, in this context, is an alternative state of consciousness in which normal patterns of defensiveness are either changed or vanish entirely. Defenses have evolved for a reason, but can become rigid and dysfunctional. Certainly, to be open and loving is not always appropriate for every situation we find ourselves in.

But the fact that defenses exist in our ordinary consciousness does not make them part of any "real" reality, and another state of consciousness, in which they don't exist, therefore a "false" reality. We could evaluate states of consciousness according to some other standard, such as: "Which state is functional to the individual?" or "Which state is esthetically pleasing?" Certainly a nondefensive, loving state would be judged useful or beautiful by many in such a context.

Of course, compatibility of partners in the MDMA state does *not always* mean that they will continue to get along well in day-to-day life. Timothy Leary, Harvard professor turned LSD guru turned computer software author, tells this story of his own courtship, and issues a warning:

> Barbara and I proceeded to a French restaurant where we consumed a delicious dinner and a bottle of Maison Pierre Grolau. Felt pretty mellow as I remember it. Then Barbara, whose goal in life is to get higher and closer, looked at me with that "let's do it, baby" twinkle in her eye. What could I do? The greatest successes in my life have come from saying

Timothy Leary, Ph.D., didn't want to wait six weeks to marry . . .

"Yes" to Barbara's invitations. We each dropped one pill. I waved to the waiter and made a signing motion. The drug hits me before the waiter returns with the check. ZAP! Barbara looks at me and laughs. "You're so lucky," she sighs. "It always hits you first."

I'm sitting there feeling better than I've ever felt in my life (and I've had some good times). "Look," I say, "you're gonna have to pay the check and take a spoon and ladle me into the cab." Barbara shoots me an envious look. We look in each other's eyes and smile. This is it. We both understand everything. All the defenses, protections and emotional habits are suspended. We realize joyfully how perfect we are

Barbara Leary.

designed to be. Apparently the only thing to do is caress each other.

Well, the experience went on and on. We started to come down after three hours and took another hit. Lots of funny things happened. We chatted away like new-born Buddhas just down from Heaven.

The next day we flew back to Hollywood. Three days later we were married. I should state here that some people have termed X-T-C the "Instant Marriage Syndrome." Lots of people who didn't know each other too well have shared the experience, activated the love-empathy circuits, and rushed off the next day to get married. In some cases, after rose-colored smoke clears, the couple realize that although they did, for a while, share the highest region of love, the practical aspects of their life were not in sync. You might say it's a cosmic summer romance. In fact, it got so bad in Boulder, Colorado that bumper stickers and T-shirts were printed saying, "Don't Get Married for Six Weeks After X-T-C!"

Although Leary advises caution, his marriage with Barbara has lasted ten years, and is still going strong.

Chapter III.
The Uses of an Entactogen

When MDMA initiates begin to describe their experience, the most common themes mentioned are interpersonal. Words and phrases that will probably be sprinkled through an account of the first journey into the world of MDMA include "communication," "love," "opened up," "contact," "deep connection," "empathy," and other terms that indicate that the individual was able to relate better with others.

Yet there is another dimension of the MDMA experience—the world within, the intrapersonal. In fact, still another term for MDMA was coin.d by David Nichols, of the Department of Medicinal Chemistry of Purdue University. He calls MDMA an "entactogen," which is a composite of Latin roots that means "allowing for a touching within." This facet of MDMA as entactogen—affecting a transformation of the inner *psyche*—has uses in therapy and problem solving, meditation, self-actualization, and creativity; and will be the focus of this chapter.

Having made the distinction between the *inter*personal and *intra*personal modes of experience, we should note that the two aspects are intimately linked. When a person feels better about others, he or she also feels better about herself or himself. Feeling better about ourselves is the inward side, and feeling better about others the outward side, of the same experience.

I noted this relationship in the last chapter when discussing what could be called a feeling of "the all-rightness of the universe." There was a concomitant experience in the interpersonal domain—"unconditional love." Here "all-rightness of the universe" and "unconditional love" are like mirror images of each other.

Each reflects the other in its own world. What exactly is this feeling named "all-rightness of the universe"? Well, normally people experience a certain amount of anxiety during day-to-day existence. Worries about various areas of life—money, sex, illness, death, etc.—cloud our ordinary consciousness. We are wrenched from enjoying the present moment by nostalgia and regret about the past, as well as uncertainty about and fear of the future.

Now imagine that the clouds lift and that blue sky breaks out, spreading until it fills the entire half-hemisphere surrounding us. The blue sky is the mind unfettered by problems. Just being alive now seems all that is necessary to be happy. All of those other conditions that were placed on happiness before—a new car, a prettier nose, a job promotion, sex with all those beautiful women/handsome men—disappear. They would be wonderful, but, as Alan Watts once said, "This is it!"

In Claudio Naranjo's The Healing Journey, which we will discuss much more fully later in this chapter, another member of the family of drugs of which MDMA is a part, MMDA, also exhibits this "all-rightness of the universe" feeling.

Naranjo states:

> The perception of things and people is not altered or even enhanced, usually, but negative reactions that permeate our everyday lives beyond our conscious knowledge are held in abeyance and replaced by unconditional acceptance.
>
> This is much like Nietzsche's amour fati, love of fate, love of one's particular circumstances. The immediate reality seems to be welcomed in such MMDA-induced states without pain or attachment; joy does not seem to depend on the given situation, but on existence itself, and in such a state of mind everything is equally lovable . . .

Much the same affect Naranjo attributes to MMDA can also be said of its close relative, MDMA.

Paradoxical Effects

In his address at the Santa Barbara conference mentioned in the last chapter, Ralph Metzner compares this intrapersonal experience on MDMA to "the ground of being, the core of our being, a still point of being."

During many Ecstasy sessions, there comes a moment of calm, of complete stillness, which some meditators have compared to the headspace achieved during the practice of meditation. Because MDMA is a modification of amphetamine, it is this stillness which drug researchers pointed to when they suggested the class of drugs represented by MDMA and MDA as having a "paradoxical effect." When someone takes an ordinary amphetamine such as dexedrine or methedrine, they most usually become agitated, restless and driven. Yet this class of amphetamine derivatives—oddly, paradoxically—brings a peaceful, relaxed, calm state upon the mind and the body.

Effects on the Individual

In the last chapter, some of George Greer's and Requa Tolbert's pilot-study results relevant to the interpersonal effects of MDMA were reviewed. The following are some excerpts of the study which discuss the main intrapersonal effects observed. The first are "some benefits" reported:

David Nichols, Ph.D., defined a new class of psychoactive compounds—the "entactogens."

All 29 subjects reported positive changes in their attitudes or feelings. Sixteen felt warmer, fresher, more alive, euphoric, or loving feelings. Ten mentioned greater self-confidence or self-acceptance, and ten felt their defenses were lowered. Two of these and five others reported undergoing a therapeutic emotional process. Five participants said they had a transcendent experience. Five noticed having fewer negative thoughts or feelings. Three felt more self-aware or self-grounded, and two reported feeling blessed or at peace.

Twenty-two subjects reported some cognitive benefit: an expanded mental perspective, insight into personal patterns or problems, improved self-examination or "intrapsychic communication" skills, or "issue resolution." Five subjects used a low dose (50 mg) to facilitate their creative writing abilities—four in a group session and one alone. All found it quite useful. Five subjects reported clear cognition or enhanced presence of mind. ("Subjective Reports of the Effects of MDMA in a Clinical Setting," Greer, Tolbert, *Journal of Psychoactive Drugs*, Oct.-Dec. 1986.)

Every subject but one in Greer's study had some purpose or goal, other than curiosity and most had multiple reasons for taking the drug. Greer reports:

> Sixteen of these [participants with goals] felt their purpose was completely realized. Four reported significant progress made toward all their goals, and seven felt that

George Greer, M.D., and Requa Tolbert, R.N., the MDMA therapy team that authored the first clinical study.

some of their goals were realized while others were not . . .

Eighteen (18) subjects described positive changes in their mood or emotional state, lasting from several hours to several weeks, and averaging about one week. Fourteen (14) reported having more good feelings. Five of these specifically mentioned euphoria or improved mood, and four mentioned an increase in energy. Eleven (11) reported feeling more relaxed, calm, detached, serene, and/or less anxious or agitated . . .

Twenty-three (23) subjects reported positive changes in attitude lasting from a week to a follow-up time of two years. Again, the average duration was roughly a week . . .

Sixteen (16) subjects reported belief changes that persisted after sessions, but rarely did two report the same specific change. All changes resulted in a more positive belief about themselves, individually or in their relation to others or to the world in general.

Implications of Early Research
with Related Compounds

As these benefits and positive changes suggest, MDMA has important uses in psychotherapy. Before going on to examine the results of the Greer study with respect to its therapeutic implications and descriptions of specific cases, let us consider why the MDMA experience is useful therapeutically. Not much has been published examining this question. Only one book to date has addressed the therapeutic uses of Ecstasy—published in 1974, *The Healing Journey* by Claudio Naranjo, M.D.

I feel quite lucky to have had Claudio Naranjo as teacher of a class that I attended in Humanistic Psychology, when I was an undergraduate at the University of California, Santa Cruz, where Narajo was a visiting professor in the Spring of 1978.

Naranjo is a Chilian psychiatrist with a Ph.D. in mathematics and a background as a concert pianist. *The Healing Journey* is about Naranjo's use of four drugs—MDA, MMDA, harmaline and ibogaine—in his psychiatric practice. He calls the first two "feeling enhancers" and the latter two "fantasy enhancers."

Although the book was completed in 1970, the work within it was carried out between 1965 and 1966 in Santiago, Chile, which is also where the MDA chapter was written and the book on the four drugs conceived. At the time, Naranjo was a research psychiatrist at the pioneering Centro de Estudios de Anthropologia Medica at the medical school of the University of Chile.

MDA, MMDA and MDMA are all members of the same chemical family. Perhaps one of the most fascinating facets of what we have learned from studying these substances is that although there is a strong family resemblance in their main effect, each also differs in a clearly distinguishable fashion; so an individual who has had several experiences with each can tell them apart. In the Appendix to this book, "The MDMA Family Tree," we will find that this variation has been named the "structure-activity relationship" and described in a paper by Alexander Shulgin published in *Nature*. In it, he shows how differences in mental effects can be predicted by varying the actual chemical structure of the molecule. This relationship will also have implications when we explore the future of these compounds in understanding and controlling the human nervous system.

Naranjo wrote that the family of "phenylisopropolamines, [i.e.] MDA and MMDA, is characterized mainly by its effects of feeling enhancement, sharpening of attention, increased fluency in associations and communication."

From there, Naranjo goes about distingushing between the two drug relatives.

MDA, according to the Chilian psychiatrist, is a "Drug of Analysis." By this, he means that its therapeutic effect is brought about by exploration of past events, similar to psychoanalysis, which emphasizes the effect of early childhood events upon the individual. Naranjo says of MDA, "regression occurs so frequently and spontaneously that it can be considered a typical effect of the substance, and a primal source of its therapeutic value."

In contrast, "MMDA and the Eternal Now" is the chapter title given the other feeling enhancer. He says of the peak experience sometimes elicited by this substance:

> It is possible to speak of both individuality and dissolution, but these are blended into a characteristic new totality. Dissolution is here expressed in an openness to experience, a willingness to hold no preference; individuality, on the other hand, is implied in the absence of depersonalization phenomena, and in the fact that the subject is concerned with the everyday world of persons, objects and relationships.
>
> The MMDA peak experience is typically one in which

the moment that is being lived becomes intensely gratifying in all its circumstantial reality, yet the dominant feeling is not one of euphoria but of calm and serenity.

Naranjo's therapy with MMDA appears to utilize two principles. First, he takes advantage of the mood of serenity and detachment brought on by the drug to explore his patient's problems. He states, "As different as spiritual detachment and healthy psychological functioning may be, I believe that the latter may gradually develop in the presence of the former, making the therapeutic implication of such a peak experience an indirect one. One of the ways in which a mood of serenity may result in further change is that it increases the possibility of insight, much as an analgesic can permit surgical exploration of a wound."

A second principle, used in MMDA therapy, is the hope that the new modes of experience achieved on MMDA will carry over into the patient's life in the days after the actual end of the session. Naranjo suggests:

> The state of mind reached under the facilitation of MMDA is not something that simply lasts for a given time and then is lost, but one that may be *learned.* Once a person has used his mind in that way, he has easier access to the same way of functioning. And in this learning, whereby a desirable attitude can be "remembered" not only intellec-tually but *functionally* (as the movements of writing and walking are remembered when we do them) after it has been adopted once, lies, I believe, one of the major justi-fications for the edification of an artificial peak experience. This could be likened to the guiding hand which holds that of a child to show him how to draw a letter, or those of the practitioner in M. Alexander's system, showing a person how to stand or sit so that he can feel the "taste" of rightness, or, in the conception of Mexican shamans using *peyotl,* the guiding hand of God. Once in possession of such discrimination or knowledge, it is up to the individual to remember it and put it into practice.

In each of Naranjo's two chapters, case histories and session reports of patients are discussed to demonstrate the relations between drug action and therapeutic effect. In the use of MDA, Naranjo employs a psychoanalytical approach to the therapy, with its emphasis on remembering and working through of childhood traumas. With

MMDA, he uses the more existential Gestalt therapy, which emphasizes a centering in the present moment. In both chapters, some remarkable breakthroughs in neurotic conditions are described.

How does MDMA compare with these other family members? First, Adam is shorter-acting than the other two. MDA lasts for 8-12 hours and MMDA somewhat shorter, but MDMA lasts only 3-4 hours. Like MMDA, MDMA is a drug that brings the user into the "here-and-now." But it also can act like MDA, to bring forth repressed experience from childhood. MDMA resembles MDA in its stimulation of speech. In fact, it is more of a stimulant than MDA and increases verbal fluency much more. In addition, the peak experience that occurs on MDMA is sometimes euphoric, thus differing from the "serenity and calm" of MMDA.

When Alexander Shulgin performed his 1976 research on the effects of MDMA on humans, Claudio Naranjo was the research psychologist on Shulgin's research team. This was described in *New York* magazine:

> "The effect (of MDMA) was much different from MDA," recalls Dr. Claudio Naranjo, who worked closely with Shulgin. "MDMA was not hallucinogenic. It seemed, too, less toxic than MDA. When administered in small doses, there were few, if any, side effects; a slight tightening of the jaw, some nausea, and those would pass in the first half-hour. And the psychological effect—it was completely different from any other drug. It was like a brief, fleeting moment of sanity."

Another unique aspect of MDMA is its emotional dimension. It is often described as "heart-opening." As I mentioned earlier, MDMA is the most purely empathogenic of this family of substances.

MDMA can induce an experience of the "eternal here-and-now" as MMDA does, and can also help in the uncovering of repressed experience from the past. Thus, MDMA-assisted therapy can combine elements of both techniques.

For example, a woman who was raped is under the constant duress of the memory of the act. She is given MDMA and suddenly feels wonderful, freed from the negative condition she has been in. This can be used by the therapist in two ways. First, the therapist might talk to the woman about the circumstances surrounding the rape while she is in a trouble-free frame of mind. This would allow her to work through the painful memories without repressing them.

In addition, the woman is given, during her glimpse of an alternative state of consciousness, a chance to see what life is like without fear. This experience of pain-free existence can be remembered by the woman in her post-session life and employed to free herself from the trauma.

Uses in Psychotherapy

The following is a real-life account of a trauma victim's psychotherapy, published on the front page of the *Los Angeles Times*, in an article by *Times* staff writer, Miles Corwin:

> San Francisco—Kathy Tamm was walking to her car following a meditation class in Menlo Park when she was abducted, taken to a wooded area, tied up, beaten and then tortured for several hours. For six months after the incident she underwent intensive therapy, but she showed little progress.
>
> She had terrible nightmares. She was terrified to leave the house. Every unexpected noise, every shadow assulted her senses and brought back visions of the attack.
>
> Tamm, 39, a San Francisco marriage and family counselor, said she was "suicidal, at the end of my rope." As a last resort, Tamm and her psychiatrist (Dr. Joseph Downing) decided to treat her with MDMA, an experimental drug that some psychiatrists had found effective with traumatized patients.
>
> "I've taken it several times, and each time I felt a little less fearful," Tamm said. "The drug helped me regain some measure of serenity and peace of mind and enabled me to begin living a normal life again.
>
> "For the first time, I was able to face the experience, go back and piece together what had happened. By facing it, instead of always burying it, I was able to sort of slowly discharge a lot of horror."

In addition to traumatic conditions such as rape, MDMA has been employed for its psychotherapeutic value in a number of other applications. These include substance abuse (addiction to cocaine, alcohol, etc.), phobias, psychosomatic disorders, neurotic disorders such as minor depression and anxiety, and terminal illnesses. The use of MDMA with terminal illness is illustrated in a case study presented by Requa Tolbert, R.N., and George Greer, M.D., in an unpublished paper in 1985, "The Clinical Use of MDMA":

John was a married man in his early seventies, father to an adult son and daughter. A retired geophysicist and gentleman farmer, he had always been a successful man, in charge of his own life. At the time of his sessions he had been told that he was among the longest-lived survivors to date with multiple myeloma: a mestatic cancerous condition of the bone marrow, which was diagnosed in 1975. He underwent group therapy for two years (predating his cancer diagnosis) to help with depression over family problems. On being diagnosed with cancer, he began therapy in a group format, where he learned deep relaxation, mediation, and visualization to combat his cancer and assist in pain control. He did, in fact, learn to achieve states where his pain was as reduced as it was with narcotics, but still endured much pain.

At the time of our first meeting, his main complaint was "movement pain" from four collapsing vertebrae, secondary to the cancer. Over the past months, the pain had increased, decreasing his physical and sexual activity, ability to go fishing, or to fly his plane. He was also troubled by the depression which usually followed the numerous fractures of his spine which necessitated confinement to bed. The goal of his session with MDMA, which he wished to take with his wife, was to cope with his pain in a better way and to receive help in adjusting to his current life changes.

During his first session, he and his wife remained in separate rooms with eyeshades and headphones on for five hours. John would hum along with the classical music being played. Shortly after his extra dose of 50 mg. of MDMA, he announced ecstatically that he was free of pain, and began singing aloud with the music and repeatedly proclaiming his love for his wife and family. He spent several hours in his rapturous state. Afterwards he said this was the first time he had really been pain-free in the four years since the current relapse of his myeloma had begun. He described his beautiful experience of being inside his vertebrae, straightening out the nerves, and "gluing" fractured splinters back together.

In a letter two weeks after his session, he stated that his pain had returned, but that his ability to hypnotically "re-anchor" his pain-free experience greatly assisted him in reducing the pain by himself. John had four MDMA sessions spaced over the course of nine months: each time he achieved relief from his physical pain, and had greater success in controlling painful episodes in the interm by returning himself to an approximation of the MDMA state. He noted in particular that the feelings of cosmic love, and especially forgiveness of himself and others, would usually precede the relief of physical pain. He describes an episode from his second session:

> "As I was finishing the meditation, time ceased to exist, my ego fell away, and I became one with the cosmos. I then started my visualization of my body's immune system fighting my cancer, of the chemo-[therapy] joining with my immune system to kill the cancer cells in my vertebrae and of positive forces coming from the cosmos to fight my cancer. Gradually I went deeper in to where the feelings of love, peace and joy were overwhelming. Although I had heard the new age music before, many details of the music became clear and more beautiful."

The results of the pilot study "Subjective Reports of the Effects of MDMA in a Clinical Setting" by George Greer and Requa Tolbert, which I have mentioned previously, had some interesting implications for the therapeutic use of MDMA.

There were nine participants in the study who had disorders that are listed in *The Diagnostic and Statistical Manual (DSM III)* of the American Psychiatric Association. This book is a list of psychological problems classified into labeled categories with groups of symptoms for each designated disorder.

Greer and Tolbert report:

> All nine subjects with [DSM III] diagnoses reported significant relief from their problems. Two subjects reported full and lasting remissions: subject No. 17 with dysthymic disorder (followup after nine months) and subject No. 23 with a postabortion simple phobia of sexuality and possible pregancy. All three participants with atypical or mixed personality disorders (Nos. 5, 9, and 13), and the four other subjects with depressive disorders (adjustment disorders with depressed mood in Nos. 6 and 22, dysthymic

[depressive] disorder in No. 17, and atypical depression in No. 16) reported improvement.

There were some other benefits reported in Greer's and Tolbert's study with respect to therapy. One was a tendency among participants for relief of low self-esteem and toward greater self-acceptance. Another use indicated by the Greer and Tolbert study is in the area of substance abuse. Half of the participants in this study reported decrease in the use of mind- or mood-altering substances after their session. One noteworthy aspect of this drop in substance use is that it took place without any specific intervention on the part of the researchers.

Thus far, we have discussed treatment of less severe mental disorders. But what about the major psychotic problems such as schizophrenia or major depressive episode? Nothing like formal scientific study has been done, but the experiences of two psychiatrists with these type of patients, given in testimony during the MDMA Scheduling Hearings, gives promise that this new psychiatric tool might have usefulness in these disorders.

The first case is reported by San Francisco psychiatrist Joseph Downing, M.D.

F.R., forty-year-old highly successful entrepreneur, was referred by his business consultant, a distinguished older woman attached to a pre-eminent consulting firm. F.R. had several depressive symptoms, a moderately severe stress syndrome, and the recurrent and obsessive thought that he would do away with himself at age 43 as had his father, also a depressive. He had seen three psychiatrists over a period of six years for these symptoms, finding the antidepressive medication prescribed ineffectual, and offensive in its side-effects. Psychotherapy had no effect. "I played good boy and bullshitted my way through with them, like I do everybody else."

He presented himself as moderately anxious, empty, resenting the general opinion that he "had life made." Comprehensive examination showed a moderate stress syndrome with hormonal depletion but generally excellent physical condition. He had taken MDMA previously. Although these experiences had not uncovered any of his past, he specified that he wished to use MDMA as part of his therapy. Knowing its general usefulness in depressive states, I agreed.

We arranged a day-long session, which produced a flood
of repressed material that emerged into consciousness; he
and his sister were very badly battered and traumatized for
many years by their father who was repeatedly jailed, placed
in psychiatric hospitals, then returned home until he
repeated his psychotic behavior. The tragic cycle ended only
when the father ended his life with carbon monoxide when
the boy was seven. I have rarely heard more vicious details
from persons who have survived physically intact and sane.

Joseph Downing, M.D., used MDMA in his therapy practice.

The man is still in treatment, making good progress with the prospect of having a normal emotional life in a few years. I can say, and I firmly believe, that this absolutely central historical material would never have emerged without the use of MDMA in a proper setting, with a therapist he trusted, and with the effect of MDMA, he was able to acknowledge this previously repressed history of abuse.

Philip E. Wolfson, M.D., is another psychiatrist who testified at the MDMA Scheduling Hearings. Currently he is on the staff of Sequoia Hospital in Redwood City, and is awaiting a faculty appointment at the University of California-San Francisco School of Medicine, where he teaches in the Psychiatric Aspects of Medicine Program. For years he has worked with individuals and families experiencing psychotic crises. The following are remarks about a man diagnosed by his previous psychiatrist as "schizophrenic":

I wish to report . . . the case of a 27-year old male whom I would describe as a "flagrant" borderline individual with long bouts of psychoses beginning in his 25th year. He was hospitalized at that time with symptoms of frank delusions, hallucinations, extreme paranoia, negativism, homophobia, and a fixed persecutory set of delusions centered on an entity called the "force." Of a well-to-do family, this individual was sent to some of the better institutions in this country in the family's quest for help. This man remained largely refractory (did not respond) to lithium, which was given to control manic elements, and to neuroleptics (major tranquilizers).

I first saw him a year prior to this report under intensive family and individual-treatment circumstances on an out-patient basis in San Francisco. His family took up residence in the city in order to work with me. He was extremely elusive, negative, lacking in insight, and extremely suspicious and guarded. He refused to use medication immediately after discharge from the hospital in Texas where he had been confined after having demonstrated his psychosis to the local police there. The parents had brought him by air to San Francisco and we began our work.

The work was successful in allowing him to continue his travels with an increased degree of safety and a reduction in paranoia. He refused to stay put and intimacy issues [prevented] a positive transference for any length of time or a positive interaction that would allow for reduction of symptoms based on increased trust. A period of re-parenting with the mother's cooperation was partially successful in re-establishing a connection that needed to be bolstered. However, he could not move from a regressed state to a more integrated ego state.

I followed his activities at a distance in consultation with the parents as he used up his money and used up his options. Hospitalizations occurred along the road. Calls from doctors would arrive shortly after he left his protective umbrella. Eventually he ended up with his brother in Denver, quickly wore out his welcome by outlandish activities, and ended up voluntarily admitting himself to a

Phillip E. Wolfson, M.D., used MDMA to treat psychotics.

state hospital after having committed some bizarre acts following their initial refusal to take him in. After several weeks of hospitalization, with his consent and his parents consent, he and they came to California and therapy was resumed, this time with the aid of MDMA.

The first session was profound in the change in this individual's sense of self. Connections of an affectional nature were made with his parents and myself and the openings of trust experience began. For the first time in two years, he experienced a glimpse of a positive self-image and loving feelings that did not panic him. The afterglow of this session lasted several days with intensity, but recognition of that positive self-image has lasted permanently. A second session ten days later consolidated his sense of difference, increased his ability to cope with the delusions that he continued to experience, and enabled him to view himself as potentially redeemable from the "ape" image that he carried of himself.

We are now in the third stage of psychotherapy, there having been a hiatus of six weeks between this last experience and the start of this new work. A considerable distance needs to be traveled. Longstanding characterological issues are in the way. Manic energy and a depressive core remain apparent. Nonetheless there is a greater sense of independence, and an ability to tolerate some degree of aloneness and perceptual-cognitive changes that allow for a new experience of the world. Much remains to be done and MDMA is a vital ally in this work. This man continues on other medications which are suspended for brief periods of time when doing work with MDMA.

Dr. Robert Masters, a psychotherapist who is also a pioneering researcher with mind-altering drugs, points to the effectiveness of MDMA in the treatment of severe depression. As he has observed it, the tendency of MDMA to eliminate negative ideations and emotions extents to even near-suicidally depressed patients. The breaking up of emotional and ideational patterns—also muscular ones—provides the "crack in the iceberg" which then allows the syndrome to dissipate—sometimes altogether and even permanently after just a single session. When only temporary relief is a result, then a second or third session with the drug might be warranted.

As with most other clinical applications, a good deal more evidence is needed to allow anyone to state that this approach is always without hazards. However, limited experience suggests, Masters says, that there may be no better therapy available when the depression is extreme to the point of causing great suffering or even endangering a patient's life.

One last possible use of MDMA that has been suggested, but, as far as I know, not tried as yet, is with autistic children. Two different authorities have independently suggested this: June Reidlinger, in the previously mentioned article in the *Journal of Psychoactive Drugs*, as well as Morris A. Lipton, Ph.D., M.D., Professor of Biochemistry and Director of the Biological Sciences Research Center of the University of North Carolina at Chapel Hill. The latter testified at the MDMA Scheduling Hearings:

> Childhood autism is an essentially untreatable condition in which the child is unable to relate to significant people in his environment. MDMA might be tried with such children, partly because this distresssing illness is otherwise untreatable and partially because the reported effects of enhancing communication among adults might be helpful in autism.

The Quest for Self-Actualization

Although the treatment of mental problems is a most important use for MDMA, Maslow and other humanistic psychologists assert that the lack of pressing mental problems is not all there is to being healthy. There is another dimension to mental health—toward increasing wellness and self-actualization. This is a use of MDMA for the rest of us.

The employment of MDMA for this purpose is not just recreational. The pursuit of self-discovery or of a spiritual path is a valid option for many who attempt to go beyond the shallow consumerism and pop veneer of modern life. These individuals are generally sound, healthy people who have an interest in becoming more creative, more loving, more effective. For these people, there is a questing after answers to the basic life questions—where did we come from, why are we here, where are we going?

Since the beginnings of our species, many human cultures around the globe have used sacred plants for healing and for spiritual insight. Shamans were the specialists of their tribe, given the role of using and administering these indigenous psychoactive substances. The goal in using these plants is to allow for transformation of consciousness, a transcendance of ordinary ways of viewing reality.

When we depart from ordinary consciousness, we find that each of us has our own hell and our own heaven within. Alternative states of consciousness can be difficult, fearful, painful places as well as pleasurable, beautiful, ecstatic regions to experience. In the Preface to *The Healing Journey*, Claudio Naranjo asserts that both realms of consciousness can be useful—"The Healing Power of Agony and Ecstasy." Naranjo favors a balanced approach, which views both types of experiences as "material" which can be used to benefit the individual if handled the proper way and viewed in the appropriate context.

With MDMA, experiences are mostly pleasant, especially for healthy people who would use the substance for self-actualization.

Abraham Maslow, who came up with the concept of self-actualizing people, also suggested that these people evolve through the achievement of what he called "peak experiences." These life episodes provide glimpses of our possible selves toward which we can grow. The experiential model that the term "peak-experience" comes from is the mountain climber who strives to reach the crest of the mountain. As the mountaineer arrives at the top after days of sweat and cold and precarious footwork, he or she looks around, takes a breath, and has—a "peak experience."

Other kinds of experiences like this include the alternative state of consciousness achieved by a long-distance runner in top form, the transcendent sexual orgasm that shatters the barriers between partners, the "aha" feeling we sometimes get when everything seems to be in harmony and working perfectly, and many other times in life when we reach an optimum place of awareness and functioning.

These peak experiences are viewed by those who have them as self-validating and self-justifying. They carry their own intrinsic value and are an appropriate end in themselves. But in addition, they have after-effects which can be therapeutic for the sick (as we saw above), as well as help the healthy toward self-actualization. Maslow, in his *Toward a Psychology of Being*, published in 1962, says of these after-effects of peak experiences:

> 1. Peak experiences may and do have some therapeutic effects in the strict sense of removing symptoms. I have at least two reports—one from a psychologist, one from an anthropologist—of mystic or oceanic experiences so profound as to remove certain neurotic symptoms forever after
> . . .
> 2. They can change the person's view of himself in a healthy direction.

3. They can change his view of other people and his relations to them in many ways.

4. They can change more or less permanently his view of the world, or of aspects or parts of it.

5. They can release him for greater creativity, spontaneity, expressiveness, idiosyncracy.

6. He remembers the experience as a very important and desirable happening and seeks to repeat it.

7. The person is more apt to feel that life in general is worthwhile, even if it is usually drab, pedestrian, painful or ungratifying, since beauty, excitement, honesty, play, goodness, truth and meaningfulness have been demonstrated to exist.

The ultimate aim of these peak experiences, according to Maslow, is to become a self-actualized person. Self actualization, as Maslow explains it in his last book, *The Further Reaches of Human Nature*, "means experiencing fully, vividly, selflessly, with full concentration and total absorption ... At this moment, the person is wholly and fully human." Maslow goes on to explain that self-actualization is an ongoing process and that it demands using one's intelligence. It means working to do well at what you want to do, always striving for excellence.

Self-actualized people, according to these theories, have more peak experiences than others. And each peak experience is a transient glimpse of what it is like to be self-actualized.

As we found earlier in this chapter, different sorts of peak experiences are common to specific sorts of empathogens. MDA has its characteristic one and MDMA has another. Empathogens, as a class, have a characteristic peak experience unique to empathogens. Claudio Naranjo, in a personal correspondence, characterized this peak as "earthly paradise in comparison to the heavenly paradise of LSD and hallucinogens of that category."

Each of these different peak experiences is a distinct insight into self and reality. Perhaps when we have mapped out peak experiences of different substances in a methodical way, we will find the particular usefulness of each to therapeutic work or self actualization.

These substances can be thought of, in the context of a quest for self-actualization, as part of a particular path toward growth. Certainly, the drug by itself is not the entire path. Any chemical can only enhance what we already bring to it, the framework that we use it within. Chapter V, "A Guide to the Use of MDMA," will elaborate how our life history and orientation, expectations, session goals, personality, the people we associate with, and our environment all help shape the course of an MDMA session. To stress this point, the experience occurs inside of human beings, and the psychoactive subtance is merely the catalyst for that experience.

How does MDMA act as such a catalyst for self-actualization? By giving us a taste of peak experience, a little model of what self-actualization is like, it gives us something to work toward. Just as an artist might see a painting in one visionary glimpse and then dedicate himself to expressing it in oils, those who experience an MDMA-induced peak experience may work toward self-actualization in their life.

A particularly good example of this is meditation. Earlier in this chapter, I mentioned that in many MDMA sessions, there comes a period when a profound calm washes over the body and the mind, which is perceived as a vivid stillness.

Many meditators spend years before they attain this level of experiencing. An article by Mark Corwin, *Times* Staff writer, in the May 27, 1985, *Los Angeles Times*, states,

> Brother David Steindl-Rast, a Benedictine monk from the Immaculate Heart Hermitage in Big Sur, tried the drug at a conference on the medical uses of MDMA. Steindl-Rast, who was a psychologist before he entered the monastery, said the drug facilitates the search for the "awakened attitude" all monks seek.
>
> "It's like climbing all day in the fog and then suddenly, briefly seeing the mountain peak for the first time," he said. "There are no shortcuts to the awakened attitude, and it takes daily work and effort. But the drug gives you a vision, a glimpse of what you are seeking."

Ralph Metzner and Sophia Adamson, in their unpublished essay, "The Nature and Role of the MDMA Experience," remark,

> One meditation teacher has suggested that the Adam experience facilitates the dissolving of barriers between body, mind and spirit—the same separation within the individual that can be observed in society . . .
>
> Mind and body can be coordinated: mind including feelings has a positive empathic attitude toward the body, which in turn feels accepted and protected. Thus, instinctual awareness as well as mental, emotional and sensory awareness can all function together, rather than one being the focus at the expense of the other. Similarly, Spirit or Self is

no longer felt as a remote abstract concept "above" somewhere, but rather one senses the presence of spirit infusing the structures of the body and images and attitudes of the mind.

Awareness is expanded to include all parts of the body, all aspects of the mind and the higher reaches of Spirit. This permits a kind of re-connecting, a re-membering of the totality of our experience, an access to forgotten truths.

A group consisting of two married couples living together have written an account of a series of MDMA experiences that they shared collectively and as separate couples between July 1984 and January 1985. The following is their evaluation of the value of these sessions in terms of working through psychological issues encountered on their road to self-actualization:

When we began co-living, we had approximately five two-hour group sessions, plus many individual sessions, with a therapist we consider extremely competent. She is a California-licensed MFCC. We have this baseline for comparing non-MDMA therapy and our MDMA experience.

One outstanding distinction is that MDMA has always moved us *immediately* to a psychological clarity and depth unprecedented in our everyday life. We immediately know with total clarity exactly what we want, what we need, and what we are ready and willing to release. We only wish non-MDMA therapy were of such power. Another difference is that we have integrated radical changes following every MDMA trip. In therapy, we felt positive changes, but progress was incomparably slower, less dramatic and often more superficial or subject to backsliding. With MDMA, each event occurs at a depth level far beyond the level at which we previously perceived the "issue," and thus issues dissolve and disappear as we are ready for that. Without MDMA, this occurs only ponderously, and depends on whether the dialogue, bioenergetics or other forms of therapy is "suited" in terms of depth . . . MDMA seems to operate without requiring that a therapist assess issues and whether others have a greater need to work with a therapist, or have issues MDMA cannot reach . . . We have stressed our intentionality and preparation. Those we have talked with who have used MDMA (about 12 people including ourselves) all have evinced intentionality and some preparation; none sees MDMA as a "recreational" drug. Three are practicing therapists and nine are not.

We are not addressing treatment of psychotic or equivalent conditions. We find MDMA an invaluable aid in going from good mental health toward our full emotional, mental and spiritual potential. MDMA is the most appropriate and powerful tool we have found for the purpose of becoming more fully human and spriritual, as sought by transpersonal and humanistic psychology.

Creativity Enhancement

When writers, artists, or inventors talk about the creative source of their invention, often they describe a sudden inspiration or vision or dream; yet this creative process is as difficult to explain for the artist as spiritual experience is for the mystic.

There are myriad examples of this. Some report having pondered a problem for months, and suddenly finding the solution while asleep during a dream, or in a creative flash while doing something completely apart from trying to solve the problem. The placement of the elements in the periodic table of elements by Dimitri Mendeleev, for example, came to him during a dream.

What is common to many of these stories of creative inspiration is that, in some way, the consciousness of the individual was altered from her or his ordinary waking state when the problem was solved. Willis Harman, James Fadiman, Robert Mogar, Myron Stolaroff, and others at the Institute for Psychedelic Research at San Francisco State College gave low doses of mescaline or LSD to 22 volunteers. These were professionals who were faced with technical problems that they were unable to solve. At the time the report was written in November 1965, six of these individuals had found concrete benefits from their experiences in their work. The report gives intriguing accounts of chemically induced inspiration. Oddly, this was the last research project completed before LSD was criminalized in 1966.

Again, as in the reports of creative experience *au naturale*, there was an altered state of consciousness in which the creative act took place. It may be that these states gave the individual greater access to the unconscious, which presumably spins away solving problems we pose to it without our paying any conscious attention. Then suddenly it disgorges the solution into consciousness.

It is often mentioned by people who take major psychedelics and

MDMA that experiences on MDMA are much easier to remember, probably because the state of consciousness accessed on Adam is not as different from our ordinary awareness as the state entered into via LSD or its relatives. Thus, creative experiences while on MDMA would be easier to remember and, perhaps, to use in our ordinary waking world. One possible drawback for MDMA in relation to creativity would be that it does not usually produce visual hallucinations. Visionary artists who use the vivid and colorful excursions into the realm of psychedelia probably would not find similar benefit with MDMA.

However, the experience of the creative writer should be different. You will remember that MDMA usually stimulates verbosity. If this increased fluidity of word production could be applied to the task of writing, then MDMA might prove to be a useful tool for the enhancement of creativity.

This writer (while MDMA was still legal) has used MDMA for this purpose with good results and has heard favorable reports from other writers as well. Greer and Tolbert were the first people to test MDMA on writing creativity somewhat formally.

Five of the subjects in the Greer pilot study used low dosages, around 50 mgs., to facilitate their creative writing abilities. Four took MDMA in a group setting, and one alone.

Greer and Tolbert report, "As mentioned previously, five subjects had low-dose (50 mg) sessions specifically for the purpose of facilitating their creative writing. All reported being satisfied with the results."

Of course, this report leaves us wondering what, indeed, the results were. Still, it is an indication that creativity enhancement might be yet another use for MDMA. Certainly, we can hope that future studies (if these are permitted) will examine this question in a more structured manner.

Especially useful would be a study which used some kind of product, an essay on an assigned topic, for example, that could be used to evaluate the results.

The Inward Journey

So it can be seen that gregarious, extroverted, empathogenic Adam has an inward side. Just as the tendency of MDMA to enhance interpersonal contact can be used, so can the introspective dimension of the experience. Although it is convenient to divide the experience, it must be emphasized that the experience with MDMA is a holistic event. Therapeutic effects reported are based on both internal and external change.

Chapter IV. Some Experiences

I swallowed, hoping to God the source was reliable; that this really was it and not some new amalgamation of PCP or even LSD . . .

Some time later I looked at my watch. Forty minutes had passed. I looked at my friend. Was she any different? Could I see into her soul as had been promised? Was I feeling great empathy and love?

No, in fact we were having an argument. Tired of the park, she wanted us to go home, while I preferred to stay there with the hilltop view of London. My heart was beating a little faster, but I put it down to anxiety.

Another twenty minutes passed. Still nothing. Perhaps the drug was just too subtle for me. Disappointed, I gave in to her wish to go home. We started down the hill. But by the time we reached the bottom I'd forgotten how to be angry. We were having a new conversation, examining our goals in life. What had we done so far? Had we *really* followed those vows of adolescence? Did either of us know what it was like to be close to another human being? For the first time in years I confessed my childhood yearnings to become a marine; she told me she'd wanted to marry Woody Allen. Defences were dropping at a rate it normally took people months to achieve. Suddenly I knew I could trust her with my closest secrets . . . strange because not half an hour before I wouldn't have cared if I never saw her again in my life. I told her this and we both laughed . . .

—Peter Nasmyth, *The Face* (1986)

Question: What are your impressions of MDM?

Well, first I was amazed. The first time I took it was the first time I had actually been able to experience a real sense of hope for all the bad

situations going on everywhere. I had always had "We need peace . . .,"
etc., but I never thought it was actually a possibility. The first time I took
it, I thought, "Oh, my God, this might just be the little tool that we
need." I think it's so good that a lot of people will probably take it and it
will probably have a really major effect upon things in the next five years
or so.

It suspends—it takes away all the silly things that we do to ourselves,
and lets us act freely and love ourselves. And when we do that, we love
everyone else and everything.

Another interesting thing about it—for a long time I thought you
really had to take it intelligently and have a big briefing beforehand and
think real hard about it, you know? Then I came into contact with a
bunch of people who had just taken it with no knowledge whatsoever
of any of the philosophical things. And I asked them about it, and they
told me the same intellectual things about it as I would have said to
them. They figured it out for themselves, which I thought was pretty
interesting. I mean, they talked about easier communication.

I don't know—it's a pretty wonderful thing. It's a thing that lets
people be their best.

The thing that it helped me with most is self-esteem. Because while I
was on it, I would notice things that I would usually do—and I just
wasn't doing them. Then, afterwards, I just thought, "Why do that
anymore?" It really improved me quite a bit. It made me more
extroverted I think.

I think generally it's just going to make people a little bit nicer to each
other. It makes people want to be nicer to each other.

Another fascinating thing—the best thing about it is that it's
completely accessible later. I mean, you can remember everything, and
in that sense it makes it a very good tool for learning. You take it, and
you can get better using it, become a better person.

As for other people I've seen using it, I've seen some pretty amazing
things! Two years ago, I knew a guy named Bill—and he was like the
most down guy. I mean, he's extremely funny—had a great sense of
humor—but he's just very cynical and very down all the time. Didn't
enjoy anything. And I saw him like two years later—about three
months after he had taken MDM for the first time—and he was just
completely changed. He was all smiles and cheerful, it was really
amazing. This was where I went back to college, and everyone said,
"Have you seen Bill? Have you seen Bill? Go see Bill, and you'll just freak
out!"

Everyone I've talked to about it, I've gotten a lot of positive feedback. People just tell all these amazing stories about it.

Parents—I know a few people who have taken it with their parents and who have felt incredible about it. My friend Andrea. Her situation with her parents—I guess they're like New York kind of socialites. Her father is a curator, and there has always been a lot of pressure on her. And she just didn't like her parents at all. I mean, just basically there was no communication going on. But she talked them into taking it with her. I was there and it was pretty amazing.

At first they started off talking about things that they had done to each other that weren't good. And then pretty soon—I don't know, I think it was her dad that said it. He just said, "Well, wait a minute. We all know that those things happened, but now we're completely conscious of it so let's just go from here." And since then, it's been a lot better. She's become good friends with her parents—that's what she told me.

The reason why they took it was that there were a bunch of us—friends of hers—and we took it there, in her house. They were home, but they didn't know. And then the next day, they were asking her, "Why was everyone acting so nice? And why was everyone giving people hugs? Why was this going on?" And so she told them. And I guess they were impressed enough by watching us the night before that they decided to do it too, which was pretty wild. That is a pretty difficult point, to convince your parents to take it.

As for difficulties, the only thing I would warn against really is making a bunch of decisions for yourself while you're on it. I think you need to take it, and then experience for yourself what happens, and then think about it afterwards. Because I know one person who took it, and then made a whole bunch of ultimatums based upon how they were feeling, and then when they came down they felt really bad because they didn't really carry through with them. So I think the thing to do is to come down and integrate the whole thing later.

The first day she was just really sort of sad because she couldn't be as great as she thought she could—something like that. But then the second or the third day after that, things started coming back, and it ended up she was quite a bit happier than she had been before. She was pretty sad for awhile.

I've never really seen a failure story, nor people who've felt disappointed. Well, actually, I know two guys who took it thinking that it was a hallucinogen—and so they were disappointed at first, but then after a few minutes they decided they liked it better than that anyway. I haven't really seen anything negative.

With LSD, it provides a really good set to begin a trip with. It takes away paranoia and all that sort of thing.

The times I take it, about the first thing I think is, "Wow, that was pretty important—I'm going to think about that for a long time." I think a lot of people have that—which is good because it keeps it where it has a really low abuse potential. Because the first reaction isn't to take it more and to take it again. But to wait, and to think. It seems like the longer you wait in between, the more incredible it is and the more you learn. That's something of my attitude toward it.

I generally use about 150 milligrams—just one dose. I don't know, taking a whole lot just doesn't appeal to me.

That first experience was an enormous release. That hope was actually possible. The war is over, and I can actually feel like a tiny part of what it would feel like if it was over. It was pretty incredible, this feeling.

Actually, when I first took it, I thought, "Oh, my God, this drug is so incredible!" But since then, having taken it a few more times, I've seen that it's actually the people you are with that makes it incredible. I mean, I pretty much always have a good time, but the depth of the experience depends on who you are with.

It can be really amazing with just one or two or various small groups of people—just really good friends. But the first time I took it was at a fairly large party with a lot of people I didn't know. And I guess that's why the focus was so much on self-esteem, because the whole night I spent just walking around talking to people and meeting them on a really core level, without being any of our superficial selves. Just the real core me. And that was just an incredible feeling—to feel free enough to just do that, without playing games. And to this day, like some of those people—I don't know where they work or what they do, but I feel that I know what they're all about. The heart, or whatever.

If you can get a large group of people who are all into group experience, and sit around in a circle or something, and tell stories or hold hands—well, we had this sort of wild theory that there's some kind of pool of love, and humans are a conduit, and our job is to get it down here to the physical world. So we had one session with that kind of idea in mind. Like the idea was to get as much of the love from out there down here to the real physical world as we could. There were like twenty people with all that same focus. And everybody got much higher than they would have, just because of the group and everybody thinking about the same thing. It doesn't really change the person, it's just really the people and if they act the way they live.

Another thing that's good about MDM is that it's not so wild—or it allows people to access mystical areas within themselves because it's not so scary as the major psychedelics like LSD. I think that's why more people will take it—because it's a lot more accessible than normal, and it helps people overcome their fear of exploring the mysticism within themselves.

—Peter, from Wesleyan University,
quoted in Peter Stafford's *Potentialities of MDM*

All the following accounts appear in *Through the Gateway of the Heart*, compiled by Sophia Adamson and available through Four Trees Publications, Box 31220, San Francisco, CA 94131 for $14.50 plus $1.00 for postage and handling.

Affirming Who I Am, Where I am Going

37-year-old female, graduate student, systems designer

Set: self-exploratory, meditative

Setting: at home, with therapist/guide

Catalyst: 150 mg. plus 50 mg. MDMA

Whatever I can say now only dimly reflects my meeting with myself under Adam's influence. These phrases and ideas from the transcript remind me of some of the highlights:

There's an opening that wasn't there before . . .

It's clear that everything I'm about, and everybody is about, is just loving God, and how to do that . . .

Guide: Does this remind you of your previous psychedelic experience?

Answer: This is quite different. Much more important. Much more personal, much more relevant. Much easier to carry back and to apply. I've got so much love and compassion that attaches itself to anything in the vicinity and tries to make it seem appropriate. That's when I forget that what I'm all about is loving God—then I try to put too much into any relationship.

There are still levels of integration to do around sexuality ... There's a real confusion of some kind ... a real split ... Now I'm listening to my inner voice—usually I tend to avoid it ... Sex can be a way to get closer to God, but I haven't been choosing in such a fashion that it's going to be ... It's been very helpful to be celibate because I can see so much more clearly and easily where my sexual energy goes, where my attractions are.

What is the source of my arthritis? Blocked energies. I need to get in touch with what I want, and let the knowledge lubricate my joints; no more stoppage of anger or love. Let it *all* flow through!

Guide: So love lubricates the joints!

Material about a sexual molestation incident—first reported during a hypnosis session several weeks ago—has had much more meaning for me since I heard the tape of the Adam session. In it I sounded like I was seven years old. The impact comes from the deep recognition of how many ways the event molded my responses to the world around me, in part because of the distrust of my parents that was focused by the incident. Reliving this incident helped to free up my energy and emotions in a number of ways; it feels like this process will be ongoing for some time to come. The understanding and resolving of this incident is not only helpful to me personally; it can be a vehicle for my reaching out to others with similar experiences.

In general, my journey with Adam affirmed who I am, what I am doing, where I am going. The affirmation was experienced through an opening of my heart rather than as a deepening of intellectual understanding, although some of that has also occurred.

The Adam, the set, the setting, and the invaluable input and support of the therapist/guide created a sense of receptivity, wonder, love, and joy. In this set and setting, with empathy for all aspects of life, learning took place whose content was easily and deeply received. My desire to access such learning is great, in part because recalling these lessons elicits the highly desirable state of consciousness in which the learning occurred. The content itself also seems to take on a certain desirability, making it more readily available than much that I have learned under more traditional circumstances. Just writing about the state now, almost a week later, still brings back the sense of wonder, love, and joy that I felt at the time.

My mind tends to scurry about, trying to give form to some of the issues that were raised on the trip, but which still seem incomplete. These include a deeper understanding of my confusion about/dissatisfaction with past relationships, sexual matters, use of alcohol, and future plans for my internship, dissertation, and profession. Despite the attention that these topics get, I am for the most part holding them lightly; I have a clear sense that my journey with Adam is far from over; much is being considered and reflected upon below the surface of my conscious awareness. To the extent that I have addressed these concerns I am very well satisfied with the understandings I have reached.

My actions as well as my attitudes have begun to shift in certain areas. I am able to perceive, receive, and respond to love in a much more open way than I did a few weeks ago. There is greater ease with respect to my dealing with and responding to my sexual energy. I seem to find it much easier to contact my feelings and, as appropriate, to express them.

Perhaps the most important after-effect has been the indwelling experience of affirmation about what I am doing. There is a sense of correctness; even when feeling muddled and unclear about what is happening, I know at a very deep level that I am moving in the right direction. However dark the path, however many shadows may appear, there is a light within me that provides warmth, illumination, and nourishment. My awareness of this indwelling light and my increased clarity of my sense of purpose has been greatly enhanced by my experience with Adam.

My First Sense of Not Being Paranoid

33-year-old male, graduate student

Set: self-exploratory, therapeutic

Setting: friend's home, with one other participant, two guides

Catalyst: 150 mg. plus 50 mg. MDMA

I went into the experience seeking greater empathy for the child I once was and still am, and to know my own emotional needs well enough that I could begin clearly to distinguish my needs from those of others. I intended to explore the feelings I had in early childhood, particularly in reference to being abandoned by my mother at five, in order finally to begin to rid myself of the burden of this depression.

I also wanted to explore the issue of work and financial survival, of how I could work at a job—to earn money—without falling prey to that kind of depression that comes from not having my needs met while serving the needs of others. This has always led to an exhaustion that I have found crippling and deeply discouraging. How am I to earn money and have my deeper emotional needs met?

The issues of emotional differentiation from my mother and of financial solvency/independence are very closely related. The connection was and is a major issue for me to explore.

For the first twenty minutes or so of the experience I felt considerable fear. I felt myself lowering down into a softer and more vulnerable place. I could feel the layers of fear peeling off of my torso and moving away into space. I felt immersed in fear for a time. Soon after ingesting the second capsule, I dropped below the fear and contacted a warm and supportive baseline feeling, a place of support that was totally without fear. This gave me my first sense of what it is like to not be a paranoid, to be like other people.

I did not return to childhood memories as I thought I would. Instead I remained in the present and experienced my issues in condensed form within the context of my current relationship. My issues of fear, financial survival, and emotional dependency all fell within the relationship. I felt very clear that I didn't want to return to childhood, that there was no need to do so. I didn't feel that I was resisting or avoiding anything; I needed and wanted instead to contact the heart and to establish an ongoing connection with it. This did happen.

When I listened to the tape of my experience I discovered that I have indeed been carrying out the intentions I had during the Adam experience. As long as I remain in contact with the heart and am open and honest with my relationship partner, I know that my childhood pain will continue to surface and to resolve itself within a context of healthy mourning, and at a pace that the bodymind will decide is appropriate to my capacity. My partner understands and accepts this.

Now I Feel the Pain as an Ally, not as an Enemy

45-year-old male, writer, arthritis sufferer

Set: therapeutic, to heal arthritis

Setting: at home and outdoors, with partner

Catalyst: 100 mg. plus 50 mg. plus 50 mg. MDMA; series of sessions

During the past three years I have been afflicted with a very painful case of spinal arthritis. Until recently there had not been a day when the pain was not present in most parts of my body. At times it has been so debilitating that I could barely move for days at a time. I have tried a number of prescribed drugs, including Motrin, but none has had the noticeable, long-term effect of easing the pain and the attendant worry, concern, and even depression.

Until recently. In February, 1984, I began to use MDMA, with the idea of easing the constricting arthritic pain. Within only a minute or so of my ingesting the substance there was a noticeable decrease in pain. As the day progressed, I felt my body become less and less constricted. For some months I had hardly been able to walk more than a few feet at a time. Now my body began to move freely; doubts and fears connected with the disease dissipated. I felt a new sense of hope as the "arthritic crystals" appeared to be breaking up, releasing the very tight constriction. For several days the pain, while not altogether gone, was greatly alleviated. For the first time, I had real hope that, with the aid of MDMA, I could reverse the pattern of living in constant pain.

Other sessions followed, with similar results. At times my body felt so free and light that I began to dance and move quickly with a suppleness that I had not known for years. On June 9 I ingested the substance and, again, within a minute, I began feeling elated, and the spinal-arthritis pain that had been great before was alleviated.

On June 23 there was another session. Seven minutes after the initial dosage the pain in my back began to disappear. Then I began to focus in on a healing spot for my arthritis—a point at the lower back that, when pressed, relieved pressure. The muscle constrictions became less and less, and I felt I was really beginning to be in touch with my body, which was in a state of fluid motion. I felt that there was a healing effect surrounding my body. Then I went into a frenzy of movement and I felt the heaviness and constriction leave the body. The hard stiffness in the lower back and knees loosened up.

During this experience time stood still as I looked at Taos Mountain with a sense of Oneness, stillness, quiet. The stillness of the mountains and the mesa became absolute, the only reality, as a consuming inner heat began to burn. I began to focus on a healing spot for my arthritis, an acupressure point at the lower right back, lower chakra. After applying thumb pressure there, I began to expand and I felt love energy from the mountain enter my heart chakra.

I felt a strong connection with space and the planets. I was part of them. My origins lay there. I played Gustav Holst's "The Planets." The music of Mars coursed through me. I was in space again, the Void. I was at home, free. Mars, the bringer of war. I saw conflagration, the history of the world in battle, but it was a cleansing. From the conflagration came a period of understanding, wisdom, and love. Pockets of deep understanding amidst the fire and conflagration.

I felt a tremendous closeness to my friend, and a great warmth. Space surrounded me. Both my friend and I were still there. We were part of space without time. I felt us billions of years in the past and billions of years in the future. We were part of the universe. A great love permeated me. My friend was a large part of it, but so are the world, universe, and beyond.

I focused in on myself and felt like a different person: consumed by warmth, with a wonderful feeling. My body was in a state of fluid motion; muscle constrictions dwindled, and I was in touch with my body.

Touching the earth and reaching for the sky had a healing effect on my arthritis. Warm, free, beautiful. Dancing, free-flowing body movements, a frenzy of movement, then quiet. I felt the body freeing up. I was literally blowing heaviness and constriction from my body. Energy was caught in my throat. The body was really free. There was a sensual feeling about it. The hard stiffness in my back began to loosen up. Energy was running up my spine, loosening the stiffness in the spinal column. I was literally bouncing to the music.

I felt the presence of space beings all around me. They were trying to impart some message, but I was not open enough yet to receive it. I felt that we all have a benevolent tide of extraterrestrial beings surrounding and protecting us. They want us to grow, to expand.

My body felt like it was opening up to something, like a clear channel. Energy attacked the jaw. I felt the beings trying to get through my body.

Still no message, though. I felt the night sky, covered with stars. I felt a real closeness to the *aliveness* of space. The arthritic pain returned; I felt a slight headache as I came down.

An additional session followed one week later. Within ten minutes of ingesting the drug, there was a considerable lessening of the back pain. Later I again went into a frenzy of movement as insights began to appear as to how to begin to control the energy flow within my body. There was a very rapid movement of my hands, and the arthritic constriction in the hands, knees, and back loosened considerably. My body moved very freely, and I felt much better. For the first time I really believed that I could be cured. Somehow I felt I was beginning to integrate a new me, free of pain. The arthritis in the knees and legs disappeared, and the back pain rapidly decreased.

During this experience I moved with awareness into my body. I felt that my body was a temple that I had desecrated. I wanted to let the body go, but I realized that I couldn't. It was telling me that it would continue to rebel. I felt as though the body were ready to explode in all directions. It felt heavy. I was very much in a "the-body-is-not-me" mode. I felt powerful eruptions from the inside. I felt I needed to go through a death experience—symbolically, I hoped, but great fear was there.

Then I felt comfort, a joyous knowing that there was no death. The body became much freer, though the arthritis pain was still there. I began a frenzy of actual, physical self-flagellation: a very rapid movement of hands, a loosening of arthritis in my hands, my knees, and my back. I lost consciousness while going through fast movements. My hands shook and I could not write. I shook violently and began to exhale rapidly; I was close to hyperventilation. My body moved exceedingly freely, my legs in particular. My body really fired up. I could tell that there was still some arthritis there.

Ferocious anger set in, and my hands started trembling again. My legs shook frantically again, particularly my knees, where the arthritis pain is centered. I breathed heavily, and I felt very, very hot. I felt that I was burning up. A feeling of death surrounded me, but a certain uneasiness and fear prevented me from experiencing it. Still, somehow I knew there was nothing to fear.

I suppose what frightened me was the feeling that I didn't want or need the body any longer. Yet I was stuck with it. Still, I was not my body. I felt an unsuspected confusion, but the fear subsided. I began to feel the eternalness of things, unseen things, the *real* things. A roar was bearing down on me, like a freight train. I felt that I wanted to do something dramatic, but I was not sure what. Consuming fire burned me, I felt that my body could burn away. I thought of spontaneous combustion.

There was something present that I had to break through. I felt that this could be the key to loosening completely the arthritic "crystals." I almost lost consciousness in another frenzy of movement and self-flagellation. I beat my breastplate. The energy had loosened considerably, and I felt much better physically. I still felt some remnants of the arthritis and it pissed me off. I was going to beat the son-of-a-bitch if I had to flagellate myself to death. Beating myself seemed to help, and now I was beating myself with a regular broom. Energy had left the breast-heart area and travelled to the back. My friend beat my back and shoulders with the broom. This brought a big improvement, and my energy freed up.

For the first time I really believed that I could be cured. I felt anger at myself and at my body, and I beat myself with a whisk broom. I felt as though I were caught in the middle of a battle, and I was determined to win. I was fighting the bastard and this felt good. The fire was burning me up, consuming me. I felt exhausted, I was coming down. There was much improvement in the body, but each little pain made me angrier at not being able to let go completely.

My body then shook fiercely, and my exhalations became heavy. I lay on the floor and frantically flailed my hands. I grasped the flesh around my midsection and pulled hard. I beat my butt against the floor, hard, shouting as it hit. Energy travelled up the body to the throat. I grasped my throat and shoulder as though I wanted to rend the flesh from my body.

I felt very hot again, and I feel great anger at myself. Damn it! I wanted to flail the body, beat it into submission if necessary. Then there was quiet. I began to feel a love of myself, for myself, course through my body. It was very, very freeing. Some pain was still there, but I was determined to get it. The pain returned to my back, and I sat in it and just felt the pain. Tears came to my eyes. There was a feeling of sadness, and perhaps of loss. Somehow I had to face this and find out what it was. I was fearful because, perhaps for the first time, I saw that I was destroying my body. Somehow that had to be overcome, for otherwise I was in danger. Perhaps that is what the earlier closeness to death was trying to tell me.

The clouds were so still and quiet. I felt a powerful oneness with space; I wanted to leave my body and join that oneness. Death felt closer and closer, and I felt resigned to it, but I drew back. I had to discover what this thing was in me that wished to die. I knew only that my body was not important, but that I couldn't drop it yet. What was this death inside me? Where was the life? Perhaps both were the same. I felt that there was a connection, a kinship between them. I felt I must experience death, symbolically, but I was afraid that it might turn into a "real" death.

I began to try to feel the death experience. I felt great sadness at first, then body movement. Surprisingly the fear left and, briefly, I passed beyond the portals of life. An encompassing, beautiful white light radiating love surrounded me and, for the first time, I knew that death was not to be feared. It was not the end-all. It was a beautiful, new beginning, a rebirthing. My friend gently massaged my back, pushing the energy up into my spinal column.

The pain is not all gone, but for the first time I know that it will be. I feel a renewed sense of life and purpose. I realize now that I had got to such a point where I was either going to let the negativity and pain kill me or else I was going to rid myself of it. I feel strongly that I have chosen the latter, though more work still needs to be done.

Oh, God, the glory of feeling, the love. For the first time I feel the pain as an ally and not as an enemy. I can use it for insight and understanding, and not for self-destruction. I no longer feel the pall, the aura, of death around me. The pain is telling me that it will disappear completely only after I have pushed that invisible "integration" button. Why? The answer comes as tears flow, and the heart, as it expands, seems to *know*. *Using* the pain with love and understanding instead of constantly fighting it with deep animosity will enable me to end it. A "bolt" from my heart caresses my pain and, strangely, I feel a deep love *for* the pain. It is my teacher. By accepting rather than rejecting it, wonderful, soothing clarity about it pours into me.

On July 18 I had an experience very similar to MDMA, without taking the substance. My feelings and actions were very much the same, however. The energy began to move through my body and I began to move—stretching, pulling, shoving, guiding the energy somehow. It did not blast through the arthritic blocks but appeared to dart around, over and under them. I felt great relief. Later in the day I began to breathe in the cool, wet, soothing wind. It had a comforting, even healing, effect on the arthritis. I exposed both my front and my back to the wind, and the effect on the pain and constriction was noticeably good, and healing. For five full days I was almost completely free of the arthritis pain—the longest stretch of pain-free time in three years!

On July 23 I had still another MDMA-like experience without ingesting the substance. Once again my body moved at a rapid pace and the constriction loosened. I seemed almost to push the constriction down and out of the body through the gut area, which became loose and free. Then I began physically to pull the arthritic pain from the lower back. It worked. The energy went to other areas of the body.

Meditation and Remembering the MDMA State

32-year-old male

Set: therapeutic

Setting: at home, with therapist/guide and two friend/participants

Catalyst: 100 mg. plus 50 mg. MDMA

I've waited a week to put my thoughts and feelings down on paper; I am just now coming out of the euphoria of the experience. This past week I have been happy, contented, loving, concerned, easy to get along with, and at peace with myself. I've made a concerted effort (and it hasn't been that hard) to retain the self I was put in touch with.

Regarding the experience itself, I had no awareness of the passing of time. Throughout I was comfortable personally and I was completely at ease with everyone present. The physical sensation was a combination of warm heaviness and mental clarity. I was totally involved in the conversation and interaction with my friends. All inhibitions and defenses were stripped away, so that I was directly in touch with my feelings and my ability to express them. My thoughts flowed with reason and purpose. I felt a genuine warmth and affection for my friends and a strong desire to express my love and concern for them. I was able to say the words I've saved for so long for fear of prying or of hurting them.

The greatest reward was the positive feedback I received, the respect for who I am and what I have done, and this has given me a far greater feeling of self-worth. Seeing myself through others' eyes has enabled me to see more clearly the good that I have to offer, and it is now easy for me to throw off the cynicism I've been hiding behind. I want to build on a new foundation of trust and openness and to accentuate the positive forces within me. I would hate for this to sound like the gushings of a Polyanna or of a recent convert to the latest cult. I honestly feel that I was given a rare opportunity to look inside myself and to gain a profound understanding of who I really am.

I feel that through self-revelation and the comments of my friends I gained a greater awareness of my strengths as an individual. The session brought out my positive aspects and these overshadowed a negative self-image. It was a profound, delightful experience that I continue to benefit from.

The experience has stimulated my interest in self-discovery. I now feel that I have a great deal of potential that is untapped. I have begun reading books of a spiritual and philosophical nature to help develop this potential. I have resumed meditation after a lapse of about six years; it has a calming, centering effect that helps me remember the MDMA state. I hope to continue meditation on a daily basis and go farther into it than I have in the past. MDMA has helped me to find my center while meditating.

I have taken steps to increase my self-awareness, and I have re-evaluated my needs for love. I think my self-confidence has increased due to the improvement in self-esteem.

MDMA Experiences Have Saved My Relationship

37-year-old male, businessman

Set: enhancing communication, relationship

Setting: at home, with partner

Catalyst: 150 mg. MDMA

What is the experience like? I address this by describing what my partner and I do. Mainly we sit on the floor facing each other and gazing into each others' eyes—MDMA is the eye-contact drug. Physical contact is also maintained, so we have eye contact, hand holding, gentle caressing of hair and face. Skin surfaces and hair feel incredibly soft (a feeling that persists well beyond the four hours). One is impressed with the preternatural beauty of one's partner. No one has ever been so fine, delicate, exquisite, or full; the sense is that she is all and everything. "I have been looking all my life for you."

I believe that the love experience on MDMA is the Divine Love spoken of by the saints. There is suddenly an openness to giving and receiving unconditional care and adoration, one feels privileged and blessed, nor do one's ordinary fears and defenses rise to quelch these powerful positive feelings. Without question the experience is powerfully intense—powerful, but unlike the overwhelming experiences on LSD or mescaline.

This intense love for one's partner leads naturally and immediately into sexual areas. I desire to undress myself and to have my partner similarly unclothed. I enjoy touching my own genitals and having them touched, and I enjoy touching my partner's. But all of this seems to be an aspect of a greater love, and the genital contact has a charge that is little different in character and degree from an exchange of glances or a facial caress. The world, too, is observed as clear and profoundly present—here and now, in Gestalt parlance. A color slide of a wall whose paint is peeling appears stunningly beautiful, as though seen for the first time.

One night my partner and I held each other while we watched the full moon rise over the ocean and reflect on the waves. We experienced closeness while we experienced the wonder of the world. In my experience, sexual consummation—that is, orgasm—is impossible until the end or slightly after the MDMA experience. If a distinction can be made between love and sex, MDMA is a love drug, and not a sex drug. This fact, taken along with its raw power, suggests that one would not want this experience with everyone, and one would not want it every day. Experiences of this significance require time to digest, so intervals of two weeks or more between experiences seem appropriate, the positive nature of the experiences notwithstanding. As this is a drug that feels sacred, one does not want to profane it by mundane usage.

Further comments are called for on the interactive qualities of MDMA, particularly on the verbal level. Conversation emerges spontaneously and comfortably from the contact and closeness. My partner and I were able to express total love for each other, and the level of articulation is reminiscent of classical love poetry: "A loaf of bread, a jug of wine, and thou . . ." The accumulated grievances of a stormy five-year relationship paled into insignificance. We didn't forget them; indeed, we talked freely about them. Yet the unpleasant memories, the laundry list of hurts, had no charge; it was just so much data, like yesterday's weather. And most touching of all are the expressions of gratitude for the gift of this beautiful life and for each other. It is this receptivity and appreciativeness that Catholic mystics call Grace.

A handful of MDMA experiences have saved my relationship. My partner and I had actually broken up, in each others' and in the world's eyes (an announcement had been made). We had been falling apart despite our love for each other, a rich family life, and an adored infant child. Under the MDMA we reconnected with our mutual caring and love, with what was important to us, and with the place of our love in the larger religious and spiritual nature of things. The lessons we learned carried well past the drug session. We have a look that we give each other that instantly takes us back to the caring place. The MDMA experiences are centerpieces of our common mythology. They are shared peak experiences. Sex is better than before.

Peace with Great Energy, Tangible, Expansive

53-year-old male, minister

Set: spiritual exploration

Setting: outdoors, desert/mountain, with two friends

Catalyst: 120 mg. MDMA

On the morning of August 18, in the presence of two others, who also took MDMA, I drank 120 mg. of MDMA. Prior to taking the substance I was handed a rose, freshly cut, and I was made to feel loved, safe, and secure. Even so I was a bit anxious, because, except for a single encounter with a psilocybin mushroom, I had never ingested a psychedelic.

After a few minutes I began to feel numb from my head to my toes. I became frightened and I looked to the rose for reassurance. The numbness gave way to a sensation of great energy. It felt as though every molecule and atom of my body had a powerful motor, and for the first time every one was turned on. The great surge of power and energy was overwhelming and I began to have second thoughts about taking the substance, but I knew that it was too late. I was at the highest peak of the roller coaster, about to descend with the speed of a falling rock. Great excitement and fear held me, and once again I looked at the rose and felt reassured.

All of this had the feeling of me versus it, and it was winning and was very much in control. Then, at some point, the struggle and fear vanished and a great feeling of peace came over me. It was not the kind that comes from not having problems or stress, but peace with great energy, super peace, tangible, expansive, a real thing, and highly prized. I sat until I was sure this state would not dissolve. I felt as though I were breathing for the first time in my life.

All the while I had been looking at the desert sand beneath my feet. Occasionally I would raise my eyes and look at the pile of wood stacked neatly beside the garage. If the wood appeared so fascinating and wondrous, what must the mountains, which were at my back, be like? I thought perhaps if I turned to look at them, that I would surely be overcome by their great beauty. So I turned very slowly, each glance being a bit longer, taking in more of them with every turn of my head until I felt confident enough to stand and have a panoramic view of the whole range. They were spectacular and *breath-taking*—literally. I was filled with joy.

I went over to my fellow travelers, with much excitement, and I exclaimed, "I knew that there must be such places as this, I knew it, I knew it." Part of this realization was from having read about such states of consciousness, but the larger part of it was that I felt at home, like the birds or fish who migrate thousands of miles because somehow they know and are called by an inner prompting to a place where they have never been, have never seen, but at last find.

Then came a flood of connections. I felt connected with some master plan. Everything seemed to have a purpose and a plan, a reason why, and I felt caught up in it and was thrilled. Life seemed to have been conspiring to get me here to this moment, to this place of love, beauty, goodness, and truth. There was no uncertainty about any of this. "Only the fool, fixed in his folly, thinks that he turns the wheel on which he turns." The greatest freedom is to have no freedom but to go where we long to be. I had been migrating for fifty-three years in order to be home at last. I knew that I had done something as great as the birds and the fish.

As the heart quickens the closer you approach your destiny, so I saw the connection between the fact that my body had uncontrollably quivered the day I had interviewed as a possible candidate for this experience, and the greatness of the experience to which I felt called and which was now part of me. I felt as though all that I was trying to accomplish in life was somehow confirmed by the experience that I was undergoing. It was a premonition, and a confirmation. I was being caught up in the mystery, and the providence, and I was able to know the feeling and the certainty of it all.

I looked at my friend and I knew that he must be an emissary for a new way of living. The feeling was one of destiny. I was enjoying my destiny for the first time. It was real and I was realizing it.

I wanted to explore, to walk out into the desert, to stand alone in that vast panorama of beauty. A few hundred yards from the house I found a huge stone, about five feet high, into which the wind had carved a seat. I climbed onto the rock ("tu es petros"—you are the rock) and sat there in the hot morning sun, looking up into the blue sky, breathing wonderfully clean, warm air, surrounded by overpowering mountains, great rock formations, and ancient boulders that, I had been told, were 25 million years old. I knew what consciousness was about. I thought of the destiny of mankind. We were going to the stars.

I walked back to the house filled with awe and wonder. I asked whether we could go swimming in the spring-filled pond, which was down a gentle slope, a few acres from the house. We nestled there amid three- and four-story-high rocks and boulders of great beauty. Here in this idyllic setting of monoliths and cattails, desert and lush vegetation, I decided that I wanted to be baptized, without ceremony, ritual, or words.

Coming out of the cool spring water I felt refreshed—cleansed inside and out, totally alive and especially privileged.

The rest of the day was spent hiking and mountain climbing, eating rich, hot soup and being fully into the here and now. The intensity of the morning had drifted into a pleasant transition of fun, closeness to one another, and to the events as they unfolded.

Sitting at night under the stars and distant lightning I knew that I had come into an awareness as unique as life and into the promise of scripture, "I have come that you may have life—*and have it more abundantly.*"

Seeing into the Beauty of One's Being

35-year-old female, businesswoman

Set: therapeutic, self-exploratory

Setting: at home, with therapist/guide

Catalyst: 200 mg. MDMA

Sunday morning: not quite 24 hours since my encounter with Adam. A new day is beginning. I feel soft. I feel present. And I am filled with my spirituality.

In many ways yesterday was a spiritual experience. I am moved by my love and by my connections with God. I think for quite some time I've been somewhat out of touch with that. I remember one morning not too long ago, as I was putting on my nylons and heels and my silk business suit, my "armor," as I refer to my work presentation, I said, "I feel like I'm losing myself." Adam was an opportunity to return to self.

It was also a completion of the past in some ways. I am moved by how clearly I saw my mother's death, and how peaceful I am with that. I am very aware of my mother's connection with God, and of her gift of love and appreciation. I'm committed to carrying that forth, and expressing it in the world. And I felt compassion and forgiveness for my father. I am really appreciating who I am in all of this, my experience of love and how all right everything is with me.

I remember when the power of Adam was at its peak, I felt that I would be carried away, that I would go unconscious. The guide told me to lie down, and I wouldn't. Maybe I didn't surrender? I felt like I was holding on. And I gripped the pillow and the sofa. What would have happened if I let go? I had intense body sensations at the peak. I felt like my brain was going to explode through the top of my head. My jaw chattered and clamped, and I chewed the inside of my mouth and the sides of my tongue with my clenched teeth. I felt for sure I was going to throw up. I remember perspiring. My face and hands were wet.

The intense part seemed quite brief. There was a fast and steep climb from the beginning to the climax and then a rather gentle and long denouement with the end coming around ten in the evening, when I went to sleep. I took the tryptophan, but I did not sleep well.

I'm more aware than ever that I have a particular model of the world. Suffering is something I'm grappling with. Yesterday I saw that my view of the world is just that, a view. Yesterday created an opening for me, an opportunity for me to shift my map of the world. Yesterday was also a completion around my experience of being a woman. This male/female thing has been an issue in my life. There's something I saw that allowed me to appreciate being a woman in a way I never had before. Again, there's an opening, and it has to do with being fully powerful, and being a woman. I also experienced compassion for men. I remember saying, "God made men, too, so they must be O.K."

I go back to work tomorrow after being off for two weeks. I feel apprehensive. This opening of the heart is lovely. As I said before, I feel soft. I have the thought that this is too vulnerable a position to be in, that I seem to need to harden up, to get my armor on, in order to go out and function in the business world.

I want to stay "opened," full of heart and love. This is where the joy is, and the possibility of life as celebration. As E.E. Cummings says, "Since feeling is first, he who pays any attention to the syntax of things will never wholly kiss you . . ."

Monday evening: I got through Monday. I felt quite emotional most of the day. I suspect it has something to do with having had an experience of Heart, of being in touch with that which we're really all about, something of essence, of spirit, of source, of our deep sensitivities, our humanity, as contrasted sharply with that which most of us interact with on a day-to-day basis: concerns about making money, treating each other shallowly, dealing with numerous seemingly unimportant details, playing political games, driving in rush hour traffic, not "connecting." What I need to do is *be* in whatever environment, whatever circumstances, full of heart, and love, and spirituality. To bring peace and joy to whatever situation. To have a light heart, an open heart.

Tuesday evening: I had a great day. Nothing particularly special happened in terms of circumstances. I realize that when I have a "bad" day, or things are not going right, I wonder to myself, "What's wrong with me?" And when I have a good day, I take it for granted, as if that's the way it's supposed to be. Today I decided to take credit for having a "good" day. Today, three days after Adam, I would say that what stands out for me is the potential Adam has as an aid in breaking up one's reality, and for seeing into the beauty of one's Being. I want to underline the importance of the context created for the experience. It would not be the same experience without a wise and loving guide.

Thursday evening: I've had a fantastic past few days. I'm really loving this new appreciation of being a woman. Something actually happened for me: I am done with trying to prove something. There's still some unsorted stuff in this area, but I do think I've shifted things. There's something I know about being a woman that I didn't know before. And this impacts on one of my goals: to appreciate myself and express myself more fully.

Springs of Enchantment

26-year-old female, student

Set: relationship communication and bonding

Setting: outside in nature; with partner

Catalyst: 100 mg. plus 50 mg. MDMA

I discovered Adam when I started an affair with this psychologist, who was using it in therapy. I broke off with my boyfriend, from whom I felt estranged and distant, even though he was very hurt and convinced that we were meant for each other. My sexual feelings became re-awakened, after a long slumber.

A few weeks later I moved to a holistic health retreat in the country, where I obtained a job, and began to study hypnosis. My former boyfriend was also there. I didn't want anything to do with him at first, even though he was very needy. Then after a while I thought it would be good if we took Adam—maybe it would help him, and it would make it easier for both of us to accept our separation.

During the session we became very close again, and I saw how he was right: we really were supposed to be together, and learn to work together. So we fell in love again. I called the psychologist friend, who was expecting to see me again, and I told him what had happened. Now he felt hurt and rejected.

He said the Adam experience reminded him of the enchanted springs in the magical forests of Arthurian legend. There was a spring, according to this legend, such that if you went there and drank from it, you would fall asleep, and when you woke up, you would fall in love with the first person you saw. There was also another enchanted spring nearby, with the opposite effect: if you drank from it you would fall asleep, and when you woke up, you would fall out of love with whomever you were infatuated with at the time.

Chapter V. A Guide for Users

When Heisenberg developed the "Uncertainty Principle" in physics, he might as well have been talking about the effects of psychoactive substances. There is no way to predict with certainty the course of an MDMA session.

Careful planning can help push things in the desired direction, but what actually occurs can vary greatly. The design of an MDMA session, therefore, is an art rather than a science. Each of the major factors which blend together to make the whole cloth of the MDMA experience might be thought of as threads. In this chapter, I will try to organize these procedural threads so that future weavers may create more elegant experiential tapestries.

Although not completely predictable, MDMA is a remarkably reliable catalyst of mental experience—especially when compared to the effects of the major psychedelics. The duration of action and required dosage vary little among users. The alternative state of consciousness produced by MDMA is quite consistent and does not depart much from our ordinary consensus consciousness.

There are differing goals for using MDMA. These objectives define the types of MDMA sessions. Each of these sessions has its own regimen and guiding principles. These session types include: (1) therapy-oriented sessions; (2) self-actualization oriented sessions, (3) creativity-enhancement oriented sessions; and (4) recreational sessions. I will discuss each of these briefly.

Therapy-Oriented Sessions

Sessions designed for therapeutic purposes must have the most careful planning, experienced guides, and controlled environment of any of the session types covered here. Obviously, people who have mental problems need more secure structures and safeguards when given a psychoactive drug.

In addition, proper screening must be done to eliminate those whose mental and/or physical conditions contraindicate the use of MDMA.

Psychotherapists, as noted in the previous chapters, have already begun work with MDMA. Of individuals who pursued experimental MDMA therapy, the only practitioners who have written extensively on work specifically with MDMA are George Greer and Requa Tolbert, from whose pilot study I have already quoted. Their papers on the conduct of therapeutic MDMA sessions remain unpublished as of this writing.

In addition to Greer, Rick Ingrasci, while testifying at the Scheduling Hearings, commented briefly on therapeutic procedures. Before going on to sketch out Greer's and Tolbert's procedure, the following is the methodology outlined by Ingrasci:

> (1) The patient or couple fasts for 4-6 hours prior to the ingestion of the MDMA.
>
> (2) The patient receives between 100-120 mg. MDMA in 4 ounces of orange juice.
>
> (3) After the onset of action of the drug (usually 45-60 minutes after ingestion), I encourage the patient or couple to talk about what they are thinking and feeling in the present moment. This gentle, non-directive process continues for the next two hours.
>
> (4) Following the formal therapeutic session with me, I have the patient spend the next two hours with their spouse and/or family members or with a close friend, someone with whom the patient would like to talk to or with in an open, intimate way. With couples, I either leave them alone to be with each other for the next two hours, or I have their children and/or other family members join them for a heart-to-heart discussion.
>
> (5) All patients are asked to write down their MDMA experience within 24 hours of the session.
>
> (6) Most patients require only one MDMA session, although some benefit from a second session 4-6 weeks after the initial session.

George Greer has written two papers on MDMA therapy procedure, "The Legal, Safe and Effective Use of MDMA," in 1984 and, with Requa Tolbert, "The Clinical Use of MDMA" in 1985. Both outline similar methodologies based on work done by Greer and Tolbert which I will attempt to present in an abridged form.

Greer and Tolbert used a rigourous screening procedure to select clients for therapy. First, they sent the prospective client a questionnaire, "informed consent" information, and an essay stating their philosophy about psychoactive medicines. The questionnaire evoked personal, medical, and psychiatric history, as well as information about the prospective client's drug use patterns. This material is also designed to orient the person toward having such a session. Questions of this type include: "What is your purpose in having a session with MDMA?" and "What are your expectations/fears of what will happen?"

After reviewing the questionnaire and finding no strong contra-indications to the session, Greer and Tolbert conducted a screening interview in their own home, where they also held most of the MDMA sessions. The screening interview comprised both a final screening and preparation for the session.

There are both physical and psychological problems which preclude the use of MDMA for therapy (or for any other purpose). Greer lists these exclusionary problems in his "Legal, Safe and Effective Use of MDMA" paper:

> MDMA should not be taken by people with the following physical conditions: hypertension, heart disease, seizures, hyperthyroidism, diabetes mellitus, hypoglycemia, glaucoma, diminished liver function, actual or possible pregnancy, and breast feeding . . .
>
> People may experience a recurrence of any psychological problems they have ever had in the past. Those with a history of panic attacks have had recurrences both during and after sessions. For this reason, MDMA is not recom-mended for people who have ever been unable to function socially or vocationally due to psychological problems unless 24-hour care by trained people is available. The person should also be fully willing to experience whatever may happen during or after sessions. This is the most important factor in screening clients. People who are not ready for anything to happen should not take MDMA because that mental set predisposes one to having a difficult time without benefiting from the experience.

It should be noted that Greer's exclusion of people with severe psychological problems does not mean that MDMA cannot be beneficial to these with psychoses or major mood disorders. We saw earlier that Wolfson used MDMA successfully with these types. What Greer is emphasizing is the need for constant supervision.

During the in-depth interview, the facilitators give an account of their personal histories and experiences, and relate the reasons why they are doing work with MDMA. Then a series of explicit agreements are made to establish a setting in which "clients must feel free to lose complete emotional and behavioral control, within ethical and safe limits." The set of agreements that Greer recommends includes:
> (1) Everyone will remain on the premises until all agree that the session is over and that it is safe to leave (including safe to drive); (2) Clients will engage in no destructive activities towards self, others or property; (3) There will be no sexual contact between facilitators and clients or between clients who are not already sexually involved; and (4) The clients agree to follow any explicit instruction given by the facilitator.

The dosage for individual sessions depends on several factors, especially the client's history of sensitivity to other psychoactive compounds. For first sessions by individuals, 75-125 mg. is the specified range. Clients can choose a "low, medium or high" dose as desired, and be given 75, 100, or 125 mg. respectively. Larger doses are recommended for single persons "wishing to explore inner space," and smaller ones for couples who wish to spend time together. A supplement of 50 mg. is offered when the effects subside, somewhere between 1½ and 3 hours after ingestion.

Greer also comments, "Sometimes Inderal (propranolol) at 40 mg. can be given every 4 hours (up to 120 mg. total dose) to partially relieve some of the side effects such as muscle tension. Inderal prevents the heart from beating faster during physical exertion, so clients may feel short of breath if they exert themselves."

In this type of therapeutic session, the facilitator does not take the drug with the client, and maintains a non-directive attitude—not attempting to work with the client, but available in case of difficulties.

After ingesting the compound, the client is asked to lie down and put on eye shades and stereo headphones. Music is played. Greer and Tolbert always recommend instrumental music except for vocal pieces in foreign languages (in some sessions of this type, clients are allowed to choose their own favorite musical selections). The style of music may be either classical, ethnic, or modern, and is based on the intuitions of the therapist. The client may decline a particular piece, or choose to have silence.

Couples or groups are encouraged to initiate their experience in different rooms, allowing them to attend to individual issues in the

MDMA state. Later in the session, after one to two hours, the couple or the group members come together for a sharing of experiences and insights.

If the clients attempt to engage in a "rambling monologue" with the facilitator, they might be asked to stop talking, or to talk into a tape recorder. It is recommended that the client make no commitments while in the altered state, nor engage in activity with outside people (making phone calls or going to public places).

Clients should have no work or social obligations scheduled the next day. This is to permit recovery from the fatigue that may result from the session as well as to allow for integration of the psychological rumblings of the previous day.

Greer gave his subjects a "Peak Experience Profile," authored by Walter Pahnke, Stanislav Grof and Francesco DiLeo, as well as a follow-up questionnaire, to be completed within three days. A facilitator was, as well, made available on a 24-hour basis for the following three days.

An anonymously written fact sheet simply titled "General Information: MDMA" has been circulated by a Santa Cruz, California group called the Psychedelic Education Center. This short, but wise essay was offered as a guide to the conduct of legal MDMA therapy in the pre-Schedule I period.

This fact sheet, from which I will excerpt passages in this chapter, outlines procedures quite similar to those of George Greer and Requa Tolbert, including the use of eye-shades and headphones, and a therapist who refrains from taking MDMA.

This sheet also recommends an alternative procedure:

> The second method is as follows: the person who is leading the experiment participates in the taking of MDMA along with his clients. No one remains outside the experiment. The amount given initially is 120 mgs., and the supplement offered, at about 1-½ to 1-¾ hours is 40 mgs.
>
> It should be noted here that just as it is generally understood by the intelligent and informed therapist or leader that under no circumstances should any person be persuaded or pressured to take MDMA, so must it be understood that there should never be any urging or persuasion regarding the taking of a supplement. The client's instincts and intuitions regarding his or her own state of body and mind are to be regarded as correct and must be respected.

In this second method, which we personally prefer, there is no isolation with earphones and music, although it is understood that anyone involved in the experiment may do anything that he or she wishes to make the experiment enjoyable and comfortable, within the obvious limitations presented by the surroundings and the circumstances.

Generally, talking and sharing insights and feelings goes on continually as desired.

Self-Actualization-Oriented Sessions

The climb up the self-actualization mountain differs in many respects from the climb out of the valley of psychological despair. Instead of the client/therapist relationship, your co-participants in the experience might be a trusted guide (for first-timers), a friend, a lover, or sometimes nobody except yourself. And your goals are not measured in freedom from symptoms, but in degrees of growth.

Screening of individuals for self-actualization-oriented sessions should observe the same rules for excluding physical ailments as in the therapy-oriented category. Presumably, self-actualizing people are free from mental disorders, and so there should be no concern in this regard.

Environments for experiences with this purpose can also be less restricted, especially after the first few sessions. A setting in nature, for example, would not normally be used in a therapy session, but could be suitable for self-actualization-oriented experiences.

As mentioned in this book's Preface, my own experience with MDMA progressed through what I perceived to be stages of growth. Perhaps future cartographers can develop precise maps of such stages for those pursuing self-actualization as a goal. Also, the use of established descriptions of psychological growth from Eastern schools like Zen Buddhism, or Western paths such as Jung's model of stages of self-realization, can be of help.

Creativity-Enhancement-Oriented Sessions

Creativity and peak experiences are not far apart. As I noted in the fourth chapter, creativity often occurs in an alternative state of consciousness and taps the wellspring of the unconscious mind. Thus, much of the same guidelines that were discussed in relationship to self-actualization-oriented sessions also apply here.

There are two methods of MDMA use that may help elicit creativity. In the first, the creative task is attempted during the MDMA session. In the second, the MDMA session is used to generate ideas that later may be applied to the creative task.

In the first method employed in George Greer's and Requa Tolbert's pilot study, a small dose of MDMA, 50 to 75 mg., is taken by one or more individuals. This reduced dose allows the individual to remain closer to their ordinary state of consciousness. After taking the substance, the experient or experients might spend some time "coming on" to the drug, processing through any initial psychological issues that might surface.

Then the experiment turns to a chosen task, which could consist of painting, writing, sculpting, music, or other endeavors to which a creative hand and mind might be applied. There would be no problem with visual distortions, as on major psychedelics, expecially at such a low dose. Also, coordination—including eye-hand coordination—is not impaired; so tasks that require such dexterity could still be accomplished.

In the second method, a full dose (125 to 175 mg.) of MDMA is taken, and the participant or participants refrain from any active involvement with their selected media. If one person is involved in the session, the person could choose to listen to music on headphones or perhaps examine past creations or masterpieces in the chosen creative area. In a pair or group, there might be some kind of "brainstorming" or idea-generating discussion which could loosen the soil of the fertile imagination.

Then, when the effects of the MDMA have subsided, creative ideas or images are applied to the final product. This type of session is particularly valuable for dealing with creative logjams, such as "writer's block." I should mention my own experiment in creativity with regard to the writing of this book, during a time when I felt somewhat blocked. I took a small dose (75 mg.) of MDMA with the idea of working on Chapter III during part of the experience. This was my first time taking the substance alone. I first went on a run along a road that follows the ocean, which is close to my house. An athletic friend had told me that he likes to run and bicycle on low doses of MDMA because it enhances his experience of his body and performance. I had decided previously that I would begin my experiment with my usual evening run to the Santa Cruz Lighthouse and back (about 4 miles).

The run was exhilarating. I completed the distance in a shorter than normal time, returned home, and immersed myself in a cedar hot tub.

A little over an hour and one half into the experience, I sat at my typewriter and attempted to write some of Chapter III. However, the most well-intentioned plans for drug experiences often have to be revised. I began to feel emotional and decided to write a letter to a close friend in Connecticut as a way of expressing the feelings I was having (as there was nobody around, and I had decided to receive no phone calls).

The letter ran to about four typed pages (single spaced). Then I returned to the planned chapter, and wrote a few paragraphs—and felt the block. I began to look over the entire draft of what I had written, however, with a feeling of precision and clarity.

Then I wrote a few more paragraphs and lost interest in writing entirely. I decided to do some reading, and soon was asleep. The next morning, I awoke and set about writing the chapter with renewed energy. What appeared like large granite blocking stones the day before were reduced to pebbles!

My experiment was not quite scientific, and certainly not a pure form of either of the two methods that I have outlined. It was its own kind of creation, as is each session. I look to future rigorous studies to see if what seems subjectively true actually occurs.

Recreational Sessions

Scenario I. The three friends sat holding hands on the sandy beach cove. An almost full moon lit the landscape as the three talked animatedly. Suddenly, they stopped talking and just sat. Waves broke on rocks. The air seemed charged with calm electricity. Their eyes met in wonder. They shared a new depth to their friendship that they had not previously realized.

Scenario II. The stereo filled the large living room with music and a group of partiers gathered together to participate in a spontaneous round of improvisations. Several of the people were theater-arts majors at a local college, and were teaching the rest of the group to do spontaneous skits. It was a special "creative-fun" moment for all of those there, as laughter alternated with applause.

Scenario III. The two lovers sat holding each other. As each looked at the other's naked body, it almost seemed that they could see streaks of energy flowing on the surface of their skin. Touch was highly sensitive and completely free of lustful grasping. Each felt that they were merging with the other yet becoming fully themselves simultaneously.

What do these three scenarios have in common? In all of them, the minds of each of the participants had been set on a new consciousness level, and relations between them were intensified by the recreational use of MDMA.

Recreational drug use has almost become a dirty word in 1988 America. Nancy Reagan's campaign against drug abuse is really a national campaign against any recreational drug use. Marijuana, heroin, and MDMA are not differentiated.

Intelligent use is not distinguished from insane abuse. Yet, if we were to compare the above now-illegal scenarios with similar situations in which the participants were strongly intoxicated on alcohol, we would perceive quite a contrast. Behavior on MDMA would appear more calm, peaceful, and sensitive.

If the three friends in the first scenario were stoned on alcohol, they might stagger along the beach, talking past each other, rather than really listening. The alcohol party might be highlighted by a drunken brawl rather than creative theater skits. And the lovers would be grasping at each other's anesthetized body in inebriated lust, rather than the aesthetic love-dance of the third scenario.

Because MDMA is now illegal, I cannot propose that you use this substance. However, from what we know about the drug underground, it is sure that many of you will.

In the following section, broad guidelines will be given for the use of MDMA. These can be applied to any of the uses of MDMA, including recreational use. Then, when I turn to "Future Potentialities" in Chapter VI, I will propose a more intelligent way for society to handle the use of recreational drugs through education and licensing.

What Determines the Outcome of an MDMA Session?

Returning to our earlier metaphor, if an MDMA session can be thought of as a piece of fabric, then the "set" and "setting" are that cloth's warp and woof. Set refers to what the drug taker brings to the situation, her or his enduring personality, as well as earlier imprinting and learning, individual history, emotional and intellectual tendencies, motivations and intentions, the procedure (preparation and programming for the session), philosophy and techniques of the therapist or guide, and the immediate expectations about the experience. Setting refers to the actual environment of the experience, both physical and interpersonal (social and emotional milieu), and to the concrete circumstances under which the drug is administered.

The importance of set and setting was first shown by two social psychologists, Schacter and Singer, who demonstrated that the same drug could produce two different effects depending on the set and setting. The drug they used was amphetamine, a simple stimulant. When the social situation was set up to be tense and uptight, the drug produced anger in their subject; when it was made pleasant, the same drug produced euphoria.

Each of the various types of MDMA sessions would have its own particular appropriate set and setting. Part of the set obviously is the purpose for which the substance is taken. Goals chosen have an important influence on where you end up. Fortunately, MDMA experiences tend to be positive and the substance can oftentimes brighten a previously dampened perspective.

As I mentioned before, settings for therapy-oriented sessions must be more secure and protected than for other purposes. The same is true for first-time experiences. Preparation is also part of the requirements of set, and will be disussed later in this chapter.

Settings should be comfortable and aesthetically pleasing to the MDMA taker, and should convey a sense of intimacy and warmth. Items in the environment should be chosen for the influence they might have. For a first-time user, a good setting would be his or her own home, where he or she is surrounded by familiar sights and sounds.

Included in the setting are the other individuals present during the session. The key issue in regard to these others is trust. You *must* trust the persons present with you when you take any psychoactive substance for the experience to be positive. Drug reactions can often amplify any suspicion or mistrust that is present in various session participants.

Perhaps the most important individual present is the person who occupies the position of session leader (sometimes called the guide or therapist). As with all those present in any session, you should trust this individual. The session leader influences the course of the session by his or her particular philosophical model with respect to MDMA sessions, the techniques they use in guiding the session, and how they conduct themselves during the course of the experience.

Finally, the number of people present can greatly influence the outcome of a session. For a first-time experience, the various guides published unanimously recommend taking the substance with one other person or, at most, a partner and a guide (or therapist). More experienced users may prefer to take MDMA by themselves or sometimes in groups. In the next section, a method for group experience will be explored.

Group Experiences

When groups of people take MDMA together, the interpersonal magic of this empathogen is often multiplied in proportion to the number who take the substance. Used for therapy, MDMA group sessions intensify the group-therapy process. An MDMA party can generate unique social forms and facilitate bonding of people for friendship or romance.

One of the best guides for the use of MDMA in groups was issued by
the Psychedelic Education Center of Santa Cruz, California. It is based on
observations of many group experiences.

> XTC [MDMA] has enormous potential as a tool for
> connecting and unifying groups of people. Although there
> are endless possibilities for application of this tool within a
> group setting, the following guidelines have proven
> invaluable in terms of creating productive sessions. People
> seem to get higher if the sessions are directed and organized.
> We see these guidelines as a point of possible departure,
> open to change and interpretation but of enough importance
> to pass this information along . . .
> A session is organized as the result of one person's
> decision to host the event. The host invites friends over,
> and prepares a space for the session that is clean, attractive,
> warm and safe.
> The participants begin by expressing their hopes, reser-
> vations and expectations for the session.
> As the effects unfold, all participants are encouraged to
> share their experience and insights with the group as an
> entity.
> Private conversations tend to disconnect the group and
> should be minimized.
> Shared silence is exquisite.
> Having pencils and papers on hand at all times allows
> people to retrieve information for use at a later time.
> Getting together the following day for a debriefing after
> the experience has dissipated is helpful to bind the things
> learned during the session into normal operating conscious-
> ness . . .
> If the session is successful, and the group wishes to get
> together again, a new host volunteers to provide the space
> for the next one, and sets a date.
> This procedure seems to work best if the majority of the
> participants are already familiar with the XTC experience,
> and first-timers are held to a few.
> Provision of the XTC itself works well if all participants
> bring their own supply to the session as much as possible.
> This relieves the host or any one person from the burden of
> providing for all, and tends to make the experience more

collective and easier to get together for repeats.

As mentioned in the "Reflections on the Nature of XTC and Guidlines for Its Use" [a companion set of guidelines covering more general principles], it is possible for people to have very difficult trips on XTC, although this occurrence is rare. Individuals most likely to react in this fashion are people with strongly suppressed negative emotions who act as if they aren't hurting when they are hurting badly. People with rigid personalities and belief systems can also have difficulties when their operational foundations crumble. Should a negative reaction occur in a group setting, the participants can best handle the situation by extending love and compassion to their brother or sister who is in trouble. What does this mean? It means supporting them in feeling whatever they're feeling, even if it's negative. On the other side of all negative emotions is love.

Experience has shown that these people often stand to gain the most from these experiences. The act of releasing themselves allows them to be reborn as more sensitive and understanding people, infused with new vigor for life. If possible, try to initiate these people in a small private session, rather than a group session, if the potential for difficulty can be recognized ahead of time. This occurrence is rare, but does happen and should be considered. It can be very intense.

XTC is a a tool for reaching out and touching others in soul and spirit. If responsibly used, strong bonds of unity and love can be forged that strengthen everyone involved.

Claudio Naranjo, in a private communication, describes his work with MDMA in groups, a decade after the experiments in *The Healing Journey*.

On most occasions my scheme of work has involved the following stages:

1. Individual interviews with those group members I have not met before.

2. Preparatory group sessions devoted to personal information, for sharing the expression of interpersonal emotions and for the clarification of individual expectations on the occasion of the session.

3. Group rules and general indications—of which the most important are:

3.1 Seeking a balance between spontaneity and non-interference.

3.2 No sexual intercourse during the psychedelic session and the night after.

3.3 Waiting for the effects of MDMA in an attitude of self-observation and goalless restful effortlessness.

3.4 Seeking not to establish contact with other group members before a sufficient time devoted to "self immersion" (ecstatic or painful).

4. **Distribution of MDMA, followed by ingestion: waiting for the effects in a meditative attitude, and the psychedelic group session proper**—six to eight hours in duration.

5. An "integrative" session, on the following day, for the retrospective sharing of experiences, group feedback and my comments or supplementary therapeutic intervention.

I usually work with 12-16 people, and meet for about eight hours after ingestion of MDMA and some four hours on the following day . . .

I will describe my manner of intervention during the MDMA therapy session proper briefly and only say that:

1. I rotate part of the time among group members, listening, sharing insights, occasionally using gestalt therapy techniques, giving advice or suggestions for group experiments (such as approaching such and such in such and such an attitude). In the course of years I find myself becoming less directive and less confrontative on this day.

2. I mostly come to people who come to me or call me, and rarely to those who seem to be avoiding me.

3. I am more a "father" than a "mother": I give my attention and perceptions but seek to mediate in such a way that the usual thirst for body contact of participants in the course of regression is satisfied by proximity to those group members who are at the time undergoing the typically warm and contactful MDMA peak experience.

Some of the things I have observed throughout my experience with MDMA groups consist of things that can be observed in individual MDMA therapy as well:

1. "Simple" peak experiences.

2. Peak experiences coupled to psychological insight.

3. Experiencing of hitherto repressed psychological pain.

Claudio Naranjo, M.D., author of The Healing Journey.

4. Age-regression experiences.

Though I have sometimes felt after sessions with "occasional" groups that some individuals might have been helped better through one-to-one MDMA therapy, on the whole I can say even these sessions proved very helpful to many, particularly when preceded by individual appointments and sufficiently long preparatory and integration sessions. Still, I have found work with more coherent groups and families most fruitful. It is particularly in these cases that it may be said that what is lost in individual attention from the therapist (in comparison with one-to-one therapy) is compensated by group dynamic factors. I have also seen in the training structure a satisfactory alternative to individual MDMA therapy.

I have on occasion brought together multiple couples groups: two families (two brothers and their wives, and a brother and sister with their spouses), one joint meeting of these two families and a multiple-team group, constituted by couples and associates. This, together with the experience of two ongoing teams (of psychotherapists) has constituted the most satisfactory part of my MDMA psychotherapy experience. The experience of teams is of a similar quality to that with couples and families, for quickly the team becomes a sort of family, and, indeed, my two groups came spontaneously to call themselves such. In all these instances, persons engaged in ongoing relationships are helped by the potential of MDMA for couples, who were helped through an enhanced ability to express themselves nonmanipulatively and to listen nondefensively to each other.

Having practiced LSD group therapy in the '60s and experimented with multiple substance groups (in which LSD, harmaline or MDA were given to different group members), I have for long appreciated the value of psychedelic group therapy, yet I can say that MDMA group therapy is that which I value most for its specifically psychotherapeutic results.

Though I would question MDMA sessions without the therapeutic context, I think that the properly prepared and properly elaborated MDMA group session is better than any therapeutic group experience that I have witnessed.

I have no follow-up study to present, no before and after testing, no statistics. I am well acquainted with the difficulties and limits in the evaluation of psychotherapy, and have neither been funded to set up that research nor motivated to undertake it without institutional support. I am consoled a bit, however, thinking that most forms of psychotherapeutic practice have been communicated through no more than the activity itself and the sharing of clinical impressions.

Session Preparation

Irrespective of the goal of an MDMA session, careful planning and both physical and mental preparation are important. Experimenters who take the time to prepare for a session will enhance the chances of a positive experience, and much more of almost all the benefits that can be gotten from such an undertaking will be attained.

Experimenters would usually plan to have the experience when participants will be free from any kind of obligations—or other constraints—on their time for the period of the session and for the next day as well, so that, while on the drug, their full-time attention should be on the experience and not on any competing task. Afterward, they will need time to integrate what has been learned.

The experience is something like a retreat. The MDMA experience is neither trivial nor casual. It can be a life-transforming experience.

George Greer says of this period, "Thorough psychological preparation before the session cannot be overstressed. The first and most important question to be answered is, 'Why do I want to take MDMA at this time in my life?' This is the most important preparatory step. This conscious purpose, along with the open willingness mentioned above, is the foundation of a client's mental set for the session."

Ralph Metzner and Sophia Adamson, in their paper, "The Nature and Role of the MDMA Experience" from the yet unpublished anthology, *Forbidden Fruit*, advise us:

The single most important foundation for a beneficial experience is intention or purpose. One should ask oneself, and discuss with the therapist or guide, "What is my purpose in entering into this altered state of awareness?" Typically, people approach the experience with fundamental existential and spiritual questions ... In addition there may be more personal and therapeutic questions . . . Some people prefer to declare an intention to explore certain areas or topics rather than posing questions. In either approach, it is a good practice to release the questions or intentions to one's higher self or inner guide, just prior to ingestion. In this way, one is not too intent merely on problem-solving which can, on occasion, tend to limit one's experience.

In addition, these authors make some other important recommendations. They suggest either meditation or some basic relaxation prior to the session. Those with shamanic bents might like to bring "objects" such as feathers, crystals, etc. Photographs of parents and other family members might be helpful in triggering early childhood memories.

In regard to physical considerations before taking MDMA, a good sleep the previous night is advised, just as is generally good physical health. It would not be a good idea to take MDMA to attempt to "heal" influenza or a cold, as the stress to the body will probably worsen the condition. Exceptions to this rule are terminal illnesses like cancer, where positive psychological benefits outweigh possible negative effects.

It would be advisable to have a lot of liquids—fruit juice, soft drinks, pure water, etc.—available for the session. MDMA increases the need for fluids. Participants would need to try to drink more than usual during the experience. Also, they would be advised not to each much food for about six to eight hours before a session. Food in the stomach will inhibit the absorption of the drug, or make its effects manifest unevenly.

Ingesting The Drug—Pharmacological Considerations

Before taking MDMA, one should be certain that the substance is really MDMA. Someone involved in FDA-sanctioned experimentation or therapy would have no worry here. A person who has gotten the drug from black market sources would have more need for concern. It would be wise to know and trust the individual who supplies any MDMA. Buying a drug on the streets from somebody courts trouble. There are cases of substitution of MDMA with MDA or, even worse, with LSD, PCP, or even "China White."

In 1985, Analysis Anonymous reported that 58% of samples received contained only MDMA. However, now that MDMA is illegal, the percentage of MDMA samples cut, adultered, or misrepresented with other psychoactive compounds will probably rise sharply.

MDMA is usually a white crystalline powder. A reddish or brownish tint is sometimes seen, and indicates the presence of manufacture by-products. The smell of the powder also gives a clue to these by-products. The strong smell of solvent indicates that the material still is damp with ether from manufacture, and the smell of sassafras indicates isosafarole that hasn't been converted into MDMA. However, experience has shown that these two impurities have little impact on the potency of the drug. Different ways of making MDMA result in crystals of various sizes, up to the size of very course rock salt. The crystals are normally ground up before marketing to a fine powdery consistency.

In addition to the crystal form, occasionally MDMA is buffered and pressed into tablets. Normally, a tablet is a single dose. The dosage specified is often not the real dosage, but there is no way of measuring this, because of the buffering material. Crudely made crystal MDMA can be disguised in a buffered pill.

Any unknown drug can be sent to a drug-testing company. The best one we know of is S.P. Lab, 5426 N.W. 79th Avenue, Miami, Florida 33166. They ask for a sample wrapped in foil or plastic, enclosed in an envelope, with a slip of paper telling the alleged content, cost and any undesirable side-effects noticed—$25.00 per sample—and a five-digit number to identify the sample. After 14 days, call (305) 757-2566 for the result.

If the drug is indeed MDMA, and it is not buffered with anything, the experimenter would need to decide on the dosage, in terms of the specific purpose the drug is being taken for and in relationship to the body weight of the individual who is using it.

The average dose for MDMA is somewhere between 125 mg. and 180 mg., depending upon weight. The more you weigh, the more you must take to have the same effect. A complicating factor is that each individual responds idiosyncratically to a given dose of MDMA. Some are very sensitive, while others might be resistant to having an effect on even very high doses. This may be due to variations in metabolism or to psychological factors.

The purpose of the session also enters into the dosage equation. A person taking MDMA for reasons of working creatively might take 50-75 mg., a threshold dose (the smallest amount that has a psychological effect). A person taking the drug for communicating with others might find a moderate dose—between 125 mg. and 160 mg.—to be appropriate. For self-exploration of inner spaces, doses in the high range of about 180 to 200 mg. would be called for.

MDMA is a peculiar drug in that there is a small ratio between its threshold dose and a dose that is too large. A larger dose than 200 mg.

will produce an MDMA experience, but one more like that of amphetamine—a jittery, anxiety-provoking stimulant high.

The paradoxical effects of the drug are lost at these higher doses. Furthermore, a very high dose might be physically harmful or even lethal. *Under no circumstances should anyone take a dose over 250 mg.*

After the initial dose, a "booster dose" can be used to prolong the experience. This dose can range in size from 40 mg. up to the size of the initial dose. **A dose between 75 mg. and 100 mg. has been used. The booster is usually taken about one hour after the onset of the first dose's** effects. Sometimes a second booster dose is taken in another hour.

But a second booster usually does not have the desired effect of enhancing the experience. Instead, the taker is often made to feel anxious, jittery, and sometimes confused by this third dose, with little of the pleasant effects of the first two. This characteristic is one of the best reasons why MDMA is not subject to abuse.

George Greer says of dosage size, "Many people feel they learn more from lower doses than high ones." This could be because their state is only slightly altered, so that the insights gained are more realistic and applicable to their usual state of consciousness.

Taking MDMA orally is the most usual and probably the best way to ingest it. It can be put in a capsule and swallowed. A more efficient way to take MDMA is to put it in a spoon and place it under the tongue— the sublingual route of administration. This allows for faster and more complete absorption into the blood. However, MDMA tastes terrible, and this practice is certainly not for everyone. A good compromise is to put it in juice or a carbonated beverage and drink it.

An alternative route of taking MDMA is nasally. This is popularly called "snorting" the drug, a slang term picked up from the cocaine subculture. Unlike cocaine, however, MDMA does not numb the nasal passages. Instead, it is quite irritating. Some people cannot tolerate the burning sensation that ensues upon snorting the drug. The effects of nasal inhalation are a shorter onset of action, with an almost immediate effect. The duration seems to be shortened, though, and the psychological impact of the experience seems less than that of an equivalent amount taken orally.

For MDMA to be taken nasally, the crystal must be chopped into a fine powder. This allows for proper absorption in the mucosa. Another method of ingesting MDMA is to inject it into either a vein (intravenous), or a muscle (intramuscular), with a hypodermic syringe. This method is rarely used, mainly because it has little advantage over the oral route. The main reason that drugs such as cocaine, amphetamine, and heroin are injected is that their psychological effects seem predicated on the rate at which the concentration in the blood is increased. This is called the cocaine "rush" or the "flash" with regard to heroin. However, MDMA does not produce a "rush" based on its rate of increase in the blood. Its "rush" is instead part of its course of action. The only difference between swallowing it and injecting it into a vein is the time it takes to feel the initial effects and the required dosage level.

Injecting shortens the time of onset and decreases the dosage requirement, mainly because no MDMA is lost in the digestive tract.

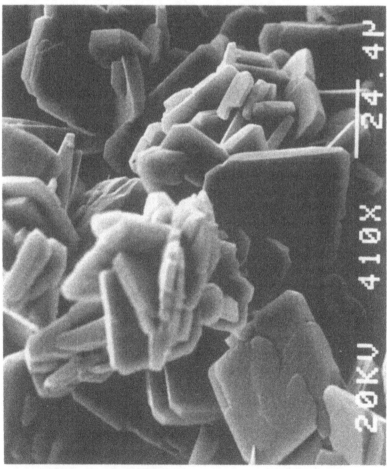

MDMA crystal magnified by electronic microscope (410 times).

Stages of a Typical Session

It has been said that no two people are exactly alike. The same individuality can be ascribed to MDMA sessions. However, in comparison to psychedelic drugs, MDMA's duration, required dosage, and psychological effects are remarkably consistent from session to session and from user to user. With this in mind, I can offer a portrait of the typical MDMA experience.

Coming on (first half hour)

As I mentioned in my Preface, and in Chapter II, the initial portion of the MDMA experience is the most profound. This period is colloquially termed the "rush," the "hit," or the "come-on."

Unlike major psychedelic substances, in which the effects appear mild and gradually become more intense, the transition to the peak of an MDMA experience happens very rapidly—about 30 to 45 minutes after the substance is taken. Its duration is between 15 and 30 minutes, followed by a gradual descent back to normal consciousness.

At the beginning of the typical positive session, there dawns a sudden clarity and intensification of experiencing. Outwardly, everything seems brighter and crisper. Inwardly, there is a feeling of ecstasy and utter happiness. Everything is perfect just as it is; everybody is lovable just as they are.

Unless you are in a therapy session, blindfolded and isolated, there is a tendency to verbalize what you are experiencing. Psychologists use the strangely awkward term "pressure of speech" to describe this phenomenon.

This increased talkativeness can be a real delight. Along with it comes a dropping of the normal defenses which we put on what we say. Many unexpressed ideas or feelings can come forth at this time. There may be a feeling of sharing your true self with others, of deep empathetic contact.

This period, if used for introspection with blindfolds or just being by yourself, can be a different kind of experence. There may be a rapid flow of ideas or emotions. Along with it, the same ecstatic awareness as in the more extroverted session may be felt. One may have a noetic perception of the world, now viewed in a completely fresh new light.

On rare occasions, there is a build-up of psychic tension, instead of the usual initial "rush" as described above.

Within 10 to 15 minutes, however, reasons for this negative experience are acknowledged, and the effects of the MDMA become apparent. This is sometimes referred to metaphorically as "bubble bursting." It is usually not experienced during any subsequent session.

The reason for the resistance involved in a negative experience is usually the surfacing of some traumatic memories. In therapeutic sessions, when the reason for giving the MDMA is to allow the individual to deal with ongoing psychological problems, the encounter of negativity in the initial session is much more common than in other session types. Many victims of violence or rape, as well as individuals with terminal disease, have a difficult time comprehending why MDMA ever was named Ecstasy.

In a therapeutic session, the therapist may encourage the encounter and reliving of traumatic episodes. But in other types of sessions, people who resist the positive effects of the substance are best told to relax, let go, and surrender to the experience.

Plateau (one half hour to 3 hours after initial effect)

Like a flat expanse on the top of a prairie plateau, there is a leveling off of experience after the initial rush. This can manifest as a peaceful calm awareness and affinity with others. The same qualities that were intensely felt at the beginning continue on. These feelings can deepen into a profound stillness, which some have likened to the realization of the goals of meditation.

During this period, coordination and movements are not impaired. It is transitions between states of consciousness that are the most dramatic manifestations of drug experience. Here, a steady new state of consciousness has been achieved. Freed from the initial "noise" of the rush, the MDMA user can now begin to explore this state's parameters.

One suggestion for using the MDMA experience for later benefit is called "future pacing." Here you conjure up, while in your alternative state, a mental image of people or situations which you would like to experience in an open and empathetic way. Then you construct an image, visual, auditory, and/or kinesthetic, of an experience of being in the MDMA state while with those persons or in that life situation. In the days ahead, your experience of that person or situation focused on might change as a result of this exercise.

Coming Down (3 to 6 hours after initial effect)

The psychological effects of the MDMA begin to shut down after about 2 ½ to 3 hours of action. The stimulant qualities of the substance can sometimes linger on for another 2 or 3 hours. For this reason, it is best if the session can be planned for the entire day or early enough in the evening that 6 or 7 hours can elapse between the taking of the drug and going to sleep.

There can be some disappointment and other negative emotions experienced at this time. This is probably best explained psychologically as the contrast between the MDMA state and baseline (ordinary) states. Physiologically, both fatigue (the result of any stimulant) and depleted neurotransmitters can account for this low after the high.

To minimize this physiological component of post negativity, some nutritional supplementation would be useful. Upon coming down from an MDMA experience, one might take 1000 mg. tryptophan before going to sleep. Then, upon rising, one might take 1000 mg. of tyrosine. Both amino acids are available at most health food and vitamin stores. These amino acids will replenish some of the neurotransmitters *suspected* to be depleted by the action of MDMA.

Psychologically, it would be a good tactic to recall the most positive moments of the experience. Looking back on these highlights and insights would help you reaccess the positive state and dispell psychic darkness.

Afterglow (the day after the session)

This is a period when you feel tired, relaxed, and open to others. There persists a residual mental clarity and positive emotional state from the previous day's empathetic and entactogenic adventure. This is sometimes called the"afterglow" and may persist for days or even weeks after a particularly beneficial session.

You might feel either somewhat fatigued or perhaps energized by the previous day's experience. As mentioned earlier, it is best to leave this day free of obligations for the reintegration of the material generated by the session into normal awareness, as well as for continued exploration of the openness you may be feeling. My own preference was to spend most of the next day at home with some time allotted to naps. In addition, I liked to get out to a public place to walk around and interact with people. I found it fascinating to see how my perceptions of people changed after an MDMA session.

Side-Effects and Adverse Reactions

There are a number of common side-effects of MDMA. These include (from a list by George Greer): jaw-clenching, eye wiggle (nystagmus), muscle tension, nausea, decreased appetite. Occasional side-effects reported less frequently are: difficulty in walking, chills, sweating, biting the inside of the cheek, headache, fainting, inability to reach orgasm, and vomiting. Also, psychosomatic symptoms can occur and these can take many forms.

This list of possible side-effects may sound horrible. However, most people find them tolerable, given the highly rewarding main effects of MDMA. None of the symptoms on the list occur in all those who take the substance.

The listed side-effects are most probably not products of the mind, but a direct result of the physiological effects of MDMA. Yet they can be minimized with psychological techniques.

As an example, take the most commonly noted side-effects—jaw-clenching and muscle tension. A good method to allay these negative symptoms is as follows. First, get a moistened washrag, and place it between the teeth of the sufferer. Tell the individual to close his or her eyes and on the count of ten, to progressively tense every muscle in her or his body and to bite down as hard on the washcloth as they can. Then slowly count to ten, instructing them to make their muscles "more and more tense" and their jaw "tighter and tighter." You might talk about the tension in each specific muscle group between counts. Then finally, on ten, tell the individual to "relax completely."

Done in a hot tub, this exercise can be doubly effective.

Hot springs and saunas would be very useful for MDMA sessions, because they help tight muscles to unwind. George Greer disagrees with me on this. He fears that hot tubs might lead to faintness or even cardiac problems.

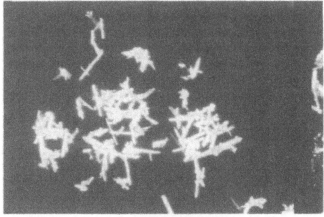

MDMA crystals.

Another technique for relieving jaw tension is to chew gum during the session.

The prescription drug Inderal (chemically known as propranolol) at a dosage of 40 mg. every 4 hours, including a dose shortly before the initial dosage of MDMA, is also helpful. Three doses is probably a good cut-off point. Inderal can relieve some of the side-effects, including tremor and muscle tension. However, Inderal is a blood-pressure medication, which prevents the heart from beating fast; so there may be shortness of breath during any activity requiring exertion.

As mentioned above, the pain of unfinished grief, or early traumatic epidodes, can arise as negative psychological bubbles that burst, transforming into an ecstatic release of tension. Sometimes, an adverse reaction will last the entire session, with no release at all. Greer, in "The Legal, Safe and Effective Use of MDMA," comments:

> The most common undesirable emotional symptom is anxiety. Depression, emotional lability, racing thoughts, confusion, and grandiose thoughts can also occur during or after the session. These other symptoms are not common. It is safe to assume that any psychological disturbance could occur.
>
> The facilitator running the session should be very experienced at handling such reactions and helping clients use them for therapeutic growth. Any physical or psychological reaction can be utilized beneficially if all parties are committed to that endeavor.

It always should be remembered that it is best not to consider sessions as "bad" and "good" sessions, but rather as "difficult" and "easy." An experience that is filled with difficult material can often prove quite useful to an individual, showing him or her areas of their *psyche* that they have repressed and avoided. By opening up to these dark sides of oneself, psychological growth is promoted.

Because these difficult sessions almost always occur during the first few exposures to MDMA, it is important to have a guide or "sitter" who will be there for support and to help the beginner through any possible negative manifestations.

Claudio Naranjo, in the Preface of *The Healing Journey*, discusses what he calls "The Healing Power of Agony and Ecstasy." Naranjo compares experiences on psychoactive substances to the situation in Dante's *Divine Comedy*, a guided tour of heaven and hell. Both the heavenly and hellish types of journey can be useful for psychological growth. The heavenly ones give you a glimpse of your potentials in growth, and the hellish sorts point to what has been repressed from conscious awareness. In terms of the *Divine Comedy*, Naranjo depicts the role of the session's guide:

> For practical purposes, though, it seems clear that the best that the therapist can do is stand by the traveler in hell as Virgil did by Dante, reminding him of his goal, giving him the courage to step ahead and see, pushing him even when he wants to retreat in fear. I believe that the realization that hell is no hell must come from inner realization and not from well-intentioned reassurance and brainwashing, so I find myself saying to patients again and again, "Stay with it." Staying with it is the best way of going through it, whatever it is.

The Changing Nature of the MDMA Experience

Of those that try MDMA, there are some who abide by the words of one fellow who remarked, "When you get the message, hang up the phone." These individuals feel that they have learned what they needed to on their initial session and don't need to repeat it. Some comment that they now hope to recapture the feelings they experienced without having to take a drug. Others initiated into the empathetic and entactogenic world are eager to repeat the experience as soon as possible.

This, of course, leads to the question: "How often can you safely use MDMA?" As mentioned earlier, MDMA cannot be taken repeatedly, or it loses its main effect and becomes a bunch of increasingly annoying side-effects. This is due to a phenomenon known as tolerance. Tolerance is the tendency of a person to build up a resistance to the effects of a psychoactive substance when taking it repeatedly. MDMA shows a type of tolerance called tachyphylaxis, which means that tolerance rises rapidly upon subsequent administrations.

Tolerance to a substance decreases with the passage of time. Physically, MDMA can be taken again in two or three days. However, the effects appear to flatten out when taken this often.

There seems to be a need to mentally digest the experience at all levels of the *psyche*. Once per week is the most often MDMA can be used without diminished effect. More sensible would be using it perhaps once per month. This would give sufficient time to integrate all the material uncovered by the experience.

One comment I have heard repeatedly is: "I never have MDMA experiences anymore like my first one" (or first ten sessions). I have noticed from my own series of sessions, over eight years, that while none of my experiences had quite the overwhelming impact of my first few, there were occasions when MDMA again seemed to break me through to a new level of communication, or self-understanding, that I had never before achieved.

This loss of quality in repeated usage might have either physiological or psychological causes. A physiological explanation, for example, is that the long-term tolerance is the result of some permanent change in the way that receptors, at the synapses of brain neurons, react to the MDMA after repeated exposures. Perhaps more likely are possible psychological explanations.

It may be that the experience becomes much more familiar and therefore does not impress us as much. Or it could be that as we integrate the state of consciousness achieved on MDMA into our ordinary state of consciousness, the difference between the two states becomes smaller. Since it is dramatic shifts in consciousness which are noticed most, these repeated experiences are perceived as more commonplace.

If sessions are taken far enough apart, there will be an upward spiraling progression from experience to experience. I leave it for future explorers to find and delineate the patterns that this psychological evolution might take.

Synergy with Other Drugs

Noted architect Buckminster Fuller developed the concept of synergism—"The simultaneous action of separate agencies which, together, have greater total effect than the sum of their individual effects." Many of you know of common synergies, both positive and negative, in the realm of recreational drugs.

A famous example of a negative synergy is the mixing of barbiturates and alcohol. Just small amounts of the two taken together—neither one of them by itself high enough to be dangerous—can combine to kill.

Combinations of MDMA and other drugs most often demonstrate the positive effects of drug synergism. One of the most important discoveries of this kind was that of the benefits to be derived from taking MDMA prior to ingestion of a major psychedelic.

When taken by itself, LSD is quite non-specific in its effects. Set and setting are critical variables in determining which direction an LSD experience will go. But because MDMA is more specific and mainly positive in its effects, using MDMA either shortly before or simultaneously with LSD can usually ensure a positive, short-term psychological set for the LSD experience. For those who normally experience some anxiety prior to taking LSD, the de-stressing, anti-anxiety effect of MDMA can be an enormous boon toward ensuring a positive initial direction to the LSD experience.

This synergistic effect of MDMA and LSD can be quite useful in LSD-assisted therapy. This sort of therapy—which has demonstrated benefits in the treatment of neurosis, alcohol and substance abuse, and terminal cancer patients—can now be practiced with a greater probability of eliciting a positive psychedelic reaction.

MDMA has been combined experimentally with another new psychedelic substance, 2-CB (2,5-dimethoxy-4-bromo-phenethylamine). Alexander Shulgin described 2-CB at a 1983 Conference, "Psychedelics and Spirituality," at the University of California, Santa Barbara:

> 2-CB . . . is a tool . . . which ties the mental process directly and constructively into the physical soma.
>
> The analgesic effects experienced with many, if not most, psychedelic drugs, are not present with 2-CB. On the contrary, there is increased body awareness of every kind, including skin sensitivity, heightened responsiveness to smells, tastes, and sexual stimulation.
>
> One experiences increased consciousness of physical health and energy, or, on the other hand, sharpened awareness of any body imbalance or discomfort.
>
> 2-CB allows for rich visual imagery and intense eyes-closed fantasy without the cluttering up of the mental field with too much elaboration . . . It is a superb tool for learning and growth.

2-CB, as of this writing, is still a legal compound (aside from the "analogs law," which is constitutionally questionable) and has been used by both psychotherapists and self-experimenters. At high doses (above 30 mgs.), 2-CB is intensely hallucinogenic, and, like any major psychedelic, can be frightening for certain people. In small doses, it becomes a mild sensory enhancer but does not have the strongly empathogenic qualities that MDMA has.

Perhaps the best use that has been found for 2-CB is as a synergist with MDMA. When taken together, the MDMA pushes the non-specific 2-CB reaction in a more warm and empathetic direction. Because

2-CB is a psychedelic drug, and therefore not fully predictable, its action can take the user in many different directions. But if the set and setting are right, 2-CB can enhance the desire for sexual orgasm during an MDMA experience. The synergy of the two substances can on occasion be a true aphrodisiac.

What about MDMA in combination with common recreational drugs, such as alcohol, marijuana, and cocaine?

While on MDMA, people can drink a lot of alcohol and not be affected as they would normally be. This is probably due to MDMA's stimulant quality. Observing recreational sessions, I have sometimes noted copious consumption of alcohol. This is not recommended—for two reasons. First, alcohol acts as a depressant, impedes MDMA's action, and produces a stupor state that interferes with MDMA's clarification of thought processes.

Second, the day after MDMA and heavy drinking is bound to be rough. It is a combination of the fatigue of Adam, mixed with the hangover of too many drinks that weren't noticed, that hits you like a ton of bricks.

The most intelligent way to use alcohol with MDMA is to have one mixed drink or a glass of wine after coming down, as a way of calming any residual anxiety.

What was just said about alcohol could almost be applied verbatim to marijuana. Sometimes, however, a small amount of marijuana can be a useful adjunct during the session, as a method of dampening the stimulant qualities of the MDMA. Remember that over-smoking marijuana can dull the experience as well as lead to post-session fatigue.

Since they are both stimulants, MDMA is sometimes compared to cocaine. But there are many important distinctions between them. Cocaine's duration is much shorter, and its effects differ greatly from those of MDMA. Cocaine is not truly empathogenic, leading to talkativeness but not real contact between people. Cocaine is euphoric, but usually does not lead to any authentic self-insight. Many cocaine abusers find regular, though relatively infrequent, use of MDMA as a way of escaping their addiction. They report that the MDMA experience was what they were looking for with cocaine, but never got.

Cocaine truly is addictive. It can be injected or smoked (as a free base), and this will produce a euphoric rush due to the rapid rise of concentrations in the blood. Tolerance builds up, but subsequently larger doses will still produce the rush. A long string of successive dosings is possible.

MDMA and cocaine should never be used together. There are

indications in the MDA literature which suggest that cocaine is negatively synergistic with MDA. Until research can be done, the combination of these two drugs should be avoided.

Chapter VI. Future Potentialities

> *"The time will come when we'll separate all our senses and
> capabilities—the visual from the auditory, the tactile from the
> sense of smell, as well as wit, intellectual capability, creativity—
> and [be able] to enhance them with drugs."*
> —Alexander Shulgin (in "Future Drugs," *Omni* magazine)

The controversy and promise of MDMA is part of a larger issue facing our society—the possibility of accessing new states of mind through the intelligent use of drugs and potential non-drug methods, as well as our freedom to do so. The development of tailor-made drugs with more specific effects will continue, as the above quote from Shulgin suggests. Our understanding of the brain, both of its chemistry and structure and of its relationship to thought and feeling, will expand as we enter the 21st century.

Only science fiction, with its broad powers to speculate and extrapolate on current trends, can touch what will someday become our reality. Now I will make an attempt to explore these possible directions, as well as point to coming choices that might lead down very different roads. A possible model for using MDMA in a more rational and less hysterical manner, to make best use of its potential, will then be proposed.

Roots in the Past

However, the future must rest on the present and the present on the past. The introduction of MDMA into our society as a popular intoxicant is part of a historical process in which every ten or twenty years American culture embraces a new drug which reflects the avant-garde ethic of its time, including its art and music, its literary style and street slang.

When someone mentions the "Roaring Twenties," for instance, we think of hip flasks and flappers dancing the Charleston. The speakeasies were packed with multitudes imbibing a very illegal drug called booze.

Then there was the amphetamine boom during World War II. The Germans developed amphetamines in the 1930's and used them to wage the "Blitzkrieg" or "Lightning War." The German slang expression for "speed" was "blitz." Their bomber pilots could stay "wired" for their long-distance runs over England.

But the American military, not to be outdone by the Germans, started packing "crank" (slang for amphetamine) into ration kits of the G.I.'s. The total use during World War II amounted to one pill per soldier per day.

In the 1950s there were the Beatniks. Beats "dug" jazz and jeans and sweatshirts and cool, reciting marijuana-inspired poetry in coffee houses and urban lofts. And they learned Indian chants with a bitter peyote after-taste. The leaders of this new movement challenged the Valium culture of Eisenhower, with its conformist in the grey flannel suit. Their drug of choice was marijuana.

Although he died in 1963, young John Kennedy—with his plans for a New Frontier, his easy-going hedonism and visions of peace—laid the groundwork for the explosive decade of the 'Sixties. The Kennedy spirit found its legacy in the flower-power of the Hippie upheaval and the anti-war sentiment that grew as the decade developed. The drugs of choice of the young and bold of those times were the psychedelic drugs—mushrooms, mescaline, LSD.

Then, the repressive atmosphere of Vietnam warrior and law-and-order champion Nixon led in the 'Seventies, and soon we had the Arab oil cartel setting off a world-wide recession. "Looking out for Number One," the self-assertive ethic of the decade, replaced the mind-expansion and laid-back ways of the previous ten years. So it came as no suprise that cocaine was chosen as drug of the decade.

During this same decade, our friend Adam (aka MDMA) was born as a social phenomenon as part of a new generation of psychoactive compounds. After a relatively quiet childhood, Adam emerged in adolescence as just the right antidote to 'Eighties paranoia.

But Adam's passage to adulthood has been troubled. Adam was branded a renegade in the anti-drug political climate of the times. When Ronald Reagan took over in the White House, he declared "War on Drugs." His wife Nancy chose to turn this war into her Holy Crusade. In this atmosphere colored by fundamentalist politics, in which any drug aside from alcohol is considered sinful, it is difficult to contend that any new substance might be benevolent and useful.

Adam's future is hard to predict. Will he grow up to be a career criminal or a therapist? What about Eve, or the next generation?

Prospects for the Immediate Future

The DEA appears determined to keep MDMA illegal, and any MDMA research frozen. It appears that the DEA intends to keep MDMA in Schedule I. Every recommendation by an independent judicial body to place MDMA in a lower schedule has been rebuffed by the DEA.

The Omnibus Drug Bill of 1986 included "the Controlled Substance Analogue Enforcement Act of 1986," popularly called the "Analogs Act." The bill lists felony penalties for the distribution and manufacture of substances that have a chemical structure substantially similar to that of a controlled substance in Schedules I or II, or which have hallucinogenic, stimulant or depressive effects which are substantially similar or greater than that of a controlled substance.

With the passage of this bill, a whole new tack has been steered with respect to drug policy. The government is sailing full-tilt into dangerous waters where laws ban states of consciousnesss rather than specific drugs.

Thus the prospects for Adam and his friends for the near future appear bleak. Unless the voices of therapists and researchers, who are a small yet vocal minority, can be heard, the anti-drug hysteria sweeping our land may succeed in throwing the baby out with the bathwater. Laws designed to curb dangerous designer drugs, like a synthetic heroin substitute that has produced Parkinsonian symptoms, will also be used by the DEA to repress the radically different sort of drugs being developed to expand human functioning.

A Model for Rational MDMA Use

Thomas Kuhn, in his *The Structure of Scientific Revolutions*, noted that it takes about one generation for a new theory to be accepted by the scientific establishment. The same is more or less true of many new ideas and practices in society.

A good example of this is gambling. A generation ago, lotteries run by the "mob" were called the "numbers racket." Today, many states run numbers rackets of their own, calling them "state lotteries."

It should also be noted that commonly accepted drugs today—such as alcohol and coffee—carried penalties in some past cultures more dreadful than that given for heroin or cocaine in our own society.

Matthew Huxley, articulate son of the late novelist Aldous Huxley, discussed the possiblities of the development of a "socially sanctionable drug" in a 1976 issue of *Interdisciplinary Science Reviews*, which I will examine later in this chapter. In a recent interview in the December 1985 issue of *Futurist Magazine*, Huxley comments on the present situation in this country with respect to drug use:

> Under this administration, hysteria about drug use is back again, much as it was in the late 1950s and 1960s. This is a reflection of the views of many of the administration's supporters, such as born-again Christians. I do not know how long the hysteria will last before a sensible approach can be taken. Let us remember that McCarthyism lasted all too long and seems, alas, to be reappearing.
>
> I do not see a trend against drug use in America, particularly among the middle-aged and the young. In fact, drug use has grown by leaps and bounds. It is the small, conservative, "moral" groups—some of whom have the ear of the administration—who are pressing for draconian enforcement measures.

If Huxley's view is accurate, then it seems inevitable that sooner or later we will have a loosening up of social restrictions on the use of drugs. As the harsh drug measures and billions of dollars poured into armies of drug enforcement personnel fail to stop drug use, the views of the man-on-the-street about how to deal with drug abuse may change dramatically.

People may begin to understand that education, rather than criminalization, is the best way to temper drug use. As I have mentioned earlier in this book, the failure to distinguish between proper use and abuse of drugs—as well as the more fundamental error of not distinguishing between drugs that are safe when used properly and dangerous drugs—led to our present mess with respect to drug use. Classes which teach young people what each drug does and how to use the more benevolent drugs—including the study of such topics as the influence of set and setting on drug exprience, the use of proper dosage, and drug purity—could help enormously in irradicating the present ignorant misuse of drugs.

Our culture is certainly not the first to use powerful mind-altering substances. The use of potent plant-derived compounds has existed in many cultures around the globe and since the beginnings of our species. Powerful psychedelic drugs like psilocybin mushrooms, for example, have been used by Indians in southern Mexico as an adjuct to healing. Shamans called *curanaderos* conduct nighttime ceremonies guided by chanting and drumming. Many other examples of tribal use of powerful intoxicants could be given.

Yet nowhere in any of these cultures can you point to drug-abuse problems that are so prevalent in Western industrial societies. The reason is that the use of drugs in tribal communities is institutionalized, and respect for the powerful sacraments of healing and religion is taught early.

To harness the potential of the newly developed mind-changing compounds, schooling on the proper use of drugs would provide a good first step. Education might be accomplished within the present educational institutions.

But even more innovative would be the development of new institutions for training people to use psychoactive compounds as well as conducting basic research in this area. These would be the central feature of a new model for the use of MDMA as well as other mind-altering tools. Within this new institution—which might be called a Psychological Exploration Center—we might see the integration of many of the growth techniques developed by humanistic and transpersonal psychologies during the past twenty-five years, drug as well as non-drug.

Licensing for the use of drugs would be part of our model for the solution of the drug problem. People would be required to take a course at school or in the Psychological Exploration Center—which might include classroom computer and video simulations of drug experiences, readings, lectures and guided drug sessions to learn to use MDMA responsibly. Then, after taking a comprehensive exam, they would be certified to use MDMA on their own.

This licensing has precedent in the way that our society presently handles the operation of a motor vehicle. Certainly there are many more people killed each year driving cars than using MDMA. There have been only five substantiated cases of human death related to the use of MDMA (all in individuals with heart arythmias and in several cases complicated by multiple drug use). Car accidents are the largest non-disease related cause of death in the United States. As mentioned in Chapter I, there are few if any individuals mentally damaged by MDMA. In spite of the hazards of operating an automobile, there is no draconian ban on the use of cars. Instead, we use education and licensing to make driving as safe as possible. This is because automobiles are tremendously useful for transportation. Society sees the casualties as an acceptable risk when balanced against its benefits. MDMA and some other new compounds, in a similar way, can be seen as useful tools for human mental development.

Licenses for various drugs would require different amounts of training. MDMA would entail a fairly simple course of study compared to the more demanding requirements for mastering of a drug like LSD.

To train and research the mastery of altering consciousness safely, a new specialization—the "Self-Exploration Guide"—might emerge from the fields of psychiatry and psychology. These individuals would be experts at managing and directing the new mental energies and behaviors catalyzed during drug sessions.

Possible Futures

When we speak of "Psychological Education Centers" and "Self-Exploration Guides," we begin to take leave of the dominion of science and enter into the more speculative realm of science fiction. Instead of describing the future of MDMA and mind-altering drugs, it might be better to talk of possible futures—each of them described in terms of potentialities rather than certainties.

In 1973, the United States Government's National Institute on Drug Abuse issued a small booklet which was quite unusual for an agency which normally publishes literature delineating the dangers of using drugs. *Drug Themes in Science Fiction*, by science fiction-author Robert Silverberg, is a short but fascinating work which begins with a lively essay on the book's topic, giving a short history of drug themes in the genre, discussing the "two distinct attitudes toward the use of mind-related drugs" (cautionary and visionary), and listing the various descriptors that are used in the book's Annotated Bibliography. These categories for drug-related science fiction stories include "Drugs as Euphorics," "Drugs as Mind Expanders," "Drugs as Panaceas," "Drugs as Mind Controllers," "Drugs as Intelligence-Enhancers," "Drugs as Sensation-Enhancers," "Drugs as Reality-Testers," Drugs as Mind-Injurers," and "Drugs as Means of Communication."

Of these categories, "Drugs as Euphorics"—"Drugs that give pleasure in simple unstructured ways through release from depression and tension, much as alcohol does in our society" [although alcohol is not, strictly speaking, a euphoric, of course], and "Drugs as Means of Communication"—"Drugs that have the specific property of opening hitherto unknown channels of communication between minds," would begin to suggest the effects of MDMA, which was virtually unknown when this booklet was written.

Silverberg states in his introduction:

A drug is a kind of magic wand; but it is a chemist's magic
wand, a laboratory product, carrying with it the cachet of
science. By offering his characters a vial of green pills or a
flask of mysterious blue fluid, the author is able to work
wonders as easily as a sorcerer; and by rigorously examining
the *consequences* of his act of magic, he performs the
exploration of speculative ideas which is the essence of
science fiction.

Each of the alternative scenarios listed in Silverberg's cartography of
possible futures describes yet another effect a drug might have on mind
and civilization. Some of these are quite amazing, and give us some
sense of possible future shapes our humankind may be molded into by
chemical influence. Yet somehow none of the compounds we have
examined in this book appear to be accurately predicted by any of those
works listed in Silverberg's book.

Perhaps the person who came closest to predicting some of the
functions of the empathogens/entactogens is Aldous Huxley. Huxley,
one of the great novelists of the 20th century, developed a deep and
abiding interest in mind-altering drugs, including their effects upon the
individual and society. As described in Appendix I of this book,
Huxley's academic interests became more worldly with his introduction
into the altered landscape of mescaline intoxication by Humphry
Osmond in 1954. After that time, Huxley took infrequent but evidently
illuminating psychedelic journeys until his death in 1963. During that
time he also lectured widely, often on the topic of visionary experience
or human potential, which included extensive discourses on mind
drugs.

In a 1962 talk entitled "Human Potentialities" at Esalen Institute
(recorded by Big Sur Tapes), Huxley made the following prediction:

One day, somebody may discover a really good euphoric.
We all know that happiness is one of two conditions that
cause people to function at a high level (the other being
crisis). Happy people do their work well. A good and
completely harmless euphoric, one that works its effects
without damaging the physical organism, might be
developed which would make people happier and more
contented.

Such a drug would lower the barriers between the

conscious mind and the preconscious, the ego and the creative self, leading to the production of great works of art or literature. The euphoric might also have another effect, to make people more moral. Bertrand Russell was fond of pointing out that contented and happy people are more virtuous and kindly toward one another than unhappy people. And here again, we may find the pharmacological tools contributing to the realization of greater potentialities.

Following this path first forged by his venerable father, Matthew Huxley has also written about the possibilities of our culture developing and legitimizing new socially sanctionable drugs which he calls "Soma." The Soma—or, in this case, Somas—of the future would be different from the ancient Soma of the *Vedas* or the Soma envisioned by Aldous Huxley in his novel *Brave New World.*

In his paper "In Search of a Socially Sanctionable Drug," published in *Interdisciplinary Science Reviews* (Vol. 1, No. 2, 1976), the younger Huxley presages the development of new drugs which would be engineered to have specific effects and which would be safe for both the individual and society.

There might be several of these new Somas, each with differing purposes. A Type I Soma "should, like alcohol, be able to enhance social situations by disinhibiting emotional expression, elevating mood, reducing anxiety levels and the like." Sounds a bit like MDMA, doesn't it?

A Type II Soma would foster "the introspective, ideational, contemplative state of consciousness in individuals alone, or in very small groups," while Type III would be sought as a mechanism for "explorations" of the sensory universe. All three types would be engineered for precise duration of effects, be fully tested and approved, and have a way to turn off the effects when doing so would be desirable. They would also be restricted in their use by sanctions on "purpose, person, place, and provider."

Understanding Consciousness and the Nervous System

Another science-fiction author who has made psychoactive drugs a part of his literary repertoire is Norman Spinrad. Spinrad, in an article in the now defunct *Head* magazine, says, "psychochemistry [has] created states of consciousness that had never existed before." His view is that "psycho-chemicals are a declaration of independence from the minds we were born with," and that hence "we will no longer be able to count on our 'naturally evolved' brain chemistry as a benchmark of sanity."

Spinrad is touching here on the idea developed in Chapter II that there exist many alternative states of consciousness, and that our ordinary state is not necessarily the only state in which we can be considered mentally healthy. The intervention of a drug into the nervous system means that different patterns of brain activity are set up, with each compound producing its own distinct mode of experiencing.

Building upon this theme is the work of psychologist Timothy Leary. In his fascinating book *Exo-Psychology*, Leary explores a model of human psychological growth in which each individual turns on and uses a series of brain "circuits" during his or her life. These circuits are distinct states of what Leary calls "contelligence" (consciousness + intelligence). Each succeeding circuit activated is a quantum leap to a new and different level of contelligence, but rests upon the foundation of the preceeding circuits.

He also postulates that humankind is itself evolving through a sequence in which much of our species will soon operate at higher levels of neural functioning. Leary states, "The person who can dial and tune the circuits of the nervous system is not just more intelligent but can be said to operate at a higher, more complex level of evolution."

The last part of this millennium may see dramatic advances in the areas of neurophysiology, psychopharmacology, and consciousness sciences. The new understandings and resultant technologies will shape future human psychological growth.

In neurophysiology, the brain is at last beginning to yield its secrets. In the last twenty years, psychobiologists have begun to describe the chemistry of brain neurons, the synapses that separate them, and the way in which signals travel through both. A number of neuro-transmitters have been isolated and studied, and their relationship to the various neuron circuits in the brain are starting to be understood.

The function of various types of neurons have also begun to be comprehended, as have ways that more complex structures in the brain act to regulate sensation, thought, feelings, and behavior.

Psychopharmacology has emerged as a distinct science during the last thirty years. Alexander Shulgin, in a talk at a 1983 Psychedelics Conference at the University of California, Santa Barbara, speculated on the implications of some discoveries in this field:

> Let us look at the history of other areas of psychotropic chemistry.
>
> A few decades ago, it was marveled on that past drugs

such as the opiates, including morphine, heroin, meperidine, could have such an exacting influence on the brain's integrity. Then it became known that there were natural factors in the brain that had these actions, and there were specific sites in the brain which were pre-designed to respond to them.

There were the enkephalins and their fragmented portions, known as the endorphins, which were derived from the cephalic process, and related to morphine; these met the person's need for the suppression of pain.

Perhaps there are the enkedelics (from the psychedelics) and the specific enescalines (from mescaline) yet to be discovered that are related to these communicative factors— which might be natural and which might be connected, eventually, to the natural receptor sites, for transcendental communication.

We can speculate that there are also receptors in the brain for MDMA, and that these have something to do with the way that empathy is expressed in the structures of the nervous system. In the future, we may find many compounds that control almost every aspect of human thought, feeling, and behavior. From the random and haphazard ways we function now, the future may see each of us as a musician playing the keys of a magic synthesizer. What may be commanded from our fleshy instrument is not just sound, but all the qualities of human experience.

In addition to our understanding of the hardware of mental functioning, we will soon learn more about the states of consciousness associated with the neurological structures. Psychologists such as John Lilly, Kenneth Pellitier, Ken Wilbur, and Timothy Leary have proposed complex maps of human consciousness and intelligence. Valle and von Eckertsberg have compiled a book listing more than a score of these maps which they call *Metaphors of Consciousness.*

Each of these systems is built on concepts drawn from science, art or religion, and sometimes from combinations of the three. They attempt to use metaphors from these fields to build models of how the human mind actually processes information and, even more mysterious, how it becomes aware of itself.

Beyond the tentative threads of today may lie a true science of consciousness, and when integrated with neurophysiology, a real scientific psychology may emerge.

Altering States of Consciousness

From the new knowledge of the nervous system and consciousness will come more powerful and precise technologies for changing the functioning of the nervous system and producing altered states of consciousness. Not all of these new technologies will be limited to pharmacological compounds, but will probably include a wide range of methods. Nor will each of these new technologies be used exclusively, but may be combined to vastly increase their effectiveness.

One of these new technologies will be biofeedback. Back in the 'Sixties, when biofeedback was first introduced, it was touted by some as the path to instant meditation, or as an "electronic LSD." Small machines that produced alpha brainwave feedback were marketed that did nothing more than convey electrical noise made by people moving their eyes.

Biofeedback devices pick up electrical waves from the surface scalp by the use of electrodes taped on the head. A device called an E.E.G. (an electroencephalograph) measures the brainwaves, which are then presented back to the person being monitored by sound (a tone, for instance) or visually (some new biofeedback devices have video monitors).

The early disillusionment with biofeedback as a method of altering consciousness may have resulted because the ultimate promise of this method could not be matched by the technology of the time. With the advent of the microcomputer, biofeedback might again move to fulfill its original potential.

Computers may help us find out exactly what electronic changes occur in response to changes in states of consciousness, and to use feedback to help make desired changes. Some of the possibilities of human/computer linkups are a future when we could buy ROM-discs which contain previously recorded desirable experiences, play them on a machine, and have the experiences. This might eventually replace movies as a form of entertainment.

Another use of biofeedback is close in its reported effects to that of MDMA. Psychologist Jean Millay has done experiments with a biofeedback device which places the brainwaves of two individuals into synchronization. Some have reported increased empathy and even telepathy while making these connections.

Other experiments being done with altered-states technologies include new ones—such as electronic brain stimulation using electrodes taped to parts of the heads to induce altered states—and older methods—such as hypnosis presented in new and more powerful ways.

Recently, "brain spas" have appeared which feature machines which alter the brain in different ways, as described in Michael Hutchison's book *Megabrain*. While there are many who claim to have been helped by these machines, it is probably best to see these as early prototypes of what will be truly useful devices ten or twenty years from now.

If present trends continue and are allowed by the conservative forces in our society to manifest, the future may see a blending of the various new altered-state technologies to radically transform the way humans function psychologically. We may find even more advanced generations of specific psychoactive drugs, electronic interfaces with computers and biofeedback devices blended with ancient methods, such as meditation and yoga, to allow individuals the freedom to change their states of consciousness at will, as well as freedom from negative states of mind.

Violent individuals might find ways to control their impulses.

Creative artists may find ways to augment their craft.

Humanity may find a key to ecstasy.

Understanding Ecstasy

Ecstasy is a transcendent emotional experience and an altered state of consciousness. The root meaning of the word comes from *ex-stasis*, literally out of, or released from, a fixed or unmoving condition.

MDMA certainly can lead to the attainment of its unique version of ecstasy. Novelist Thomas Pynchon, author of *Gravity's Rainbow*, says of the action of MDMA: "the circuits of the brain which mediate alarm, fear, flight, fight, lust, and territorial paranoia are temporarily disconnected. You see everything with total clarity, undistorted by animalistic urges. You have reached a state which the ancients have called nirvana, all seeing bliss."

Nirvana and ecstasy are here synonyms for an experience that is often attained through the prudent and responsible use of MDMA. Robert Masters, head of the Institute for Mind Research and author of *Varieties of Psychedelic Experience* (with his wife Jean Houston), compares MDMA to the mythic drink of the ancient Greek gods, *Nepenthe*—the banisher of sorrows. The state of transcendent ecstasy temporarily dispels our psychic darkness, filling us with the light that heals. The therapeutic effects of this modern *Nepenthe* has its origin in the capacity to banish the mental traumas and depressions that cloud minds, giving us a glimpse of what it's like to be truly happy.

Appendix I.
MDMA's Family Tree:
Chemistry & Physiological Effects

The family tree to which MDMA belongs is large and varied, heavy with psychoactive drug fruit of every description. The main trunk is alkaloid drugs and, further up, the tree forks. We follow up the branch of the compounds called phenylalkylamines and, still higher, the tree branches again into the phenylisopropylamines. The methoxylated phenylisopropylamines are found on a small top branch from which hangs a cluster of MDA-like fruit—including MDMA as well as a bud or two.

MDMA is a semi-synthetic drug. It is related to several substances found in plants, but is also a member of a large family of psychoactive compounds that are synthesized in chemical laboratories.

The vegetative ancestry of MDMA is found in the essential oils of more than half a dozen familiar herbs, roots, and spices, which contain substances from which MDMA and its relatives can be derived. The list of plants containing these precursor volatile oils include nutmeg, mace, sassafras, saffron, calamus, crocus, parsley, dill, and vanilla beans. Of these, nutmeg, mace, and calamus have long histories of use as psychoactive plants.

Calamus (botanically *Acorus calamus*) contains the active essential oil asarone, which is a natural precursor of the psychedelic TMA-2, which will be discussed later in this section. Because of this psychoactivity, calamus under other names such as "rat root," "sweet flag," etc., has been used by many cultures—including those of India and China—as a medicine, and by the North American Indians for the relief of fatigue and in their puberty initiation rites.

Peter Stafford, in his *Psychedelics Encyclopedia*, recounts some of the lore surrounding nutmeg and mace:

> Nutmeg, which in the U.S. is mainly used as a garnish during Christmas festivities, is the dried kernel of *Myristica fragrans*, a tree native to the Spice Islands, near New Guinea. Now cultivated in many places, the tree grows to about fifty feet high and bears seeds for up to sixty years. Its fruit looks much like a peach, and contains a brownish-purple, shiny

kernel encased within a bright orange-red or red covering. The covering, or aril, is used for production of mace; the seed, dried in the sun for about two months and turned over each day, becomes nutmeg. Both the kernel and its covering contain psychoactive components within their oils.

Most of the natural substances that contain compounds similar to MDA have a history of use for their medicinal properties and their psychoactivity. The *Ayurveda* of ancient India refers to nutmeg and mace as *made shaunda*, generally translated as "narcotic fruit." An 1883 *Materia Medica* from Bombay records that "the Hindus of West India take Myristica as an intoxicant." Nutmeg has been used for centuries as a snuff in rural eastern Indonesia; in India, the same practice appears, but often the ground seed is first mixed with betel and other kinds of snuff. Restrictions on hashish in Egypt have brought about periods when nutmeg was used as a substitute.

Nutmeg appears in the Hindu Pharmacopoeia as a treatment for fever, asthma, and heart disease. Since the seventh

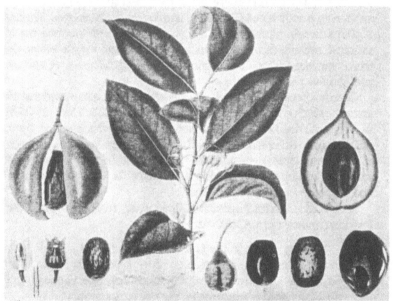

Nutmeg, a psychoactive spice, is the dried seed within the fruit of an East Indian tree, Myristica fragrans.

century A.D., Arab physicians have used it for digestive disorders, kidney disease, and lymphatic ailments. Yemeni men are said to consume nutmeg to increase and maintain their sexual vigor.

Nutmeg and mace weren't known to the Greeks or Romans. They were not introduced to the West until 1512, when the Portuguese reached the Banda, or Nutmeg, Islands. The earliest record of nutmeg's mental effects comes from 1576, in the description of a "pregnant English lady who, having eaten ten or twelve nutmegs, became deliriously inebriated" (she was lucky not to have died).

In the seventeenth century, nutmeg became an important article in the spice trade which the Dutch monopolized for a long while with their naval superiority.

Use of this commonly available substance as an inebrient has continued into this century. "Confirmed reports of its use by students, prisoners, sailors, alcoholics, marijuana-smokers, and others deprived of their preferred drugs," write Shultes and Hofmann in *The Botany and Chemistry of Hallucinogens*" are many and clear. Especially frequent is the taking of nutmeg in prisons, notwithstanding the usual denial of prison officials."

Nutmeg's essential oils include safrole, which is similar to MDA, and myristicin, which is related to MMDA. Conversion of these non-amine oils in the presence of ammonia into the amine forms (e.g. MDA and MMDA) has been demonstrated in the laboratory, giving rise to speculation that a similar process occurs in the body to produce mental effects.

In the chemical laboratory, these essential oils can be aminated (converted to the amine form) to produce their semi-synthetic relative. notably *Myristica fragrans* (nutmeg) can be aminated to make MDA. Indeed, the simplest chemical process for manufacturing MDA is to combine safrole with the basic gas ammonia. There are some other, more complicated laboratory methods for the making of MDA—including the manufacture from Heliotropin, used in the perfume industry to make the scent of hyacinths.

These semi-synthetic compounds are part of a larger family of chemicals known as the alkaloids. Shulgin, in his chapter "Psychotomimetic Drugs: Structure-Activity Relationships" in *Handbook of Psychopharmacology, Volume 11*, states:

These are basic, nitrogen-containing organic chemicals from the plant kingdom, and they represent a bewildering array of structural variations. A consistent theme found through most of the alkaloids is the separation of the nitrogen atom from an aromatic system, by two carbon atoms.

This relationship can be found through most of the known family of alkaloids and has been the mainstay for

Myristica (nutmeg): 1, Penang nutmegs. 2, Round West India nutmegs. 3, Banda nutmegs. 4, Longitudinal, cross and a broken surface of the seed. 5, Upper part of the seed. 6, Base of the seed. 7, Wormy seed.

the thousands of synthetic drugs that have been based on some alkaloid model.

From the alkaloid trunk, there are many branches reaching skyward. Among them are two branches of compounds, the phenylalkylamines and the indolealkylamines, which have within them most of the drugs variously called psychedelic.

The phenylalkylamines are alkaloids with a simple benzene ring in the position of the aromatic system. The indolealkylamines are alkaloids with the more complex indole ring in the position of the aromaic

Sassafras is a botanical source used in synthesizing MDA-like compounds.

system. On the phenylalkylamines branch (also sometimes called the substituted phenylethylamines) are also a number of stimulants and our friends, the empathogens. The indolealkylamines fork into three branches—the tryptamines (of which psylocybin, the active ingredient in magic mushrooms, is a prototype); the lysergic acid derivatives (of which LSD is the prototype); and the beta-carbolines (of which harmaline, the most active ingredient of the South American vine from which the psychedelic drink *yage* is made, is the prototype).

Structure/Activity Relationships

Structure/activity relationships are the ways that (1) the members of

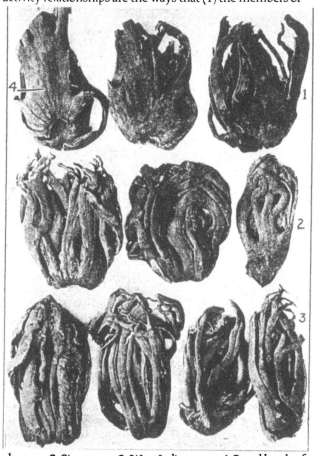

Macis: *1, Banda mace. 2, Siam mace. 3, West Indian mace. 4, Broad bands of Banda mace.*

a family of compounds compare structurally to each other, and (2) correlation of these differences with observed differences in the potency and the effects of the compounds. What is amazing is how slight changes in a position of a carbon atom on a benzene ring, for example, or the addition of an "alpha-methyl tail," can make such dramatic changes in the nature of the "high" or the duration of the experience of various psychoactive substances.

These structure/activity relationships have been systematically mapped by chemists and pharmacologists. For those who would like more technically detailed descriptions (I can imagine some readers objecting that all of this is already too technical), I suggest looking at Roger Brimblecombe and Roger Pinder's *Hallucinogenic Agents*, or Alexander Shulgin's "Speculations on Structure/Activity Relationships" as noted above.

Among the indolealkylamines as a class, structure/activity relationships have been mapped with some success. But the greatest demonstration of the significance of variations has been with the phenylalkylamines. Shulgin divides the phenylalkylamines into two subgroups, the phenethylamines, of which mescaline is the prototypical example, and the phenylisopropylamines, of which TMA is the primary representative.

Mescaline and the Phenethylamines

On the bottom of the phenylalkylamine branch is 3,4,5-trimethoxyphenethylamine, commonly known as mescaline. Mescaline is the prototype of the phenethylamines. Mescaline is a psychedelic drug and the primary active component of the cactus *Lophophora williamsii*, generally known as peyote. This small cactus has been used for perhaps as long as 3,000 years by the Mexican Indians in religious rites and healing ceremonies. Mescaline was first isolated from peyote in 1897 by Arthur Heffter, and first synthesized by Ernst Späth in 1919.

Mescaline is normally taken as a sulphate or hydrochloride (chemical forms that make it active when taken by mouth).

The compound appears as a powder composed of long white needle crystals. The active dose is about 400 mg., and the inebriation lasts for about 12-15 hours. Perhaps the most influential account of a mescaline experience was by novelist Aldous Huxley, in his short book *Doors of Perception*, published in 1954. Huxley reported on his initial mescaline experience and speculated on the nature of such radical mental transformations.

One individual who "took a day from my professional work in

industry to explore the catalytic effects of mescaline" was Alexander Shulgin. Shulgin comments, in his chapter "An Ever-Changing Quest," in Grinspoon and Bakalar's *Psychedelic Reflections*, on this experience:

> The impressions of the experience are best expressed in the flow of events that followed that day. There began what might be called a quest of curiosity. I realized that the mind, and the senses that provide inputs to the mind, were all grossly under-utilized faculties in the study of the world around us; and that it was irrational to ascribe to a small quantity of chemical the intrinsic power to provide this sensory augmentation. I found it hard to accept that such a simple, unsophisticated molecule, containing barely 30 atoms, could carry within its structure such complexities of thought patterns, of sensory license, of visual magic.
>
> It was inescapable that the molecule didn't do anything itself, but rather, allowed the human mind to make these changes. It could only serve as a catalyst, unleashing and promoting channels of mental processes that were native, that lay inculcate in the normal brain. And why should a modest cactus contain such an effective catalyst, expressible only in man?
>
> Psychologists might be able to dissect the nature of the changes, and physicians might be able to define the sites of action, but my background in chemistry and biochemistry limited me to the atoms and bonds of this catalyst, and the compelling inquiry into their function by the simple strategy of changing them and observing the changes in effect that resulted. I felt that by providing in a single process both the structural change and the subjective evaluation of the results of such change, a pattern might emerge that would tie together the definitions of the catalyst and the process being catalyzed.

Alexander Shulgin's methodical investigation—changing various parts of the molecule related to his initial catalyst, mescaline—has yielded many new psychoactive compounds, members of MDMA's extensive family tree. Many of these new compounds are much more potent and have quite different effects than the prototypical mescaline. As we will see, Shulgin has been the discoverer of almost all of them.

Shulgin developed several noteworthy compounds in the same classification of substituted phenethylamines as mescaline. These include escaline, which has a substituted ethyl group and proscaline, which bears a substituted propyl group, both in the "four position" on the benzene ring—demonstrating how changing things at this important place in the molecule can increase the potency of a compound. Both have effects almost identical to those of mescaline, but escaline is about five times as potent and proscaline ten times as potent as mescaline. Their durations of action are also somewhat shorter than mescaline.

Two other substituted phenethylamines with potential for clinical and other applications are the substitition variants of mescaline, 2-CB and 2-CD. These are also known chemically as the 2-carbon homologs of the phenylisopropylamines DOB and DOM. In Chapter V, I discuss 2-CB in more depth, describing its usefulness in combination with MDMA.

There are several more active compounds in this group, some with potencies greatly exceeding mescaline and some with bizarre mental effects.

TMA and the Methoxylated Phenylisopropylamines

On one branch higher up on our psychoactive tree, we find phenylisopropylamines. One bunch of drug-fruit on this branch are the methoxylated phenylisopropylamines. The prototype of this cluster is the first psychedelic drug to evolve from a planned and systematic use of the principles discovered in the study of the relationship between chemical structure and biological activity—TMA (3,4,5-trimethoxy-phenylisopropylamine). First synthesized in 1947 by Hey, his enthusiastic report on the euphoric properties of the substance provoked Perez and a group of Canadian coworkers to investigate further. They discovered that the experience on low dosages was pleasant and there were no complaints aside from some initial nausea. Later experiments with higher doses showed TMA to be a "hallucinogenic drug with some undesirable features." What was important, however, was the two-fold increase in potency due to the connection of an alpha-methyl group to the nitrogen in the mescaline molecule.

The addition of the alpha-methyl group to the nitrogen atom in phenethylamine gives rise to the compound amphetamine, a powerful stimulant. Thus, many of the compounds that have this transformation have, in the past, been called psychotomimetic amphetamines or psychedelic amphetamines.

But the name "amphetamine" properly belongs only to one

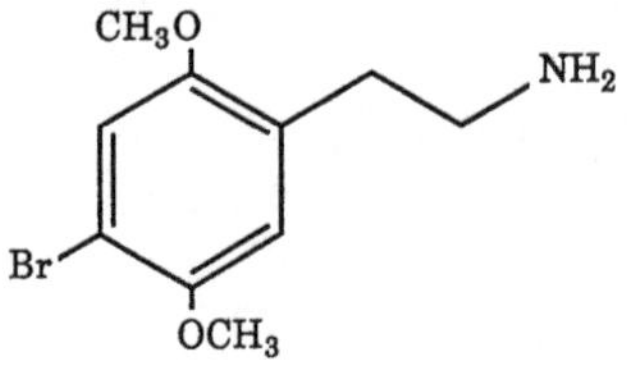

2-CB

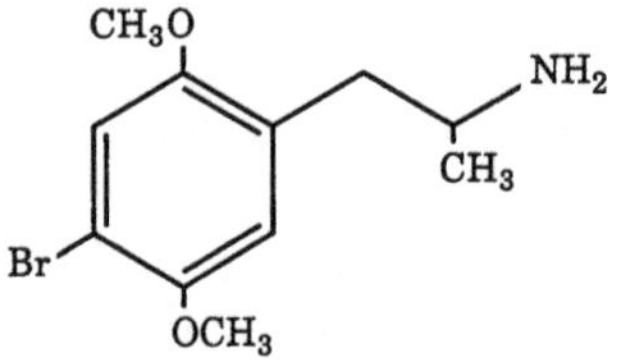

DOB

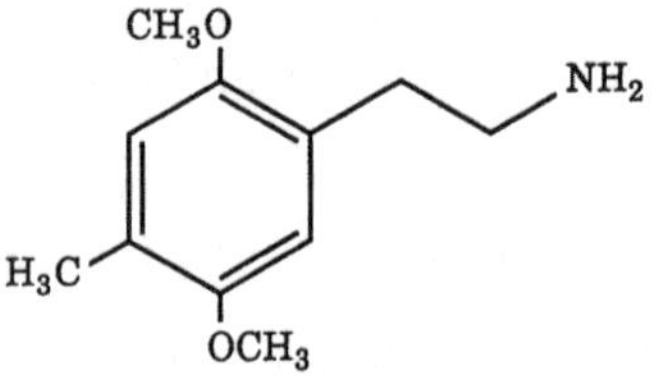

2-CD

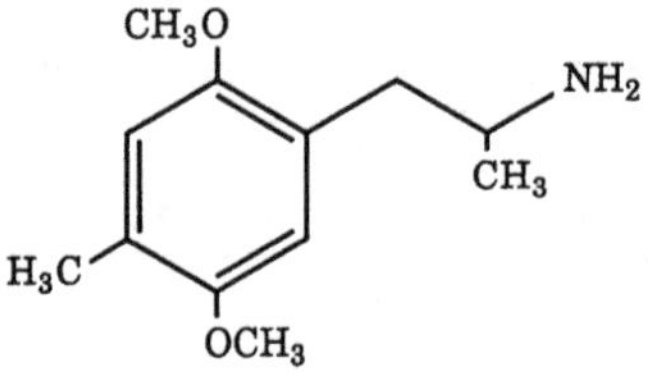

DOM

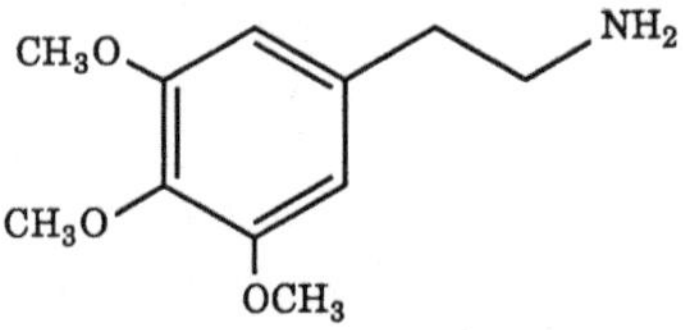

MESCALINE

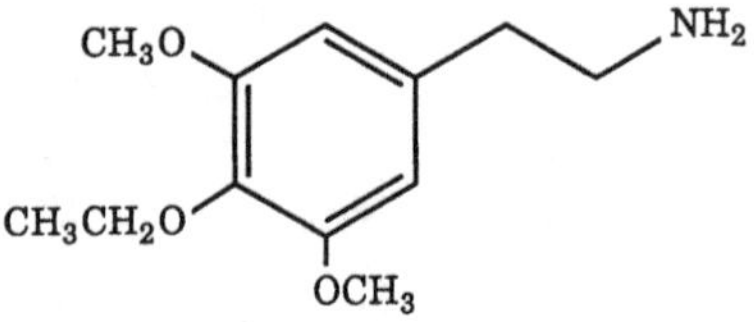

ESCALINE

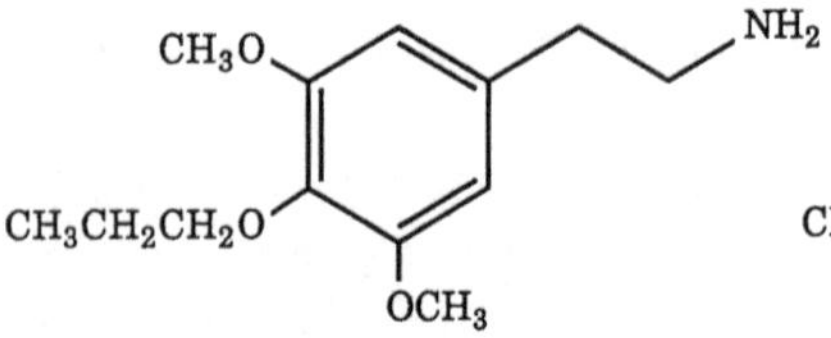

PROSCALINE

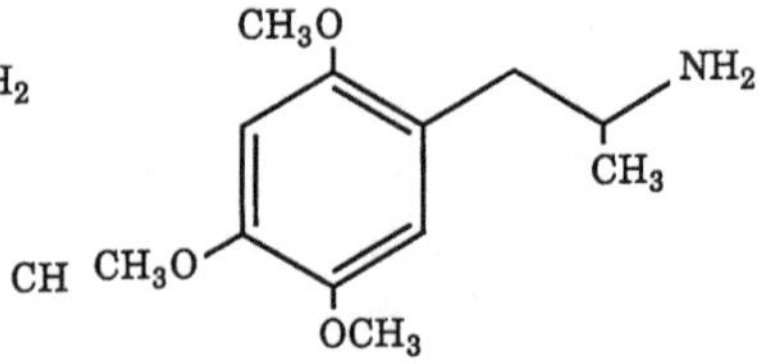

TMA-2

Chemical Structure of Mescaline and the Phenethylamines.

substance, 2-amino-1-phenylpropane—the well-known stimulant. There are many psychoactive substances in this group, and many of them have effects very different from those of the stimulant amphetamine. Instead, let's call this class of substances the phenyl-isopropylamines.

The number of psychoactive substances in this group is large. There are, for example, six types of TMA. I will mention only the most noteworthy.

In 1962, Shulgin aminized the essential oil asarone, contained in calamus—with TMA-2 (2,4,5-trimethoxyphenylisopropylamine) being the result. It had been synthesized earlier, but Shulgin was the first to discover its psychoactive effects. What he found was that the re-arrangement of the molecule from the configuration of mescaline to a different substitution pattern (2,4,5 instead of 3,4,5) had increased the potency ten times over that of the first TMA! Reports of extensive nausea during the experience should deter use of this strong hallucinogen.

DOM and the Alkylphenylisopropylamines

A second dangling collection of psychoactives on the phenyliso-propylamine branch is the alkylphenylisopropylamines, represented by their prototype DOM (2,5-dimethoxy-4-methyl-amphetamine). DOM was first synthesized in 1963. In 1967, a new drug was introduced to the counterculture under the name STP. Although this fact wasn't clear for some time, STP and DOM turned out to be the same drug. 5,000 tablets of STP, 10 mg. each, were distributed at the first hippie "love-in" in San Francisco's Golden Gate Park.

The experience was intensely hallucinogenic, and there were a number of panic reactions. Some claimed that the experience lasted for three days, although later studies indicated that it can last only up to around 24 hours. STP rapidly lost popularity after this rocky debut.

Actually, DOM, taken in the dosages that Shulgin and his colleagues first used in exploring the compound (around 3 mg.), has euphoria and enhancement of self-awareness as its main effects, while being free of strong physiological changes or perceptual distortions. But the first doses of street STP contained 20 mg. of DOM, later halved to 10 mg. At this dosage level, DOM becomes a powerful hallucinogenic drug lasting up to 24 hours. A chemical relative of DOM, DOET (2,5-dimethoxy-4-ethylphenylisopropylamine) is very similar in its effects to DOM, but is experienced as milder until it reaches dosages that would be hallucinogenic for DOM. At dosages around 4 mg. the effects are similar

Chemical Structure of MMDA Series.

MDMA

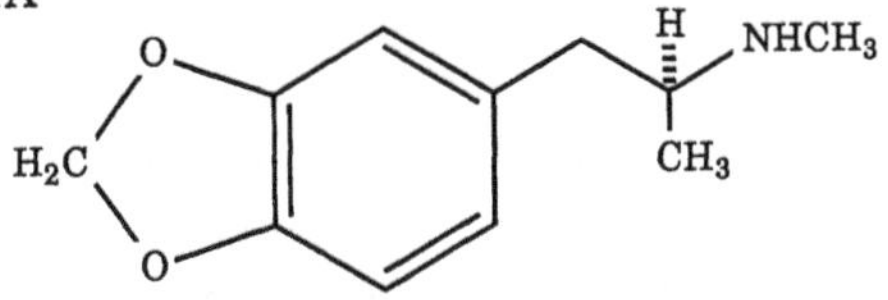

MDE

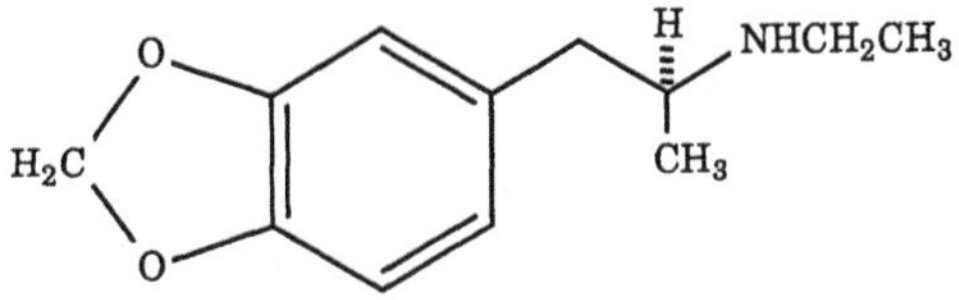

MDA

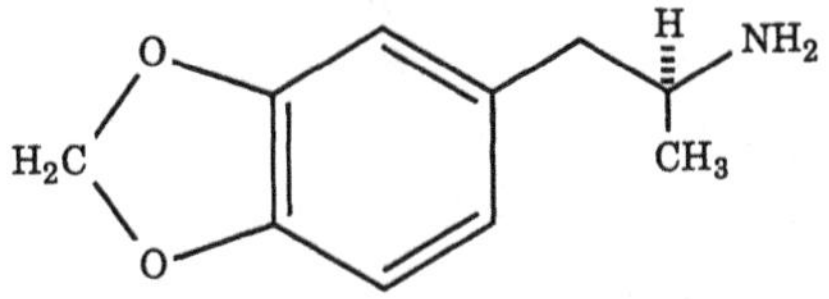

MBDB

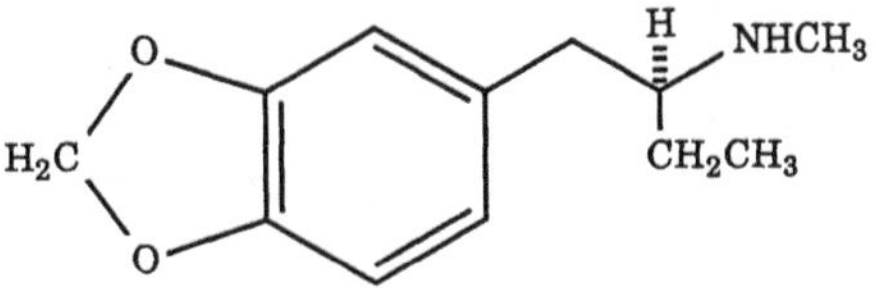

MMDA

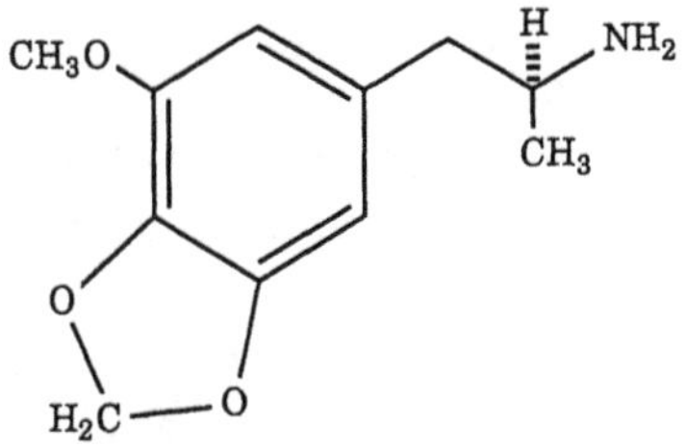

Chemical Structure of MDMA and it Variations.

to those listed above with low dosages of DOM.

MDA and the Methylenedioxyphenylisopropylamines

Do you find the above word a tongue-twister? Now you know why I put this discussion at the back of this book.

MDA (3,4-methylenedioxyphenylisopropylamine) was first synthesized by German chemists G. Mannish and W. Jacobson in 1910. Yet it wasn't until 1939 that the first animal studies were conducted, when the team of Gunn, Gurd, and Sachs became interested in the substance while conducting adrenaline studies. Two years later, another team—Loman, Myerson, and Myerson—thought this compound might alleviate Parkinsonism, but abandoned the concept when the single patient tested experienced muscular rigidity. Also about this time, MDA was rejected as a possible weight-reduction agent and as an antidepressant by the Smith, Klein, and French Co., because pronounced though not "hallucinogenic" effects interfered after a few days with the patients' ordinary routines.

Then, in the mid-'Fifties, Gordon Alles, the UCLA researcher who had discovered amphetamine in 1927, became interested in MDA and a related compound because of their similarity to ephedrine, the standard drug for testing central nervous system stimulation during the 1930s and 1940s. Peter Stafford, in his *Psychedelics Encyclopedia* describes the details of Alles' examination of MDA:

> He decided that he would conduct what he called a "double-conscious" test of these substances—meaning he would synthesize, measure, and take them himself in order to compare their effects with what he knew about how ephedrine affected him. "I was quite well-calibrated," he remarked later, "with 50 mg. doses of ephedrine and with similar doses of amphetamine."
>
> After tests with dogs, which indicated that these two compounds were one third to one half as active in their peripheral effects as mescaline and amphetamine, Alles swallowed 36 mg. of MDA. During the following two hours, he noticed neither physical nor mental sensations. He then took an additional 90 mg.
>
> Within a few minutes, he "realized that a notable subjective response was going to result." The muscles of his neck became markedly tensed, and he was closing his jaws tightly and grinding his back teeth. He perspired quite a bit

and noted a slowed respiration rate. His pupils were "markedly dilated . . . I had never seen such dilation of the pupils in animals or man to such an extent."

About 45 minutes after the second dose, smoke rings filled the air, moving in slow motion about him. In a closed room on the sixth floor of a university building, there "was no possible source of smoke rings." Yet,

> an abundance of curling smoke rings was readily observed in the environment whenever a relaxed approach in observation was used. Visually, these had complete reality; and it seemed quite unnecessary to test their properties because it was surely known and fully appreciated that the source of the visual phenomena could not be external to the body. When I concentrated my attention on the details of the curling gray forms by trying to note how they would be affected by passing a finger through their apparent field, they melted away. Then when I relaxed again, the smoke rings were there.

Talking about these smoke rings later, Alles commented, "I was as certain they were really there as I am now sure that my head is on top of my body." These visual effects only introduced what lay ahead.

Looking at his "almost entirely black eyes," he had been fearful momentarily but thereafter had "a general feeling of well being," accompanied by a switch in his perception of the location of his consciousness.

> When I was very relaxed, my thinking became introspectively speculative. Awareness of the body and of its functionings became subject to a detached spatial consideration, and the reality of the place of detached observation for a time seemed clearly transposed out of the body and to a place above and to the right rearward. I was compelled to turn my head several times and look into the upper corner of the room in wonder at what part of me could be up there and observing the subjective situation and behavior as if from that point. I observed this phenomenon from where I was seated.

Alles recounted this experience before a Josiah Macy Jr.
Foundation conference in 1957. In 1959, his account was
published as part of the proceedings of the conference as
Neuropharmacology: Transactions of the 4th Conference (edited
by Harold Abramson).

By the mid-'Sixties, MDA began to show up in the subculture—
nicknamed "the Love Drug" or "the Mellow Drug of America." Because
of its high profile at the time of the Comprehensive Drug Abuse
legislation of 1970, it was placed in Schedule I.

As I noted above, safrole, the essential oil in a number of plants, most
notably *Myristica fragrans* (nutmeg) can be aminized to make MDA.
Indeed, the simplest chemical process for manufacturing MDA is to
combine safrole with the basic gas ammonia. There are a some other,
more complicated laboratory methods for the making of MDA—
including its manufacture from Helitropin, used in the perfume industry
to make the scent of hycacinths.

MDA is actually two distinct drugs. Each is a mirror image of the
other, and thus classified by the direction in which they bend light. The
dextro,or right-handed, version and the *levo*, or left-handed, form of
MDA each exhibit unique drug effects but are often blended together in

Gordon Alles, discoverer of the psychoactive effects of MDA.

a 50% mix called "racemic" MDA.

Clinical studies performed by Shulgin have shown that the *levo* isomer of MDA possesses properties that occur with the use of the racemic mixture. On the other hand, the *dextro* isomer of MDA does not possess such properties, but rather has been characterized by Shulgin as "more benign and peaceful," when compared with racemic MDA.

The pharmacologically equivalent dosages for the first three forms are 70 mg. for the *levo*, 125 for the racemic, and 225 for the *dextro*. It is clear that the *levo* isomer is responsible for most of the activity of the racemic mixture.

It has been noted that discoveries in science often occur at about the same time to two or more researchers working independently of one another. Another case of such synchronous discovery is the production of MMDA (3-methoxy-4,5-methyldioxyphenylisopropylamine) by both Gordon Alles and Alexander Shulgin, at about the same time. Both produced MMDA through the aminization of another of the essential oils of nutmeg, myristicin.

MMDA is effective as a hydrochloride salt at 120-150 mg. In addition to the original MMDA, there are five other MMDAs numbered in a manner similar to the six TMAs and varying molecularly in somewhat the same fashion (although there is no MMDA corresponding to MMDA 6, but, instead, a MMDA-3a and MMDA 3b). Each of these MMDAs has its own distinct set of effects, and these vary in potency, with MMDA-2, MMDA-3a and MMDA-5 with the highest potencies, about three times as powerful as MMDA.

Now we reach the top of the tree, stretching high to grasp two globes of fruit at the end of a small top branch. Does it not seem odd that these two "N-methyl derivatives of the phenylisopropylamines" have been called Adam (MDMA) and Eve (MDE)—two fruits from the tree of wisdom in our psychotropic garden?

It is structurally analogous to MDA in the same way that meth-amphetamine is analogous to amphetamine. This "N-methylation" of MDA shortens the course of the experience, increases the required minimum dosage, and changes its effects in the ways already described.

MDMA (N-methyl-3,4-methylenedioxyphenylisopropylamine), the focus of this book, is one of these two derivitives of MDA.

Like MDA, MDMA has both a right-handed and a left-handed version. However, it is the *dextro* or right-handed isomer that is active, while the *levo* or left handed version is substantially without activity. David Nichols, who discussed this topic at length during 1986 MDMA hearings, has speculated that it is "N-methylation" (the addition of an N-methyl group to MDA) that makes the action of MDMA so different. Nichols goes on to suggest that the N-methylation renders the *levo* 'isomer inactive while leaving the *dextro* isomer unaltered in its effects. This would account for the lack of a hallucinogenic component to MDMA's effects.

MDE (N-ethyl-3,4-methylenedioxyphenylisopropylamine) has come into some prominence since the banning of MDMA—under the nickname "Eve." Still an unscheduled substance as of this writing, MDE is somewhat similar to MDMA, but is slightly faster-acting and shorter-lived than MDMA. According to Shulgin, its action is just about completed at the end of the second hour of its action. It is also said to be 25% less potent than MDMA. Eve has been described by some users as lacking MDMA's ability of unlocking the emotions. Instead, it is said to be more of a stimulant than a feeling-enhancer.

One largely unexplored fresh bud on a branch at the very top of our tree is the newly reported compound MBDB, or N-methyl-1-(1,3-benzodioxol-5-yl)-2-butanamine. David Nichols has described MBDB in a paper in the proceedings of the 1986 MDMA Conference held in Oakland published in the *Journal of Psychoactive Drugs* with the long but informative title, "Differences Between the Mechanism of Action of MDMA, MBDB, and the Classic Hallucinogens: Identification of a New Therapeutic Class: Entactogen."

3,4-METHYLENEDIOXYMETHAMPHETAMINE HCL

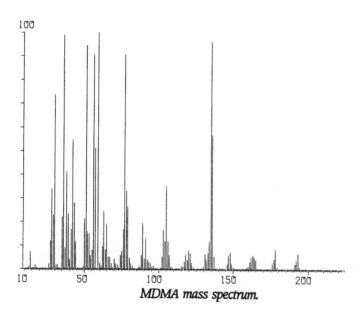

MDMA mass spectrum.

Although less potent than MDMA, MBDB has qualitative effects in humans very similar to MDMA. Furthermore, it has the *dextro*-isomer that was more active, similar to MDA and in contrast to the hallucinogenic amphetamines. In rats trained to discriminate LSD from saline, MBDB did *not* have LSD-like actions.

MBDB represents a structure that combines two separate structural features that abolish or attenuate hallucinogenic activity: N-methylation and alpha-etheylation. All the logic of structure-activity relationships derived from substituted amphetamines argues that the synergistic attenuation provided by these two structural features should render MBDB totally inert as a hallucinogen. Yet, MBDB *is* biologically active. It generally has the same effect on emotion and empathy as MDMA. Clearly, one is not dealing with the pharmacology of hallucinogens anymore, but with some different category of psychoactive drug.

Inasmuch as MBDB represented the first molecular structure that could definitely be placed outside the structure-activity definitions of the hallucinogenic amphetamine class, it was designated as the prototype of a new pharmacological class. That is not to say that MDMA—or even MDA—does not exert this same action to some degree, but only that MBDB is the clearest example, based on a structure-activity relationship argument that cannot be classified as a hallucinogen.

Nichols goes on to name this class of psychoactives the "entactogens." MBDB has been reported by early users to be milder in its action than MDMA because it lacks the stimulant-like euphoria at the beginning of the experience. Instead, the experience is a more subtle yet purer version of the empathogenic-entactogenic qualities attributed to MDMA.

MDMA and the Brain

The question of what MDMA does in the brain remains largely unanswered at the present time. Much more is known about the psychopharmacology of psychedelics, such as LSD, and stimulants, such as amphetamine.

Only one paper has thus far been published on the subject of MDMA's brain activity, by David Nichols and others in the *Journal of Medicinal Chemistry*. In this study, the release of serotonin, a brain neurotransmitter, was studied in "whole rat brain synaptosomes." The results suggested that MDMA's activity might be due to the release of the serotonin transmitter.

In order to understand what this means, I should tell you something about the brain and the way psychoactive drugs work in them.

Brains are made up of neurons, cells which transmit electrical signals through them and to one or more other neurons with which they are interconnected. These chains and networks of neurons make up the circuitry by which the brain does such complex tasks as receiving sensory information, thinking and reasoning, and sending commands to muscles.

The way that neurons transmit this information is complicated, but what is important here is that their transmission involves an electrical charge traveling down the length of the neuron and triggering the release, at the end of the neuron, of a bunch of chemicals into a gap (called a synapse) between the transmitting end (dendrite) and the receiving end of the next neuron (called an axion).

The chemicals, called neurotransmitters, then travel across the gap and fit into little molecular keyholes (imagine that the neurotransmitters are keys) called receptor sites. When these keyholes are fitted with keys and "turned on" they trigger a charge to be passed down the stimulated neuron to other dendrites. These stimulated neurons might then, in turn, trigger other neurons, this process continuing to form long neural cirucits, networks of activated brain cells.

Many of these neurotransmitters resemble psychoactive drugs. The two principal neurotransmitters for one of the neuron systems (the cholinergic system), dopamine and norepinephrine, are similar to the prototypical mescaline of the substituted phenethylamines. Serotonin, the principle transmitter of the indolic system, looks an awful lot like the powerful psychedelic drug DMT and its close relative psilocybin.

Psychoactive drugs can affect systems of neurons in several different ways. They can imitate the neurotransmitters themselves and plug into receptor sites just as the neurotransmitter native to the brain might. This could stimulate a firing of the affected neuron, or it might just tie up the receptor, keeping it from being activated by the brain's native neurotransmitters.

Psychoactive drugs can also keep neurotransmitters from being recycled once they are used. This is called blocking "reuptake." Or they might stimulate the brain's natural neurotransmitters to be released.

It is this last possibility that Nichols and his colleagues are suggesting occurs with regard to MDMA. They also have contrasted this action with that from MDA, which they speculated may stimulate neurotransmitters directly affecting receptor sites.

The neurotransmitter systems affected may also differ between MDA, MDMA, and MBDB. Both MDA and MDMA have significant effects on dopamine pathways in the brain, while MBDB does not. However, MDMA's effect is an order of magnitude less than that from amphetamine. Thus, MDMA and MDMB cannot be considered stimulants as amphetamine is.

MDMA and the Human Body

One of the most often expressed fears about the use of MDMA centers on its effects upon the body. Indeed, what does MDMA do to our fragile human shells?

Since MDMA has not undergone the usual trials required by the FDA for approval of a new drug, there is little hard information to report. The controversy surrounding the possibility of brain damage has already been discussed at some length. I have also noted some of the short-term psychological side-effects that may occur during an MDMA session in Chapter V. In that chapter as well are listed medical conditions with which MDMA should not be used. The most important of these is heart arythmia, to which five human deaths have been attributed.

The only physiological study of MDMA was reported by Joseph Downing. This report is summarized by Rick J. Strassman, M.D., in *MDMA:*

> He (Downing) describes the effects of MDMA (0.8-1.9 mg./pound), given orally, to 21 experienced MDMA users as well as their responses on a screening questionnaire. All subjects were free of significant medical and/or psychiatric disturbances. Ages ranged from 20 to 58 years (with an average of 31), with educational experience being, on the average, four years of college. There were 13 men and 8 women. During the drug administration part of the study, various physical parameters were monitored. Cardiovascular responses, including an increase in systolic and diastolic blood pressure, and an increase in heart rate, usually occurred with minimal levels attained within 30-60 minutes.
>
> No subjective symptoms were noted in this regard. Blood pressure was less than pre-drug values within six hours, and often was less than pre-drug values 24 hours after drug

exposure. No hypotensive reactions or complaints were noted. No effects of MDMA on blood chemistry were noted.

From the report itself, here are some excerpts of the study's conclusions:

This experimental situation produced no observed or reported psychological or physiological damage, either during the twenty-four hour study period or the three-month follow-up period. Thus, while our subjects are in no way typical of the general population, our findings support the general impression among knowlegeable professionals that MDMA is reasonably safe, produces positive mood changes in users, does not cause negative problems, is used sparingly and episodically, and is without evidence of abuse.

Certainly, any drug that causes ataxia and elevates blood pressure and pulse is potentially unsafe. We can say little about "safety" when we study effects and side-effects for twenty-four hours, then obtain blood cytology after three months. "Safety" must exclude long-term toxicity. DES and Thalidomide were safe in acute toxicity studies, but had

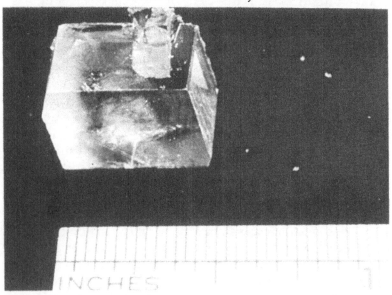

An unusually large MDA crystal grown in ethanol.

serious long-range toxicity. We do not know enough about MDMA's long-range effects other than random anecdotal evidence supplied by unselected and unsupervised users.

From the information presented here, we can only say that MDMA, at the doses tested, has remarkably consistent and predictable psychobiological effects which are transient and free of clinically apparent major toxicity. The experimental subjects believed that MDMA is both safe and beneficial, but there is insufficient evidence to judge accurately either harm or benefit . . .

ECSTASY

The MDMA Story

Expanded Second Edition

For great books by

Timothy Leary

John C Lilly

Robert Anton Wilson

Visit RONIN Books-for-Independent-Minds online

www.roninpub.com

APPENDIX II

Report on MDMA Neurotoxicity and Current Research

Rick Doblin

This second edition of *Ecstasy: The MDMA Story* is being released in 1993, slightly in advance of the imminent, historic initiation of the Food and Drug Administration's approval for human studies with MDMA. The third edition, which I fully expect to be published in due time, will thus be able to report on scientific findings from human studies that are currently being planned by psychiatrists, psychotherapists and researchers around the world.

What I will report on now are results from some recent research about MDMA neurotoxicity, as well as the historic recommendations concerning human psychedelic research from the Food and Drug Administration's Drug Abuse Advisory Committee and National Institute on Drug Abuse's first Technical Review meeting on hallucinogens in fourteen years. These recommendations encouraged the Food and Drug Administration to approve human studies with MDMA after seven years of prohibition. I will also report on how the FDA-approved Phase 1 MDMA safety studies in humans will be designed and conducted, and what the initial design of the subsequent Phase 2 MDMA psychotherapy studies will probably look like. Finally, I'll discuss MDMA research in Switzerland (the only place where human studies are currently underway), MDE research in Germany, prospects for MDMA research in Russia, and MAPS's role in MDMA research.

MDMA Neurotoxicity Update

Ever since the Drug Enforcement Administration made MDMA illegal in 1985, thereby giving the Food and Drug Administration

the task of regulating all human MDMA research, the potential
risk of MDMA neurotoxicity had been cited by the FDA (until
recently) as their rationale for forbidding all scientific studies in
which MDMA would have been administered to volunteer human
subjects. The political nature of the use of the neurotoxicity rationale
for prohibiting all human studies of MDMA research can be deduced
when one realizes that there has never been even one single confirmed case in the literature of anyone suffering functional neurological consequences as a result of MDMA neurotoxicity, nor is
there ever likely to be one.

   To attempt to resolve the neurotoxicity controversy, MDMA
research in the United States from the period of 1985 to the present
(May 1993) has been focused almost exclusively on the question of
MDMA neurotoxicity and almost all the research has taken place
in animals. The most notable exceptions have been two human
studies funded by the National Institute on Drug Abuse: a sociological study of MDMA users that attempted to evaluate MDMA's
abuse potential, and a retrospective physiological and
neuropsychological study of MDMA users that focused on the
issue of neurotoxicity.

   In the first edition of *Ecstasy: The MDMA Story*, published in 1989,
I reported on the latest research findings about MDMA neurotoxicity and pointed to three critical questions about MDMA neurotoxicity that remained to be resolved. Does MDMA cause neurotoxicity
at normal recreational and therapeutic doses? Does MDMA neurotoxicity have any functional or behavioral consequences? Is MDMA
neurotoxicity temporary or permanent? At the time of the first
edition, the answers were unclear but a review of the literature
suggested that MDMA caused little if any neurotoxicity at normal
recreational and therapeutic doses, that even massive MDMA neurotoxicity resulted in little or no functional or behavioral consequences, and that, in rats, MDMA neurotoxicity was temporary.

MDMA Neurotoxicity "No-Effect Level"

   At the time of the first edition, research conducted by Dr. George
Ricaurte and partially funded by Multidisciplinary Association for
Psychedelic Studies, Inc. (MAPS) had established that a single oral
dose of 5.0 mg/kg of MDMA given to squirrel monkeys produced,
in the thalamus and hypothalamus regions of the brain, minor long-

term (greater than two weeks) reductions in serotonin levels, an effect considered to be a marker of neurotoxicity. This finding was of some concern because the standard human therapeutic (and recreational) dose of about 1.5–2.0 mg/kg was rather close to 5.0 mg/kg and the relative sensitivities of the primate brain to the human brain were not known (and still are not). Ricaurte had also demonstrated that a single oral dose of 2.5 mg/kg had no effect on serotonin levels, however only two animals were tested and the neurotoxic effect, if there really was one, might have been too small to detect.

In an effort to better evaluate whether 2.5 mg/kg of MDMA was at or below the threshold level for neurotoxicity, a larger and longer study has been recently conducted by Dr. Ricaurte, also partially funded by MAPS. Six primates, three experimentals and three controls, were orally administered a dose of 2.5 mg/kg of MDMA or placebo once every two weeks for four months (for a total of eight administrations of MDMA or placebo). Eight brain regions were examined for 5-HT and 5-HIAA content. There were no significant differences between experimental and control animals in any of the brain regions studied. Since Ricaurte had previously shown that a single oral dose of 5.0 mg/kg causes neurotoxicity only in the thalamus and hypothalamus, this study demonstrates that the primate no-effect level lies somewhere between 2.5 and 5.0 mg/kg, above the human therapeutic dose level.

Further new data about MDMA neurotoxicity comes from a study conducted by Dr. Rick Strassman. He recently completed an FDA-approved human study in which the physiological and psychological responses of eleven subjects to various intravenous doses of DMT were studied. Physiological measures included ß-endorphin, ACTH, prolactin, corticol, growth hormone, baseline and maximum rise temperature and pupil diameter responses. Psychological measures included the Profile of Mood States (POMS) and Hallucinogenic Rating Scale (HRS) developed specifically for this experiment.

Subjects were divided into two groups, "MDMA Positive" and "MDMA Negative." The "MDMA Positive" group included six subjects who had taken MDMA 5 or more times. Not including that one of those had taken MDMA 75–100 times, the average exposure for the MDMA Positive group was about 10x. The MDMA Negative group included the remaining five subjects who had taken MDMA never or only once, with an average exposure of less than 1x.

Analysis of the physiological measurements revealed no significant differences between the groups in ß-endorphin, ACTH, prolactin, corticol, growth hormone, baseline and maximum rise temperature responses, across all four doses of DMT and placebo. The
standard analytic tool was ANOVA with repeated measures. The
only significant difference between the MDMA Positive and
MDMA Negative groups was that the maximum change in pupil
diameter relative to baseline was less in the positives than the nega-
tives, across all doses of drug/placebo. Dr. Strassman noted: "If
one believes that 5-HT2 receptors in the eye mediate the effect of
DMT on pupil size, then this is opposite of what one would expect;
i.e., if 'denervation hypersensitivity' occurred, one would expect
more robust pupil dilation. The pupil data was the least complete
(people were reluctant to open their eyes during the period of
DMT intoxication), thus ANOVA without repeated measurements
was used as a less than ideal tool."

Analysis of the psychological data showed no significant differences in the Profile of Mood States given both before and after the
injections of DMT. Regarding the Hallucinogenic Rating Scale, no
differences were noted in responses for any of the six factors between the "MDMA Positive" and "MDMA Negative" groups across
all doses of DMT/placebo; neither were there any interaction effects.

Another recent study, conducted in rats by Dr. James O'Callaghan
of the Environmental Protection Agency, further reduces concern
about MDMA neurotoxicity as a result of therapeutic doses of
MDMA. Dr. O'Callaghan's research demonstrated that serotonin
levels, which had been used as a marker for MDMA neurotoxicity,
could fluctuate without any corresponding neurotoxicity and could
return to baseline after a period of months. This finding suggests
that previous data associating serotonin changes to neurotoxicity
needs to be reevaluated. Dr. O'Callaghan noted: "An MDMA dosage regime sufficient to produce a large and long-lasting decrease in
5-HT was not sufficient to induce an astrocyte reaction characteristic
of neural injury." To produce neurotoxicity, extremely large
amounts of MDMA were required.

These three recent studies, one each in rats, primates and humans, suggest that there is little or no neurotoxic risk to experimental subjects from normal doses of MDMA. However, because
there is certainly individual variability in sensitivity to MDMA

neurotoxicity and because some recreational users take more than the normal dose levels, it is important to address the second critical question I posed in this book's first edition. Does MDMA neurotoxicity have any functional or behavioral consequences?

Functional or Behavioral Consequences of MDMA Neurotoxicity

Recent studies of the functional and behavioral consequences of MDMA neurotoxicity have been reassuring. Even when massive amounts of MDMA are given to rats and primates, and reductions in serotonin levels reach 80–90%, little or no behavioral consequences have been found.

One fascinating study by V. E. St. Omer looked at whether the administration of MDMA to pregnant rats would have functional or behavioral effects on the newborn rats. Dr. Dennis McKenna summarized this experiment as follows: "Groups of pregnant rats were administered varying doses of MDMA on alternate gestational days 16–18. Gestational duration, litter size, neonatal birth weights and physical appearance at birth were unaffected by MDMA treatment. Pregnancy weight gain was significantly reduced by MDMA. Progeny growth, maturational parameters, surface righting reflex, swimming performance, forelimb grip strength, milk induced behavior, passive avoidance behavior, figure-8 maze activity, and the density of 5-HT uptake sites, 5-HT, and 5-HIAA levels were unaffected by MDMA treatment. Olfactory discrimination was enhanced in both male and female progeny, and negative geotaxis was delayed in female pups. In the dams, MDMA caused significant reductions in 5-HT and 5-HIAA levels in discrete brain areas. It was concluded that prenatal exposure to MDMA causes only subtle behavioral changes in developing rats, while the dams are at risk for the characteristic spectra of serotonergic changes."

At the July, 1992 meeting of the FDA Drug Abuse Advisory Committee meeting, Dr. Lewis Seiden, one of the leading experts on the functional and behavioral consequences of MDMA neurotoxicity, addressed the question of the lack of research findings. He cautioned the Committee to avoid concluding that the lack of demonstrated consequences from MDMA neurotoxicity meant that there were no such consequences. He suggested that additional studies were needed that would investigate even more subtle cognitive and behavioral tasks. While Dr. Seiden's caution is appropriate, his comment highlights the fact that there is little reason to fear that normal therapeutic (or recreational) doses of MDMA will result in harmful functional or behavioral consequences.

Regeneration of the Serotonin System

The jury is still out on whether all brain regions that have suffered from MDMA neurotoxicity can regenerate. There is clear evidence that there is regeneration in rats but there is not yet enough information about primates. The uncertainty about the regeneration of serotonin systems will hopefully be resolved before publication of *Ecstasy: The MDMA Story*'s third edition.

The Historic FDA and NIDA Meetings on Psychedelics

For the first time in fourteen years, on July 13 and 14, 1992 in Bethesda, Maryland, the National Institute on Drug Abuse (NIDA) convened a Technical Review meeting on "hallucinogens." In an impressive display of interagency synchronization, NIDA's Technical Review immediately preceded the July 15 meeting of the FDA's Drug Abuse Advisory Committee. The FDA Committee reviewed general policies regarding "hallucinogenic" research and specific issues concerning the MDMA research protocol of Dr. Charles Grob that MAPS helped to develop.

The consensus of the experts at these two meetings was that there were significant scientific benefits to be gained by administering psychedelics to human subjects in order to research the brain's basic physiological mechanisms and their psychological correlates. Most importantly, the experts thought that these scientific benefits outweighed the estimated risks to subjects and society from conducting the research. The FDA's Drug Abuse Advisory Committee recommended that psychedelic research protocols be required to meet the rigorous scientific standards that the FDA applies to studies involving any other drugs.

A brief review of these meetings is important to help explain why the FDA finally approved human studies with MDMA.

The NIDA Meeting

Fourteen years had elapsed since NIDA had last scheduled a Technical Review on "hallucinogens." This lengthy hiatus was

largely due to the paucity of scientific advances, since human studies had been essentially prohibited by the government. There were,
however, several important reasons for NIDA to have convened a
Technical Review at this time. Unlike human studies, animal studies had been permitted all along and had yielded some tantalizing
clues about the basic functioning of the brain, in particular of the
serotonin neurotransmitter system. Furthermore, out of a frustration
with the success rates of traditional drug-treatment methods,
NIDA's Medications Development Division was beginning to investigate the possible use of psychedelics, specifically the African
root ibogaine, in the treatment of drug addiction. NIDA was also
concerned about the use of psychedelics outside legal contexts that
had not disappeared under ever tougher drug laws but is reported
instead to be on the increase, according to NIDA's Household
Survey data and DEA reports.

On July 13 and 14, 1992, NIDA gathered together almost twenty
scientists for a two-day meeting. Among these were three researchers
familiar to many MAPS members: Rick Strassman, a psychiatrist at
the University of New Mexico who has conducted basic research
with DMT; Sasha Shulgin, an independent researcher who co-
authored with his wife Ann the book *PIHKAL*; and David Nichols,
a medicinal chemist at Purdue University who manufactured the
MDMA that was used in the pre-clinical animal studies used by
MAPS to open its FDA Drug Master File on MDMA at the FDA.

Rick Strassman focused on findings from his work with DMT in
eleven human volunteers. He reported that it took him about two
years of effort to receive final FDA approval to evaluate DMT's
physiological effects and develop a questionnaire to measure the
psychological effects of DMT and other hallucinogenic drugs. His
groundbreaking research clearly demonstrated that human studies
with psychedelics could be conducted safely and that valuable scientific data could be generated.

Sasha Shulgin's presentation reviewed the work he and his wife
Ann have written about in *PIHKAL* in which he synthesized hundreds of novel psychoactive compounds and tested them for activity in himself and a team of twelve research associates. He emphasized the incredible subtlety and unpredictability of the relationship between the structure of a compound and its psychoactivity.
He cited instances where data from animal studies was contra-

dicted by data from human reports and made an impassioned plea for more human studies. He mentioned the use of psychedelics to produce experiences of a religious, mystical nature and asked the assembled researchers and government officials to tell him how they would ever get rats to provide sufficient data on those matters. The response was, of course, only laughter. One subsequent speaker, however, prefaced his talk on the effects of psychedelics in animals by acknowledging the courage of Sasha Shulgin and Rick Strassman in gathering human data, which he felt provided essential clues in interpreting the animal data.

At the conclusion of the meeting, Dr. Geraline Lin, the chairperson of the meeting, asked the group for a summary of their sense of the current state of research and of future directions to explore. The scientists felt confident that animal models were useful in helping to predict the psychoactive characteristics of novel compounds and in understanding the structural and functional aspects of the brain's serotonin neurotransmitter system. However, most scientists felt that animal studies had limited relevance unless correlated with human data and they were generally supportive of further studies in humans.

The FDA's Drug Abuse Advisory Committee Meeting

Since the Federal Advisory Committee Act of 1972, the FDA has used expert advisory committees to provide guidance and advice on important matters coming before it. Such matters include the final review of data concerning the approval of a drug for marketing (called a New Drug Application) and more rarely on the approval of a research protocol (called an Investigational New Drug application). The FDA has created about 17 different advisory committees, each composed of eleven members who serve for several years and meet about once or twice a year. The meetings are always tape-recorded, often filmed, and transcripts are made of all comments. Though the FDA retains final authority to make decisions, the recommendations of the committee are almost always taken. The most widely publicized recent use of an FDA Advisory Committee concerned the review of the safety of breast implants.

After almost two years of preparation, Dr. Charles Grob had submitted to the FDA's Pilot Drug Evaluation Staff a protocol designed to investigate the use of MDMA in the treatment of pain and distress in end-stage cancer patients. The Pilot Drug Evaluation Staff suggested several significant changes in the protocol design and chose to present the Investigational New Drug, along with their critique and Dr. Grob's response, to its Drug Abuse Advisory Committee.

The Pilot Drug Evaluation Staff also gave the Advisory Committee the task of considering policies for "hallucinogenic" research in general. Within the last year, the Pilot Drug Evaluation Staff has approved several applications for psychedelic research with DMT and LSD and will soon be presented with applications to research ibogaine and psilocybin. Since there is renewed scientific interest in the field of psychedelic research, the Pilot Drug Evaluation Staff felt a need for the guidance and backing provided by the Advisory Committee.

Procedurally, the Committee met in open session to discuss general policies toward psychedelic research. It then went into closed session for the discussion of the MDMA protocol, allowing in only other government officials from NIDA, the DEA, the White House Office of Drug Control Policy (the Czar's office) and participants specifically invited by Charles Grob.

To aid the Committee in its deliberations, the Pilot Drug Evaluation Staff arranged for six expert witnesses to address the committee in open session. These included MDMA neurotoxicity experts Dr. Lewis Seiden (U. of Chicago) and Dr. George Ricaurte (Johns Hopkins), esteemed researchers Dr. Reese Jones (UCSF) and Dr. Murray Jarvik (UCLA), and Rick Strassman and David Nichols, both of whom were also at the NIDA meeting. Charles Grob was given an opportunity to address the Committee during the closed session concerning details of the MDMA protocol design.

From the opening moments of the meeting to the conclusions reached at the end, the participants were privileged to witness the triumph of science over ideology. The first person to address the Committee was NIDA's Dr. Geraline Lin. She reported on the Technical Review meeting and indicated that the participants had reached consensus on the need to conduct human studies with "hallucinogens" for two basic purposes, to investigate their biological correlates and therapeutic utility. She stressed the need for well-controlled, objective human studies that would enable regulators to balance therapeutic uses with risks, toxic and otherwise.

The real star of the meeting was, however, Dr. Reese Jones. He began cautiously by pointing out the problems involved in obtaining genuine informed consent from research subjects. He recommended that the therapists conducting the studies not conduct the initial subject screening because the delicate nature of any therapeutic relationship they might develop with the potential subject could give them undue influence. He pointed out the difficult issue of ensuring that psychiatrists conducting psychedelic research be properly trained in the administration of psychedelics.

He then switched gears and reminded the Committee that psychedelic researchers are pioneers without the large resources of pharmaceutical companies behind them. He urged the Committee not to demand that they conduct the ideal protocols the first time out, but rather let them begin by conducting more limited but nevertheless scientifically rigorous studies. He strongly criticized alarming interpretations of MDMA neurotoxicity data. He conjectured that since MDMA-related serotonin depletion in animals was seemingly without harmful behavioral and physiological correlates and human users reported beneficial effects from MDMA, serotonin depletion, if it even occurred, could as easily be considered advantageous as dangerous. He quipped that a pharmaceutical company with a drug that produced beneficial effects that people desired with possible permanent brain changes would prominently feature the brain changes in advertisements and make them a major selling point.

Rick Strassman spoke about his DMT work, summarizing the data that he had reported more fully at the NIDA meeting. He primarily made the point that human studies could be safely conducted.

When George Ricaurte discussed some of his concerns about neurotoxicity, he was aggressively questioned by Reese Jones who opined that MDMA neurotoxicity reminded him of the LSD chromosome damage scare of the 1960s, which helped generate fear of LSD and contributed to the cessation of LSD research but was later proved groundless. This interchange was rather dramatic, a snippet of which was broadcast around the world in CNN's television news story on the meeting.

The MDMA Protocol Discussion

The meeting then went into closed session. It began with a presentation by Charles Grob. His sincerity and his careful preparation were evident to the Committee. He had chosen to strongly rebut some of FDA's protocol critiques, a delicate task. In addition, he was asking to make a major change in the protocol and proposed separating the study into two parts, a neurotoxicity safety study in normals and an efficacy study in cancer patients. Though he was willing to conduct spinal taps on cancer patients if the FDA insisted (the oncologist working on the study had no objections to this), he much preferred not to. He argued that the neurotoxicity data would be better in any case if he eliminated the confounding effects of the patient's terminal illness and instead used healthy normals for that study.

Dr. Curtis Wright, the FDA official directing the review of the protocol, asked George Ricaurte what he thought of the extent of the neurotoxic risk to the proposed subjects from MDMA. After considered reflection, George Ricaurte stated that the doses called for in the experiment would not pose a large risk to the subjects, either in the cancer patients or the normals.

The Committee then discussed various aspects of the protocol and suggested several changes. Curtis Wright suggested that the Committee not get bogged down in details, which the FDA staff could better handle at a later time, but should consider two basic questions. First, should human studies with MDMA and other psychedelics be conducted? And if so, was psychedelic research sufficiently unique such that a new set of standards and procedures needed to be created to evaluate the studies?

The Committee decide that the benefits of gathering scientific information about MDMA and other hallucinogens through the use of human studies warranted the risks to subjects and society of conducting such research. The Committee also felt that research into the medical uses of hallucinogens was most appropriately regulated in the same manner and held to the same rigorous scientific standards for safety and efficacy as medical research with any other drug that the FDA would be asked to review. Finally, the Committee suggested that the FDA assist Charles Grob in the design of two studies, a standard Phase 1 study to investigate the safety of MDMA in healthy subjects and a standard Phase 2 study to investigate the efficacy of MDMA in the treatment of pain and distress in end-stage pancreatic cancer patients.

The Phase 1 MDMA Research Protocol

In late October 1992 the FDA informed Dr. Charles Grob that his application to conduct a basic Phase 1 human trial of the physiological and psychological effects of MDMA had been approved. This decision of the FDA marked the first time that it had ever approved human studies with MDMA; five previous applications had all been denied citing concerns over MDMA's neurotoxic risk.

The FDA's historic decision to permit human volunteers to be administered MDMA in an experimental context was based on several key factors. Foremost among them was the July 1992 recommendation of the FDA's Drug Abuse Advisory Committee to approve human studies with MDMA. Also of critical importance was recent scientific evidence suggesting that the risk of MDMA neurotoxicity from therapeutic doses was smaller than previously feared, coupled with the record of safety established by the small group of Swiss psychiatrists who had legally administered MDMA to their patients without observing any evidence of MDMA-related harm. Finally, the FDA was influenced by the scientific interest in MDMA research that had not diminished since MDMA had been made illegal but rather had grown stronger and more vocal.

As the FDA's Drug Abuse Advisory Committee recommended, MDMA research was to be held to the same rigorous scientific standards and procedures that were applied to any other pharmaceutical drug. In practice, that essentially meant that only data gathered from FDA-approved studies would be considered in assessing MDMA's risks and benefits. All of the knowledge gained by the therapeutic community prior to MDMA's scheduling in 1985 was basically to be ignored. In effect, researchers were instructed to design studies that would gather preliminary safety data before any therapeutically oriented studies could begin, regardless of the fact that tens of thousands of doses or more of MDMA had been already used safely in therapeutic contexts.

After FDA permission was in hand, Dr. Grob was still required to apply for three additional approvals prior to the commencement of the experiment. The first additional approval was from the UC Irvine Human Subjects Committee, which needed to review the revised experimental protocol. While it had approved the earlier study design of MDMA in the treatment of cancer patients, it also needed to specifically approve the Phase 1 study, notwithstanding the fact that it was a smaller and much less risky study than the cancer patient study. This approval was granted on December 11, 1992.

With FDA and UC Irvine Human Subjects Committee approval in hand, Dr. Grob was able to make the final two applications. The first was to the DEA, which checks to make sure the researchers themselves can be trusted to handle Schedule 1 drugs and that the hospital has adequate storage facilities for the drugs. DEA review is now underway and permission is expected by late 1993. The second application was to the California Research Advisory Panel, which reviews all Schedule 1 research carried out in California. Formal approval was obtained in April 1993.

Study Design

The first MDMA research protocol approved by the FDA is extraordinarily cautious in design and scope. For one thing, the protocol involves only six subjects. The restriction of the study to six subjects obviously limits the number of people exposed to MDMA to a very small number.

Further restrictions are that all of the subjects must be psychiatrists or people in the health-care professions. This restriction was actually proposed by Dr. Grob for several reasons, primarily because the FDA would have a harder time rejecting a study proposal with physicians and health-care professionals as subjects because, in the history of medical research, physicians have been allowed to assume great risks upon themselves in their pursuit of expanding medical knowledge and improving patient care. Psychiatrists and health-care professionals are presumed to be the most able of all potential subjects to understand the risks they are taking by participating in the experiment and are thus most able to give an informed consent.

Furthermore, all subjects must have self-administered MDMA at least once. This restriction is included so that the FDA can feel comfortable that they are not expanding the total number of MDMA users and exposing new people to the risks of MDMA. The fact that the subjects had previously self-administered MDMA means that they have already willingly assumed the risks of taking MDMA and the fact that they are still working in the health-care field implies that they were able to handle the abuse potential of MDMA and are not likely to fall apart personally or professionally as a result of their participation in the experiment.

Additional restrictions have to do with conservative contraindications for the use of MDMA. Subjects who have a history of schizophrenia, bipolar affective disorder, delusional disorder, paranoid disorder, or schizoaffective disorder will be excluded, as will any subjects who exhibit psychotic symptoms or have a history of epileptic seizures. Subjects who currently have a substance-abuse disorder, or who have severe cardiovascular problems will also be excluded. This list of contraindications is not meant to imply that people with these disorders should not be administered MDMA in therapeutic conditions; for example, MDMA has been effectively used to help treat substance abusers. Rather, the contraindications just mean that extra caution should be used in working with people with these conditions and the first human trial of MDMA is not an appropriate context within which to work with people coming to grips with difficult emotions. After all, people will be coming at the subjects with needles to draw blood, with questionnaires to probe their psychological status, and with pain tests designed to see just how much pain they can stand.

Female subjects who are pregnant or who are not utilizing effective means of birth control will also be excluded, as they are from all experiments using drugs that have not been positively determined to have no effect on fetal development. While there is no evidence that MDMA will be harmful to a fetus, and the rat data suggests that MDMA does not harm fetal development, neither has it been conclusively proven that MDMA will do no harm.

The final restriction is for subjects over the age of 55. This restriction is put in place because MDMA raises heart beat and blood pressure and people over the age of 55 are statistically more likely to have heart problems than people under the age of 55. This restriction is another example of the FDA's extreme conservatism regarding this experiment.

In addition to restricting the number of the subjects and their characteristics, the protocol also restricts the amount of MDMA that can be administered. In this study, subjects will be administered a total of three doses in random order about two weeks apart. One of the doses will be a placebo and will contain no MDMA at all. Another dose will contain an amount of MDMA so small it is predicted that subjects will not be able to distinguish it from the placebo. This dose is called a below-threshold dose and is calculated to be .15 milligrams per kilogram (mg/kg). For a 150-pound person, the dose will be about 10 mg, about 8–10% of a standard dose. The third dose is calculated to be the threshold dose, the least dose at which the subject will be able to experience subtle hints of the classic MDMA effects of emotional acceptance, peacefulness, enhanced attention and insight, and emotional empathy. This dose is calculated to be .75 mg/kg. For a 150-pound person this would be about 50 mg, or 40–50% of a standard dose.

Study Objectives

This study is designed to examine MDMA's basic physiological and psychological effects and to help determine the threshold level for its psychological effects. This is a preliminary study that will be repeated almost exactly as designed with six additional subjects at doses in the normal therapeutic range and somewhat above.

Specific objectives include testing MDMA's effect on organ and immune systems through blood tests, and measurement of heartbeat, blood pressure and temperature. The inclusion of the temperature measure is in direct response to the reports from England of the deaths of several people who danced all night at raves and died from heat-stroke. Animal studies into MDMA neurotoxicity have shown that MDMA strongly effects the hypothalamus, the part of the brain that influences temperature regulation. Therefore, we would like to know to what extent, if any, MDMA affects body temperature in subjects who are not exercising. The study will also look at pain sensitivity so that we might learn how to better schedule the pain reduction tasks once we begin working with cancer patients.

Neurotoxicity studies, which we considered, are almost certainly not going to reveal anything since we are using such small doses. Because neurotoxicity tests are intrusive and expensive, they were omitted from this phase of the research. They will be conducted in later phases of the experiment when subjects are repeatedly administered full doses. However, a full battery of neuropsychological tests will be administered to subjects in an attempt to determine if there are any functional or behavioral consequences resulting from the administration of MDMA.

Pharmacokinetics tests will also be administered but only at the time of peak concentration of the MDMA and its metabolites.

Since MDMA pharmacokinetic studies have already been conducted in Switzerland, we will be attempting to confirm previous findings rather than break any new ground.

A series of psychological tests will be administered to determine MDMA's acute effects while the subjects are experiencing MDMA. An interesting comparison of two different tests designed to measure MDMA's acute effects will be conducted: both the Hallucinogen Rating Scale developed by Dr. Rick Strassman and used in the U.S., and the Altered States of Consciousness scale developed by Dr. Dittrich and widely used in Europe, will be administered to subjects. Given the difficulty in measuring the subjective effects of psychedelics, a particularly valuable part of this experiment will be to compare the results of the two tests, thereby providing data that can be used to improve the scientific methodology utilized in psychedelic research.

A standard set of psychological tests will be used to determine whether our experimental regimen of small doses of MDMA has any long-term effects. These tests will be administered two weeks before the first experimental session and two weeks after the last session.

Stated as plainly as possible, the primary objective of this study is not to kill anyone or cause any political scandals so that we can move into testing higher doses and eventually proceed into the study of MDMA's therapeutic potential in the treatment of pain and distress in end-stage cancer patients.

The Phase 2 MDMA Efficacy Study

The Phase 2 study, which has already basically been designed, will be modified somewhat depending upon the findings from the Phase 1 study. Assuming that there are no surprising findings, the most likely situation since MDMA has been widely used and studied prior to the Phase 1 study, the Phase 2 study will look almost exactly as it is currently designed. It is my hope that the FDA will permit this study to begin in late 1993 or early 1994.

The study is designed to be carried out in pancreatic cancer patients who have an average of six months to live post-diagnosis. Pancreatic cancer is such a severe condition that nothing at all can be done for about half of the patients except the administration of pain medication. It is our hope that MDMA-assisted guided imagery can help patients both to control their own pain and to deal more effectively with the devastating emotional consequences of their illness. In addition, we hope MDMA will help patients to explore the ability of their own minds to stimulate their immune systems in fighting their cancers.

Study Design

The study will involve 24 patients, each randomly assigned to one of two experimental groups. Subjects in one group will receive two sessions of guided imagery, preceded by a pill containing MDMA, and subjects in the other group will receive two sessions of guided imagery, preceded by a pill containing a placebo. Psychotherapy and training in guided imagery will be provided to all patients prior to the experimental sessions as well as for several months afterward. If successful, additional studies will try to separate out the effect of MDMA without guided imagery.

All patients will need to be suffering from pain that is incompletely mediated by standard pain medications. Much of the exclusion criteria used in the Phase 1 experiment will also apply; for example, subjects with a history of schizophrenia, bipolar affective disorder, delusional disorder, paranoid disorder, or schizoaffective disorder will be excluded, as will any subjects who exhibit psychotic symptoms or have a history of epileptic seizures.

Study Objectives

This study is designed to determine if MDMA offers any therapeutic potential and also to determine what MDMA's side effects are in terminal cancer patients. The main objective is in the area of pain relief and will be measured by various pain scales as well as by simple observation of the amount of pain medication that is consumed by each patient. The secondary objective is to measure the psychological effects of MDMA and to determine if there is any correlation between psychological effects and pain reduction. The same set of acute and long-term psychological tests used in the Phase 1 study will also be used in the Phase 2 study. The tertiary objective is to determine if there are any quality-of-life improvements experienced by the subjects or their families and a series of quality-of-life tests will be administered both to patients and, where appropriate, to their families.

Various physiological measurements will be conducted, especially those focused on the immune system. Out of respect for the patients and their weakened condition, however, as many of the necessary physiological tests as possible will be conducted on the healthy volunteers participating in the Phase 1 study and not on the cancer patients in the Phase 2 study. For those patients willing to donate their brain tissue for analysis, neurotoxicity studies can be conducted. Otherwise, physically stressful spinal taps and tryptophan challenge tests will not be administered.

International Research

When the Drug Enforcement Administration criminalized MDMA in 1985, and the over 100 member countries of the World Health Organization's International Convention on Psychotropic Substances followed suit in 1986, most everyone thought that MDMA research would never be allowed in their lifetime. Yet a little-known provision of the International Convention known as Article Seven and the efforts of a small group of dedicated doctors and researchers around the world have prevailed and have brought about the renewal of human studies with MDMA.

Article Seven of the International Convention provides a mechanism whereby member nations can allow scientists and researchers access to a Schedule 1 drug as long as the governments keep tight control over all usage. When the WHO's Expert Committee on Drug Dependence urged the nations of the world to criminalize MDMA, they also "urged countries to use the provisions of Article Seven of the Convention on Psychotropic Substances to facilitate research in this interesting substance."

As one of the people who went to Geneva in 1985 to bring scientific information about MDMA to the attention of the Expert Committee, I saw references to Article Seven as a hollow, symbolic victory of no substance. I saw their recommendations at the time as a complete defeat even though the chairman of the Expert Committee, Dr. Paul Grof, filed a formal dissent to the recommendation of his Committee and insisted that the final recommendation note that he opposed international scheduling until data on MDMA's therapeutic usefulness could be gathered. Like many others, I had little hope that a footnote from an Expert Committee would ever sway government regulators in the midst of an international War on Drugs hostile to medical research with Schedule 1 drugs.

Yet only a few short years later, in 1988, the government of Switzerland faced increasing pressure from an organized group of Swiss psychiatrists interested in administering MDMA to their patients. Though Switzerland is not a member of the United Nations and thus is not a member of the World Health Organization nor a party to the International Convention of Psychotropic Substances, the Swiss Federal Health Authorities nevertheless decided to consult the WHO, headquartered in Geneva, about MDMA. What they found, to their surprise, was encouragement to approve research with MDMA. Though the Swiss Federal Health authorities were very reluctant to be the only government in the world to legally permit psychiatrists to administer MDMA to their patients, the recommendation of the Expert Committee provided them with important legitimacy and support for the position that they eventually adopted.

From 1988 to 1990, a small group of psychiatrists were able to administer MDMA to their patients without restrictions. The Swiss psychiatrists, unwilling to compromise their patients' treatment with the restrictions and interruptions of scientific research, gathered case histories but not scientific data from controlled trials. The Swiss government was pressured to change this situation in 1990 after a French patient of one of the Swiss psychiatrists died unexpectedly after the administration of the African root ibogaine. From 1990 to 1992, all use of MDMA in Switzerland was halted while investigations into the ibogaine death were conducted. In early 1992, after it was finally determined that MDMA had nothing to do with the ibogaine death, the Swiss doctors were again permitted to work with MDMA but only in those patients previously treated with MDMA who had not made sufficient progress in the intervening years without it.

The Swiss health authorities have already permitted an MDMA pharmacokinetics study to take place, though only in subjects previously treated with MDMA. The study was conducted by Dr. H. J. Helmlin at the Pharmaceutical Institute of the University of Bern and results are expected in early 1993. These results will be used to guide the pharmacokinetics portion of the Phase 1 trial to be conducted by Dr. Charles Grob at UC Irvine.

The group of Swiss psychiatrists interested in MDMA have initiated negotiations about treating new patients. However, the Swiss authorities are insisting that new patients can be treated only within the context of scientific protocols. The Swiss psychiatrists have decided to work with the Swiss health officials toward the initiation of clinical trials. At a meeting in early January, 1993, the Swiss psychiatrists reviewed various options for scientific protocols and discussed what experimental protocols they would submit to the Swiss health authorities. They hope that an experiment testing for MDMA's therapeutic potential will be underway in Switzerland by late 1993.

MDE Research in Germany

While the United States has passed an Analogue Bill, which criminalized drugs that are similar in structure or effect to drugs already on Schedule 1, such a law has not been adopted internationally. Therefore, MDE is illegal in the U.S. but not in most other countries. Psychiatrists in Germany were thus able to conduct a series of experiments with MDE in 1990 and 1991 without having to obtain permission from the authorities. MDE was specifically made illegal in Germany in 1992 and all research has consequently stopped. Nevertheless, a great deal of fascinating research was completed.

The main MDE researchers are Dr. Leo Hermle of the Department of Psychiatry at Christophsbad in Goppingen and Dr. Euphrosyne Gouzoulis of the Department of Psychiatry on the Medical Faculty of the RWTH in Aachen. They have conducted a series of comprehensive physiological and psychological studies of MDE. These studies involve an examination of sleep EEG patterns of people administered MDE before falling asleep (who wake up once the MDE effect is strong enough), and studies of MDE's neuroendocrine, cardiovascular and psychological effects. Subjects in these studies are almost always physicians, as in Dr. Grob's MDMA Phase 1 study, and were administered placebo or one full dose of MDE (140 mg), unlike the small doses to be used in Dr. Grob's study.

A finding of great interest is that MDE (and according to the researchers probably MDMA as well) seems to have unique physiological and psychological effects suggesting it is a member of a new class of substance distinct from the stimulants or hallucinogens. The German researchers prefer to call this class of drug "entactogens," a word coined by Dr. David Nichols meaning "to touch within."

The German researchers also hope to initiate MDMA research in 1993.

MDMA Research in Russia

For the last seven years, Dr. Evgeny Krupitsky of the St. Petersburg Regional Dispensary of Narcology (a 600-bed government-run in-patient alcoholic treatment center) has been using ketamine to treat alcoholics. He is very interested in testing the usefulness of MDMA in treating alcoholics and neurotics and, after two years, is very close to getting official permission to conduct MDMA research.

The Role of MAPS in MDMA Research

The Multidisciplinary Association for Psychedelics Studies (MAPS) is a membership-based nonprofit research and educational corporation that is working to develop MDMA's medical potential as well as that of other psychedelics. MAPS has spent about $75,000, donated by our members, on preliminary FDA-required 28-day MDMA toxicity studies in the dog and rat. These studies were submitted to the FDA as part of MAPS's MDMA Drug Master File. The FDA sent investigators to the research laboratory where the study took place, conducted an investigation, decided the data was valid and reliable, and accepted it into the Drug Master File.

Any researcher interested in conducting human studies with MDMA must either submit to the FDA data from required preliminary toxicity studies or reference data that is already in a Drug Master File. Almost all Drug Master Files are owned by profit-making pharmaceutical companies, which are competing with other pharmaceutical companies to bring a product to market. Usually, these companies will not share their data with anyone nor can the FDA legally confirm that a Drug Master File exists.

Because MAPS is a nonprofit corporation, it has made its Drug Master File available to responsible researchers interested in applying to the FDA to conduct human studies with MDMA.

When Dr. Grob (and all five previous researchers) applied to the

FDA to conduct Phase 1 research with MDMA, MAPS provided them with written permission to cross-reference its MDMA Drug Master File. This document saved Dr. Grob from having to reproduce the toxicity data, a hurdle that would have been prohibitively expensive. MAPS will also facilitate international research on MDMA by making its Drug Master File data available to researchers in Germany, Russia and other countries.

MAPS has spent an additional $125,000 on pilot studies into the effect of MDMA on the serotonin levels of humans, on MDMA neurotoxicity studies in the primate, and on protocol design for Dr. Grob's Phase 1 and Phase 2 human studies. All of this research had been funded by MAPS members who make tax-deductible contributions to MAPS and receive a newsletter.

The FDA is treating MDMA like any other drug any normal pharmaceutical company is interested in making into a prescription medicine. This means that the standard set of pre-clinical animal toxicity studies establishing safety is required before human studies can begin, that the standard set of Phase 1 human safety studies is required before Phase 2 human efficacy studies can begin, that the standard Phase 2 studies are required before large scale Phase 3 trials can begin, and that a whole spectrum of additional animal studies are required before applications can be made to the FDA to approve MDMA for marketing.

The function of MAPS is to conduct MDMA research just like any pharmaceutical company would that was interested in making MDMA into a prescription medicine. The critical difference is that MAPS makes our data available for free to responsible researchers to help advance the field of MDMA research. In this way, duplication of expensive required studies is eliminated and researchers can focus on research rather than fund-raising. The only way this strategy works is for individuals to become members of MAPS. For information, write to Rick Doblin, MAPS, 1801 Tippah Avenue, Charlotte, NC, 28205, or call (704) 358-9830 or fax (704) 358-1650.

APPENDIX III

Bibliography

Books

The Clinical, Pharmacological and Neurotoxicological Effects of the Drug MDMA, Klower (New York) 1990, Ed: S. J. Peroutka

E for Ecstasy by Nicholas Saunders (London) 1993

PIHKAL [Phenethylamines I Have Known and Loved]: A Chemical Love Story by Alexander and Ann Shulgin, Transform Press (Berkeley) 1992

Psychedelics Encyclopedia by Peter Stafford, 3rd edition, Ronin Publishing, Inc. (Berkeley) 1992

Through the Gateway to the Heart by Sophia Adamson, Four Trees Publications (San Francisco) 1985

Monographs

Exploring Ecstasy: A Description of MDMA Users: Final Report to the National Institute of Drug Abuse by Jerome Beck, Deborah Harlow, Patricia Morgan, and L. Watson, September 15, 1989, Grantee: Institute for Scientific Analysis, San Francisco

MDMA by R. B. Seymour, Haight Ashbury Publications (San Francisco) 1986

The MDMA Controversy: Contexts of Use and Social Control, Ph.D. Thesis for Doctor of Public Health by Jerome Beck, U.C. Berkeley

Articles

"The Agony and the Ecstasy" by Peter Nesmyth, *The Face*, October, 1986

"The Background Chemistry of MDMA" by Alexander Shulgin from *Journal of Psychoactive Drugs*, Vol. 18/4, 1986

"Can Drugs Enhance Psychotherapy?" by Lester Grinspoon and James Bakalar, *American Journal of Psychotherapy*, 1986

"Characterization of Three New Psychomimetics" in *The Pharmacology of Hallucinogens,* Eds. R. C. Stillman and R. E. Willette, Perganon Press (New York) 1978

"Ecstasy on Trial" by Richard Seymour, *High Times,* November, 1986

"Ecstasy: Towards an Understanding of the Biochemical Basis of Actions of 'The Facts about "Ecstasy," A Talk with Andrew Weil'" by Richard Goldstein, *The Village Voice,* February 7, 1989

"Ecstasy: The Truth About MDMA," *High Times,* November, 1985

"The Ecstatic Cybernetic Amino Acid Test" by Cynthia Robins, *San Francisco Examiner Image,* February 16, 1992

"Getting High on 'Ecstasy'" by D. M. Abramson, *Newsweek,* April 15, 1985

"The Looming Menace of Designer Drugs" by W. Gallagher, *Discover,* July, 1986

"MDMA" by Marcus Rattray, *Essays in Biochemistry,* Vol. 26, 1991

"MDMA and Human Sexual Function" by John Buffum and Charles Moser, *Journal of Psychoactive Drugs,* Vol. 18/4, 1986

"MDMA — Non-Medical Use and Intoxication" by Ronald Siegel, *Journal of Psychoactive Drugs,* Vol. 18/4, 1986

"MDMA Reconsidered" by Robert Leverant, *Journal of Psychoactive Drugs,* Vol. 18/4, 1986

"MDMA — The Dark Side of Ecstasy" by Gregory Hayner and Howard McKinny, *Journal of Psychoactive Drugs,* Vol. 18/4, 1986

"Meetings at the Edge with Adam: A Man for All Seasons?" by Philip Wolfson, *Journal of Psychoactive Drugs,* Vol. 18/4, 1986

"The New Drug Underground" by J. Adlar, *New Age,* October, 1985

"The Neurochemistry and Neurotoxicity of 3,4-Methylenedioxymethamphetamine (MDMA, "Ecstasy"), by Dennis McKenna and Stephen Peroutka, *Journal of Neurochemistry,* Vol. 54, 1990

"Phenomenology and Sequellae of MDMA Use" by Dr. Mitchell Liester, Dr. Charles Grob *et. al., Journal of Nervous and Mental Disease,* 180.6, 1992

"The Psychological and Physiological Effects of MDMA on Normal Volunteers" by Joseph Downing, *Journal of Psychoactive Drugs,* Vol. 18/4, 1986

Reflections on Drug Enforcement and Drug Use" by Lynn Ehrnstein, *Psychedelic Monographs and Essays*, vol. 2, 1987

"The Scheduling of MDMA: A Pharmacist's Perspective" by June Riedlinger, *Journal of Psychoactive Drugs*, Vol. 17, 1985

"The 'Seven Deadly Sins' of Media Hype in the Light of the MDMA Controversy" by June Riedlinger and Thomas Riedlinger, *Psychedelic Monographs and Essays*, Vol. 4, 1989

"Subjective Reports of the Effects of MDMA in a Clinical Setting" by George Greer and Requa Tolbert, *Journal of Psychoactive Drugs*, Vol. 18/4, 1986

"A Trip into the Unknown," by Alison Abbot and David Concar, in *New Scientist*, August 29, 1992

"The Trouble with Ecstasy" by C. G. Bowling, *Life Magazine*, August, 1985

"Turn On, Tune In, Go to the Office Late on Monday" by Peter J. O'Rourke, *Rolling Stone*, December 19, 1985

"Twenty Years on My Ever-Changing Quest" by Alexander Shulgin, in *Psychedelic Reflections*, Eds. Lester Grinspoon and James Bakalar, Human Sciences Press (New York) 1983

"Why MDMA Should Not Have Been Made Illegal" by Marsha Rosenbaum and Rick Doblin, in *The Drug Legalization Debate*, 1991, (Newbury Park) Inciardi, Ed.

Index

PSYCHEDELIC 2-4-1 SALE

The "Xochi Speaks" full-color 2' x 3' print combines cutting-edge art, science and spirituality. Xochipilli, the Aztec deity of altered states, is shown with the twelve major psychedelics explained and depicted as 3-D molecular models. Completing this at-a-glance mini-course is the 16 page "Guide" with easy-to-digest information on nutritional support, brain chemistry, pharmacology, plus suggested readings and related resources. A must-have for psychonauts. And now, while supplies last, buy one, get one free! Money orders only. $25.00 ppd / $30.00 foreign. (CA add local tax.) Send SASE for latest catalog.

LORDNOSE!

POB 170473E San Francisco, CA 94117

Bruce Eisner, author of ECSTASY: The MDMA Story

About the Author

B RUCE EISNER was born February 26, 1948 in Brooklyn and raised in Los Angeles. A child of the baby boom, he first went to college in 1966 at California State University Northridge, majoring in Political Science. He left at the end of his third year to become a full-time "hippie." Later, he became a journalist, writing for "underground" newspapers with his first article appearing in 1971 in the *Los Angeles Free Press*. In 1977, he became a contributing editor of *High Times* and in 1987 a contributing writer for *Omni*.

Bruce was awarded a B.A. in Psychology in 1979, and a Master's degree in Personality Psychology from U.C. Santa Barbara in 1981, where he also worked as a teaching assistant. He began a Ph.D. program focusing on Consciousness Studies at Saybrook Institute and left the program short of his dissertation in 1987 to launch the *Mindware Catalog*—featuring computer software "for the mind."

In February 1989, he authored the first edition of *Ecstasy: The MDMA Story* and in 1990, he founded The Island Group, an organization named for the Aldous Huxley novel, *Island*, and is editor of *Island Views*, the group's quarterly newsletter. Bruce has organized conferences focused on psychedelics including the 1977 LSD—A Generation Later event at U.C. Santa Cruz, the 1991 Bridge Conference at Stanford University, and LSD—50 Years and Beyond in April 1993 at U.C. Santa Cruz. Currently Bruce is living in Santa Cruz, California and is about to launch a new publication, *Upgrade Magazine*.

Opium Poppy Garden
Griffith. 1993. This is the only book available that describes the cultivation, harvest, and pharmacology of opium in a format that combines literary and instructional writing. Includes a story and a technical appendix, providing the reader with a working knowledge of this valuable plant.
Ronin 96pp.
OPIPOP

Ecstasy: The MDMA Story
Eisner. 1989. Legal issues, psychotherapy, history, use, chemistry, 27 illustrations, health risks, 60pp bibliography, index. "Remarkably complete, courageous and well researched work."
　　—*American Book Review*
Ronin 228pp.
MDMA

Legal Highs Gottleib. 1991. Concise encyclopedia of relatively unknown legal herbs and chemicals that posess psychoactive properties. How the substances are obtained, how they are used and what the known effects are.
And/Or 64pp
LHIGH

Psychedelics Encyclopedia
Stafford. 1991. With a new foreword on recent developments and an appendix on Ecstasy, this edition is a mind expanding archive of the psychedelic age. Includes information on botany and cultivation; effects and pharmacology; LSD, cannabis, peyote, mushrooms, famous psychedelic users and events.
And/Or 420pp.
PSYENC

Controlled Substances
Shulgin. 1991. Definitive reference on illegal drugs. Lists every controlled drug with chemical formulas and drug code. Chemical abstracts number, known synonyms, charts, tables, definition appendices. "Makes accessible chemical and legal facts."
Ronin 448pp.
CONSUB

Growing the Hallucinogens
Grubber. 1991. Presents simple methods for cultivation of hallucinogenic and psychoactive plants, from seeds and cuttings, indoors and outdoors.
And/Or 96pp
GHAL

Brain Boosters: Foods & Drugs That Make You Smarter Potter & Orfali. 1993. Fascinating look at foods and drugs that are reported to make the mind work better. For professionals, business people, seniors, people concerned with Alzheimer's and other neurological impairments, as well as students, athletes and party goers who want to improve mental performance.
Ronin 256pp.
BRABOO

Drug Testing at Work
Potter & Orfali. 1990. Comprehensive guide to drug testing in the workplace. Testing technology, programs, legal issues and methods used to foil the tests. For medical staff, educators, attorneys, legislators, and public and private employees.
Ronin 230pp.
DTW

Laughing Gas Shelden. 1992. Only book on the recreational use of nitrous oxide. History, personal accounts, making and obtaining the "air of paradise."
And/Or 96pp.
LGAS

Books by Phone ████████████ (800) 858-2665 (510) 548-2124